AF806134

The Autocrat's Predicament

The Autocrat's Predicament

The Political Peril of Economic Upgrade in Single-Party Authoritarian Regimes

Timothy R. Heath

LEXINGTON BOOKS
Lanham • Boulder • New York • London

Published by Lexington Books
An imprint of The Rowman & Littlefield Publishing Group, Inc.
4501 Forbes Boulevard, Suite 200, Lanham, Maryland 20706
www.rowman.com

86-90 Paul Street, London EC2A 4NE

Copyright © 2024 by The Rowman & Littlefield Publishing Group, Inc.

All rights reserved. No part of this book may be reproduced in any form or by any electronic or mechanical means, including information storage and retrieval systems, without written permission from the publisher, except by a reviewer who may quote passages in a review.

British Library Cataloguing in Publication Information Available

Library of Congress Cataloging-in-Publication Data Available

ISBN 978-1-66694-739-7 (cloth)
ISBN 978-1-66694-740-3 (electronic)

Contents

Acknowledgments vii

Introduction: The Political Challenge of Intensive Growth Policies 1

1 The Theory of the Enabling Condition 17

2 China 1991–1997: Deng Xiaoping's Triumph and a Toxic Political Legacy 41

3 China 2004–2010: Hu Jintao: Professionalization Fails to Convert Opposing Elites 67

4 China 2013–2020: A Fragmented Public Impair Undermines Xi's Strategy to Dominate Elites 101

5 Taiwan 1973–1979: Success Amid a Looming Threat of an Elite-Led Popular Mobilization 129

6 Soviet Union 1985–1990: Weak Central Leadership, Strong Elite Opposition Dooms Perestroika 145

7 Comparative Analysis 169

Conclusion 187

References 197

Index 217

About the Author 223

Acknowledgments

This book could not have been possible without the invaluable mentorship of my dissertation committee members, Drs. Ming Wan, Jack Goldstone, and Eric McGlinchey. My deepest thanks to Joseph Fewsmith, Bruce Dickson, David Lampton, Judith Blanchette, Howard Shatz, Meg Rithmire, Ming Xia, and Peter Martin for their invaluable help and advice.

Introduction

The Political Challenge of Intensive Growth Policies

China has achieved remarkable growth over the past four decades, but whether the country can ascend to the ranks of upper-income countries remains a topic of intense debate.[1] China's economy has decelerated in recent years as its exports saturated global markets, rising wages eroded the competitiveness of its industries, and mounting injections of state-directed investment yielded diminishing returns. Since 2017, China's annual GDP growth has averaged between 6 percent and 7 percent, and it is expected to decline further in the coming years.[2] While high by the standards of mature economies, these rates represent a significant drop from the preceding two decades.[3] Moreover, analysts warn that if no adjustments are made to the country's economic policies, then the compounding effects of mounting debt, low productivity, and demographic aging raise the risk of long-term economic stagnation.[4] The slowdown occurs as China continues to grapple with the legacy costs of worsening inequality, severe pollution, an underdeveloped social safety net, and rampant corruption.[5] Indeed, scholars with the Lowy Institute now estimate that China's GDP growth rate could slow to 2–3 percent on average through mid-century.[6]

Beijing's quest to improve its economy's performance faces daunting odds. Single-party authoritarian states have rarely succeeded in building highly productive, prosperous economies. The correlation between "consolidated" liberal democracies and the wealthiest economies is well established, although the reason for the correlation remains debated.[7] By contrast, authoritarian regimes have shown some variation but generally underperformed their liberal democratic counterparts.[8] The economic performance of the Soviet Union and the communist bloc during the Cold War proved notoriously disappointing, with Soviet per capita GDP barely reaching a fraction of that of the United States in the 1970s. The low productivity and inefficiency of economies led by communist parties owed in large part to their ill-conceived statist policies. But even when these regimes embraced market-friendly reforms, their economies have tended to feature low productivity and considerable inefficiency. Despite China's phenomenal growth rates, for example, its industrial sector has only achieved a fraction of the productivity experienced by the most advanced economies.[9]

China's prospects appear to dim further in light of the puzzling political strategies undertaken by its rulers. Most single-party authoritarian states have failed, but impressive exceptions have occurred amid liberalizing changes. Most famously, the Asian "Tiger" economies of South Korea, Taiwan, and Singapore followed a modernization paradigm in which liberal reform accompanied spectacular gains in growth and productivity. By contrast, China's leaders have clearly rejected this path. In fact, the leadership's ambitions to improve the economy's performance have coincided with a considerable increase in centralizing, coercive, and repressive measures.[10] In March 2018, China's national legislature voted unanimously to abolish presidential term limits, paving the way for Xi Jinping to serve indefinitely in that capacity.[11] The move capped a steady accumulation of power in the hands of Xi and his allies.[12] Xi has overseen a sweeping anticorruption campaign, which by 2020 had reportedly resulted in the disciplining of over 1 million Party members, including several high-level officials.[13] Reviving practices not seen since the days of strong men like Mao Zedong and Deng Xiaoping, the official media have promoted a fawning Xi Jinping "cult of personality."[14] Authorities also carried out a ruthless crackdown on anyone who might question these developments. According to the activist group Amnesty International, human rights in China are at their worst level since the Tiananmen Square massacre.[15]

Many western political scientists and commentators regard these moves as counterproductive and deeply misguided. Reflecting a view commonly held among China watchers, David Shambaugh, a professor at George Washington University, warned, "Only a substantial political liberalization will afford China a good chance of not becoming indefinitely bogged down."[16] Susan Shirk, a professor at the University of California, warned that Xi Jinping had failed to follow a "modernization" pattern in which authoritarian regimes "move from strongman dictatorial rule to [a] collective leadership" that is "more rule-bound" and "more institutionalized."[17] Carl Minzer, a professor at Fordham University, has declared that China's "reform era is over."[18] What is it about China's current political economy that might incentivize its leaders to coerce elites and increase repression of the public? What, if anything, might Xi's politics have to do with the country's quest for improved economic performance? This book hopes to shed light on such questions.

EXTENSIVE AND INTENSIVE ECONOMIC GROWTH

China's economic situation is a vexing but familiar one. To understand why requires a grasp of the country's principal economic challenge. As any basic course in economics teaches, growth, or the output in the value of goods and services, stems from two primary sources: (1) Increases in the inputs of labor and capital and (2) increases in the efficient use of those inputs. The first, sometimes called "extensive" growth, increases in proportion to the inputs, and thus is subject to diminishing returns as the volume of those inputs decline or the economy's ability to use those resources diminishes. Economies that grow based on increases in population, investment, and territory are examples of such input-driven growth.

By contrast, the latter type, also called "intensive" growth, is driven by the more efficient use of existing resources.[19] Economic prosperity generated by "intensive" growth is more attractive to policymakers because of its potential to significantly increase per capita GDP and enable sustained growth without massive infusions of labor and capital. Economies powered by intensive growth are less subject to the problem of diminishing returns and more likely to experience sustained expansion. However, even economies powered by intensive growth eventually experience slowdowns when they exhaust the potential of existing capacities or experience stiffer competition from rival economies.

Intensive growth is fundamentally driven by increases in productivity.[20] Productivity, the measure of output per input, may be determined by many factors. Labor productivity measures the efficiency of workers, and this can be increased through skills training and education. But other factors can affect productivity as well, such as the quality of technology used in factories, policies and institutions that incentivize work, access to new markets, and other factors.[21] Slowdowns in productivity account for a significant share of economic sluggishness. According to Barry Eichengreen and his colleagues, declines in productivity accounted "for about 85 percent, or 3 percentage points, of the absolute reduction in the growth rate of GDP per capita" for fast-growing, non-oil exporting countries (i.e., instances in which a country averaged GDP growth of 3.5 percent or higher for seven years) experienced since the 1960s.[22]

Although the benefits of highly productive economies are clear, achieving intensive growth has proven elusive for many countries, especially for those that have already moved from a low to a middle-income status. Even among the richest economies today, productivity has generally stagnated.[23] And although experts debate the concept of the "middle income trap," consensus has emerged on the problem of low productivity in many low and middle-income countries.[24] Indeed, some scholars have argued that the so-called "middle-income trap" is more accurately labeled a "low-productivity trap."[25]

China, like many developing countries, suffers from low productivity. Following a well-established precedent set by other industrializers, China enjoyed years of rapid, "extensive" growth through the mobilization of labor and capital. But its ability to squeeze growth from such methods is rapidly diminishing. China's workforce has already peaked and has been in absolute decline since 2011.[26] Moreover, rising wages since the early 2010s have rendered an economic strategy based on low-cost labor increasingly untenable.[27] Investment-driven growth has reached its limits as well. To maintain high growth rates, the country has piled on debt and wasted resources through unnecessary construction and the maintenance of an inefficient state sector.[28] To grow in the future, China will need to increase its productivity. As experts have pointed out, China's economy has considerable potential for more "intensive" growth. Its industries are only about 30 percent as productive as the most efficient, or "frontier," economies, and its productivity has actually declined since the global financial crisis in 2008.[29]

How to improve productivity depends on the particular characteristics of any given economy. Prescriptions that work for a low-income country will not work for more mature economies. For countries that have undergone a basic level of industrialization, common policy prescriptions include better education (especially higher and technical education), greater savings and investment, and modernized infrastructure. Experts disagree on the value of industrial policies, but all agree on the need for institutional strengthening, especially the administrative capacity to deliver public services and regulate effectively.[30] Finding ways to move up the value chain to provide higher value services and innovation is also critical. According to a 2012 World Bank study, middle-income countries can achieve higher productivity through a "shift to high-value services and the promotion of homegrown innovation," rather than continuing to rely on imitation of foreign technology.[31] These policy prescriptions share much in common with those espoused by Chinese leaders themselves. At the Third Plenum of the 18th Party Congress, for example, central leaders outlined ambitions to strengthen and improve public services, safeguard fair competition, promote sustainable development, expand social welfare services, and improve the country's ability to innovate.[32]

Enacting policies to upgrade an economy's performance requires more than the right economic prescriptions, however. The pervasiveness of low productivity among developing and developed countries alike, despite incessant pledges by the same governments to deliver higher quality growth, suggests the remedy may be harder to achieve than it appears. A primary reason rests in politics.

The political dimension of intensive growth can be illustrated with a closer look at some of the institutional reforms commonly prescribed. Countries could bolster productivity in part through the creation of institutions that incentivize people to consume and carry out the type of creative, enterprising work that can energize economic activity. Examples include the expansion of social welfare services, the provision of higher quality education, the establishment of a fair and equitable legal system, and the control of corruption. All of these require responsive, effective governance.[33] However, creating these institutions may require authorities to curb the arbitrary rule of government officials, control corruption, and transfer resources from less productive state-owned enterprises to a more productive non-state sector. These changes entail an unavoidable diminishing of rent for powerful elites and their clients who benefit from existing arrangements, changes that those individuals, some of whom may have amassed considerable wealth and influence, could be expected to resist.

The political requirements for the implementation of intensive growth policies can accordingly be quite demanding. To manage the opposition of elites and minimize the risks of political conflict, the central government must make clear the stakes and mobilize interested parties to pressure recalcitrant bureaucracies and interest groups to comply.[34] Increasing coordination between the central government, relevant bureaucracies, and other interested actors is also important. Policies to improve productivity often also require the sharing of information and cooperation among disparate parties in businesses, labor, and the government.[35] In short, the pursuit of intensive economic growth in middle-income countries is an intensely political process.[36]

THE POLITICAL RISKS OF ECONOMIC UPGRADE

These political tasks are demanding for the most politically nimble states, but they are even more formidable for single-party authoritarian regimes. Before explaining why, I will explain what I mean by a "single-party authoritarian" regime. There are many types of political regimes dominated by a single party, ranging from "hegemonic" parties that dominate an otherwise liberal democratic political system, as the Liberal Democratic Party has done in Japan, to personalistic regimes that rely on a single political party structured around patronage with little regard to ideology, such as Mexico's Institutional Revolutionary Party. But since one purpose of this book is to better understand China's prospects, such political regimes are not the focus of this analysis.

The regimes most similar to China's consist of ruling parties that reflect some adherence to Leninist organizing principles. These ruling parties adhere to Leninist principles in the sense that they claim, per political principles espoused by Vladimir Lenin, to serve as a "vanguard" political party made up of professional cadre who represent the interests of the masses. Such a party penetrates and controls the government and virtually all other forms of social and economic organization. It is a "closed" regime in the sense that no organized political opposition is tolerated. Instead, the party-state monopolizes economic and social power in society and retains full discretion over policy initiatives. The ruling party generally bases its political discipline on some sort of ideology—often of a Marxist variant, though not always. The Kuomintang (KMT), which ruled Taiwan in an authoritarian manner from the 1950s to the 1970s, organized itself loosely along Leninist lines and upheld a vague nationalist ideology but opposed Marxism. These features distinguish China's mode of single-party authoritarianism from other "less ideological" variants in which ideology may be absent or downplayed, opposition tolerated, and party penetration of organizations limited.[37] Throughout this book, the term "single-party authoritarian" regime will refer to this type of closed, Leninist-based political system.

A key feature of such regimes is the autocrat's dependence on elites embedded in the party-state bureaucracy to manage economic growth and governance. The unavoidable dependence of central leaders on elites provides the latter with a tremendous advantage. Theorists of policy implementation have noted the asymmetric advantage that bureaucrats in all societies have in preserving their interests and resisting change. Scholars have found, for example, that bureaucracies can manipulate their superior expertise and access to information to frustrate policymakers.[38] Compounding the problem for single-party authoritarian regimes is the lack of independent courts or organized political opposition. Indeed, such single-party authoritarian regimes by design deny the formation of independent institutions, apolitical bureaucracies, or organized opposition. These features may facilitate party control, but they also leave the ruler with few means of holding elites accountable.[39]

The depoliticized nature of the public poses a second disadvantage. In their formation, single-party authoritarian regimes often demonstrated an impressive ability to mobilize the public for revolutionary purposes. Mao Zedong, Vladimir Lenin, and Ho Chi Minh successfully led insurrections in large part due to their superior ability to mobilize populations. Charismatic leaders like Mao and Joseph Stalin also wielded the threat of mass violence to terrorize their own bureaucrats and cow elite rivals. Once in power, however, these governments have often found sustained mobilization politically destabilizing and economically damaging. The bloody violence and economic calamities of China's Great Leap Forward and of the Cultural Revolution provide vivid examples of what can befall a single-party authoritarian regime that keeps its people politically mobilized. To avoid these dangers, autocrats have eventually pursued political demobilization. Authorities tend to instead direct the people to focus on work and personal advancement, as Deng Xiaoping did when he introduced the reform and opening policies in the late 1970s. A depoliticized public aids political stability because it is less likely to challenge the ruling party's monopoly on power. But while an apolitical public might facilitate political stability, it removes a potential ally for disciplining elites.

These structural weaknesses become serious liabilities when leaders seek intensive growth through the reduction of wasteful and inefficient practices that often provide a major source of rent for elites. Measures to improve a country's *economic* prospects may require major *political* changes that the regime, with its political liabilities, is ill-equipped to carry out. Leaders of single-party authoritarian states who seek to improve their economy's performance through intensive growth policies thus face a painful dilemma.

On the one hand, the autocrat has many incentives to improve the economy's productivity. Higher quality growth could bring more revenue for the autocrat and his cronies and satisfaction for workers who benefit from higher paying jobs. Failure to improve the economy's performance could result in diminishing prospects, greater instability, and, eventually, economic frailty or collapse. On the other hand, the same changes may carry enormous political risks. Achieving intensive growth may require the reduction or elimination of wasteful and unproductive practices that provide rent to well-resourced elites and their clients.

This suggests a political challenge quite different from that posed by conventional analysis of economic incentives in authoritarian regimes. The whole logic of Bruce de Mesquita's influential "selectorate" theory rests on the notion that paying off powerful elites is critical to an autocrat's survival.[40] In the dilemma outlined, however, the autocrat is not buying political support through payoffs but instead seeking more of the opposite: He is demanding elites take steps to curtail their own sources of wealth and privilege. From this formulation, it is obvious elites have little incentive to comply and a strong one to resist.

The issue of elite compliance or noncompliance is at the heart of the predicament that confronts autocrats who pursue intensive growth policies. Autocrats face a serious principal agent problem in that they must entrust the implementation of policy to agents who are incentivized to undermine the same policy.[41] If the ruler presses too hard, he could antagonize the elites and maybe even provoke a violent reaction. Finding ways to compel elite compliance in a manner that minimizes the risk of intra-elite violence is a critical political challenge that autocrats must resolve.

There are two main ways to resolve the dilemma. An autocrat may decide to forego intensive growth policies. This offers the advantage of maintaining political stability by accommodating the interests of elites. Doing so carries the cost, however, of diminishing long-term prospects for the nation and, eventually, the autocrat. The savage repression and crushing destitution overseen by North Korea's brutal regime provide a contemporary illustration of the extreme lengths dictators must be willing to consider if they hope to indefinitely forestall the political risks of economic change.

The other option is for the autocrat to force the implementation of intensive growth policies over elite opposition. This is the option most autocrats gravitate toward in light of the bleak and doubtful prospects offered by the first option. However, since it antagonizes well-resourced elites, autocrats who contemplate this route must be prepared for the possibility of political instability and violence.

Central leaders who accept the challenge of antagonizing well-resourced elites have several options. One option is to preempt a potentially violent reaction with violence. Brutal autocrats such as Joseph Stalin and Mao Zedong relied extensively on terror, torture, and executions to compel officials to carry out policies they might otherwise resist. But the extremely high risks of intra-elite conflict have historically led single-party authoritarian regimes to abandon such a sanguinary and volatile style of rule. After the initial charismatic leader has passed, these regimes have tended to institutionalize procedures for cadre management. This has in most cases resulted in greater stability and longevity for the regime, but it also removed a potent instrument to discipline and control elites. In a situation featuring "normal" politics, elites feel less pressure to carry out policies that they oppose.

A "normal" state of politics buys political stability for the regime at the cost of considerably weakening the autocrat's authority, especially during times in which the central leadership seeks to carry out policies opposed by elites. The information asymmetry inherently available to frontline managers of policy grants elites an immense advantage over distant central leaders who lack expertise on local affairs. Elites also have the advantage of numbers, since the number of party-state cadres far exceeds the ability of a small central leadership to monitor them, especially in large countries such as China. Above all, the elites have the supreme advantage of holding the reins to legitimacy. They are responsible for managing the day-to-day operations of the economy, governance, and stability maintenance, all of which are critical to keeping the autocrat in power. Antagonizing elites risks potentially upsetting the economy and the nation's stability.

Central leaders may be at a disadvantage, but they are not powerless. Even in a period of normal politics, the defiance of any authoritarian leader carries substantial risk. Autocrats, even weaker ones, still have the power to arbitrarily seize and injure any citizen, including members of the elite. Open defiance could result in arbitrary imprisonment or worse.

Open defiance is often unnecessary, however, because the advantages enjoyed by elites are so considerable. Cadres outside the central leadership can outmaneuver the autocrat by simply feigning compliance while avoiding actual implementation through time-tested methods such as stalling, lobbying, and slow-rolling.[42] Obfuscation and feigned compliance are effective because they capitalize on the autocrat's near total dependence on elites and his need for the illusion of control. It also complicates the problem of oversight because it offers partial, if deceptive, evidence of obedience even as elites fundamentally undermine the same policies.

If violent coercion is too risky and routine bureaucratic procedure are ineffective, is there any way that the autocrat can compel elites to carry out upgrading policies that they oppose? There is a third option. The most promising way is to mobilize public pressure. Many theories on policy processes have highlighted the importance of involving outsiders, such as the public, in the successful implementation of major policies.[43] Scholars of upgrading policies have shown the importance of public demand for carrying out difficult and costly initiatives that may not provide an obvious immediate benefit but can improve an economy's long-term prospects.[44] The history of communist states and other revolutionary governments is also full of examples in which charismatic leaders mobilized popular pressure against recalcitrant elites to carry out policies of dubious value, as Mao did during the Cultural Revolution.

An engaged public can help the central leadership by providing a strong demand signal for change. A politically mobilized public can signal its disapproval of elite misbehavior. A strong public backing can also help the central leadership politically withstand challenges from elites. How to involve the public in pressuring elites without provoking political instability stands as a key task for central leaders who pursue intensive growth policies.

OVERVIEW OF THE BOOK

In the following pages, I will outline a theory that explains why central leaders require a favorable political condition, which I call the "enabling condition," to carry out intensive growth policies. I will explain the theory in more detail later but will here provide a brief summary.

This theory states that a favorable political configuration composed of a strong central leadership, a weak elite opposition, and a cohesive public is necessary to implement major intensive growth policies. The strength of the central leadership consists of the leader's control of the nation's security forces, ability to command obedience from subordinate levels of government, and relative control over the ruling party. The strength of elite opposition can be judged by the elite's share of national wealth, the degree of collusion, and its disposition for or against the proposed policies. I use the term "cohesive" to refer to the potential of the public to be politically mobilized. A cohesive public is one characterized by formal employment, industries with strong linkages, meaningful opportunities for political participation, and a sense of shared identity and purpose.

The enabling condition allows the central leadership to compel elite compliance in a manner that minimizes the risk of political violence by mobilizing public support behind the autocrat's goals. A firm control of the government bureaucracy increases the likelihood that directives will be carried out by subordinate levels of government. Similarly, strong discipline in the party enables the central leadership to confidently rely on procedures and processes to discipline defiant elites in a manner that upholds the legitimacy of the party.

Strong control of the security forces is important for the autocrat to control the risks of political conflict. A firm control of the security forces by the top leader reduces the risk of a coup. And the dominance of the political party by the autocrat undercuts any effort by elites to contest the central leadership's authority through a countermobilization of hostile factions in the party-state machinery.

Weak elite opposition lowers the risk of political violence because elites are less likely to risk disobedience when vulnerable. By contrast, a powerful elite opposition dramatically increases their willingness to contend with the autocrat. The strength of elites can be judged by their share of national wealth and the degree of vertical and horizontal collusion. A modest share of national wealth limits the ability of elites to fend off the central leadership and protect their positions through bribes, payoffs, and the co-optation of relevant actors, including the military, media, and others. An elite riven by divisions and lacking strong horizontal and vertical linkages further constrains the ability to pool resources. It also leaves them vulnerable to divide and conquer tactics by the central leadership. But the strength of elites is not alone decisive. The disposition of elites toward proposed policies matters greatly as well. Powerful, wealthy elites will foil policy implementation when it threatens to cost them dearly. By contrast, elites, might in some cases, support economic initiatives that offer lucrative opportunities to line their pockets.

In an enabling condition, a cohesive public plays an important role in controlling political risks. If the central leader can effectively direct their mobilization, then the public's support could pressure elites to carry out the assigned tasks and deter them from challenging the central leadership. Cohesiveness may be measured economically, politically, and socially. An economically cohesive public is mostly employed in the formal sector, which has industries with strong downstream and upstream linkages. It is more likely to adhere to agreements between government, labor, and business since it has some degree of formal integration into the economy. A politically cohesive public has opportunities for meaningful political participation and is easier to mobilize. A public with social cohesion has a moderate level of inequality and shared social and cultural identities with the autocrat. They are more likely to support his goals than a highly stratified and deeply divided public that shares few values in common with the autocrat.

SIGNIFICANCE OF THE TOPIC

Although the theory of the enabling condition can apply to many types of political systems, this book focuses on the experiences of single-party authoritarian regimes. Why these countries? Authoritarian regimes led by Leninist-organized political parties are a dying breed, if not nearly extinct. Even the few that exist have largely abandoned the messianic ideologies that they were created with. Yet there are several important reasons to consider this topic. Methodologically, the analysis of a group of states with similar political characteristics minimizes problems of confounding variables. Similarities in the structure of single-party authoritarian regimes permit a detailed comparative analysis that is difficult to achieve through comparisons of countries with extremely different political systems.

The experiences of late-modernizing single-party authoritarian regimes could also help us understand China's potential growth trajectory. Whether China's leadership can succeed in overturning established wisdom by charting a repressive path to high income status carries important consequences for international peace and the possibilities for economic development. A successful China that relied on repressive political strategies to upgrade its economy could grow immensely wealthy and powerful. A rich and powerful China under a repressive CCP leadership could pose as a strong and perhaps more ideologically motivated challenger to the United States. It would also raise important questions about the future evolution of an international order featuring dominance by an authoritarian government. Moreover, Chinese success would also raise questions about the role of coercion and repression as instruments of economic development. While rejected by mainstream economic opinion today, a prosperous China that relied extensively on such repressive politics would set a disturbing new model of illiberal development.

Finally, analysis of the experience of single-party authoritarian regimes could provide insight into the much broader problem of failed efforts to implement intensive growth policies. Low productivity is a pervasive problem that has afflicted economies at all levels of development. Understanding how interactions between central leaders, elites, and the public operate in single-party authoritarian regimes could help deepen our understanding of how other political systems, such as those of liberal democracies, grapple with similar problems.

BOOK OUTLINE

To illustrate the theory's application, this book relies on a comparative case study method involving a sample size of five cases. The book proceeds in the following manner. Chapter 1 introduces the theory of the enabling condition. It explains the importance of a strong central leadership, weak elite opposition, and cohesive public for the successful implementation of major intensive growth policy initiatives. It also provides an overview of the methodology employed in the comparative case studies. Chapters 2 through 5 apply the theoretical framework to three instances in China's history over the past three decades, providing an opportunity for a time-series comparison. The three leaders, Deng Xiaoping, Hu Jintao, and Xi Jinping, adopted different political strategies to maintain power and carry out economic upgrading policies. Each faced different challenges and experienced varying levels of success, but I will explore the incentives and political logic that underpinned their decisions. Deng started from a position of apparent weakness that belied his real political strength. He and his successor, Jiang Zemin, successfully exploited that potential to shape favorable conditions for achieving rapid growth through a political strategy that tolerated considerable elite misbehavior. Hu Jintao inherited a more daunting political situation, which he tried to overcome through noncoercive measures. His conciliatory approach toward the elites and inability to build a supportive coalition among the public directly contributed to disappointing outcomes. Successor Xi Jinping attempted to correct Hu's mistakes by strengthening central power and breaking elite opposition. He succeeded in strengthening his power but only marginally curtailed the power of opposing elites, who continued to find ways to subvert the central leadership's intent. Moreover, Xi's inability to overcome the deep economic and social fragmentation of the public constrained his ability to coerce elites. As a result, China experienced an incremental improvement over his predecessor's efforts but stalled in the face of intractable elite resistance. In chapter 5, I examine the case of Taiwan in the 1970s, which successfully carried out an economic upgrade. Taiwan succeeded in part due to an unusually favorable political economy that made it easier for the top leader, Chiang Ching-kuo, to achieve the enabling condition. However, the prosperity yielded by Taiwan's success, compounded by international developments, resulted in a surprising evolution of the political situation. Chapter 6 considers the example of the Soviet Union in the era of Glasnost. Severe structural weaknesses resulted in a highly unfavorable environment, which President Mikhail Gorbachev proved helpless to overcome. Chapter 7 provides a comparative analysis across all five cases, noting commonalities and differences. Chapter 8 offers some concluding thoughts, including implications for China's prospects as a rising power as well as economic development policies.

NOTES

1. Yiping Huang, "Can China Escape the Middle Income Trap?," *China Economic Journal* 9, no. 1 (2016): 1–17.
2. International Monetary Fund, *China's Economic Outlook*, August 9, 2019.
3. *World Bank website*, "China Overview," January 9, 2021, https://www.worldbank.org/en/country/china/overview.
4. Derek Scissors, "A Stagnant China in 2040, Briefly," *American Enterprise Institute*, March 16, 2020.
5. Andrea Boltho and Maria Weber, "Did China Follow the East Asian Development Model?" *The European Journal of Comparative Economics* 6, no. 2 (2018): 267–86, https://pdfs.semanticscholar.org/a23d/717e19ca011b92b2d05309b79579a0952c45.pdf
6. Roland Rajah and Alyssa Long, *Revising Down the Rise of China* (The Lowy Institute, March 14, 2022).
7. Ricardo Hausmann, "Why Are Rich Countries Democratic?," *Project Syndicate*, March 26, 2014.
8. Daron Acemoglu and James A. Robinson, *Why Nations Fail: The Origins of Power, Prosperity, and Poverty* (New York: Crown Publishing, 2012); Dani Rodrik, "The Myth of Authoritarian Growth," *Project Syndicate*, August 9, 2010.
9. Min Zhu, Longmei Zhang, and Daoju Peng, "China' Productivity Convergence and Growth Potential," IMF Working Paper 19/263, 2019.
10. Arthur Kroeber, "Xi Jinping's Ambitious Agenda for Economic Reform in China," *Brookings*, November 17, 2013.
11. Chris Buckley and Steven Lee Myers, "China's Legislature Blesses Xi's Indefinite Rule. It Was 2,958 to 2," *The New York Times*, March 11, 2018.
12. *South China Morning Post*, "How Leading Small Groups Help Xi Jinping and Other Party Leaders Exert Power," January 20, 2014.
13. *BBC News*, "China's Anti-corruption Campaign Expands with New Agency," March 20, 2018.
14. Philip Wen and Christian Shepherd, "China Cranks Propaganda, Xi Jinping's Cult of Personality into Overdrive Ahead of Party Congress," *Business Insider*, October 12, 2017.
15. *South China Morning Post*, "Human Rights under Xi 'worst since Tiananmen Crackdown': Amnesty," November 17, 2017.

16. David Schambaugh, "Contemplating China's Future," *Washington Quarterly* 39, no. 3 (Fall 2016): 121–30.

17. *China File*, "Does Xi Jinping Represent a Return to the Mao Era?" June 16, 2015.

18. Carl Minzer, *End of An Era* (New York: Oxford University Press, 2018).

19. Gene Tidrick, "Productivity Growth and Chinese Industries," *World Bank*, SWP 761, July 2010.

20. Enrico Marelli and Marcello Singorelli, "Employment, Productivity, and Models of Growth in the EU," *International Journal of Manpower* 31, no. 7 (2010), 732–54.

21. Norwegian Energy and Environment Consortium, "China's Productivity Imperative," 2012. As of August 5, 2020, http://www.neec.no/uploads/China-Productivity-Imperative_en[1].pdf.

22. Barry Eichengreen, Donghyun Park, and Kwanho Shin, "When Fast Growing Economies Slow Down: International Evidence and Implications for China," National Bureau of Economic Research, Working Paper, No. 16919, March 2011.

23. *Reuters*, "Productivity Stagnant Despite Global Stimulus: WEF," October 8, 2019.

24. OECD, *The New Development Traps*, 2019.

25. Pierre-Richard Agenor and Otaviano Canuto, "Middle Income Growth Traps," World Bank, Policy Research Paper, No. 6210, World Bank, 2012, 4.

26. *Washington Post*, "China's Workforce is Expected to Start Shrinking in Next Few Years," May 31, 2011.

27. *Wall Street Journal*, "Rising Wages Pose Dilemma for China," May 17, 2013.

28. *Financial Times*, "China Locked into Investment-Led Growth by GDP Targets," July 22, 2019.

29. Zhu, Zhang, and Peng, "China' Productivity Convergence and Growth Potential."

30. Eva Paus, "Escaping the Middle Income Trap: Innovate or Perish," Asian Development Bank Institute, No. 685, March 2017.

31. Agenor and Canuto, "Middle Income Growth Traps," 4.

32. *Xinhua*, "CPC Announces Decision on Comprehensive Reform," November 13, 2013.

33. Michael Pettis, "How Much Investment Is Optimal?" *Carnegie Endowment for International Peace*, June 10, 2013.

34. Paul Sabaltier and Christopher Weible, "The Advocacy Coalition Framework: Innovations and Clarifications," in *Theories of the Policy Process*, ed. Paul Saultier (New York: Routledge Press, 2017).

35. Richard Doner and Ben Ross Schneider, "The Middle Income Trap: More Politics than Economics," *World Politics* 68, no. 4 (2016): 608–44.

36. Alejandro Foxley and Fernando Sossdorf, *Making the Transition: From Middle-Income to Advanced Economies* (Carnegie Endowment for International Peace, 2011), 2.

37. Juan Linz, *Totalitarian and Authoritarian Regimes* (London: Lynne Rienner Publishers, 2000).

38. Scott E. Robinson, Foun'say Caver, Kenneth J. Meier, and Laurence J. O'Toole Jr., "Explaining Policy Punctuations: Bureaucratization and Budget Change," *American Journal of Political Science* 51, no. 1 (January 2007): 140–50.

39. Ibid.

40. Bruce Bueno de Mesquita, Alastair Smith, Randolph M. Siverson, and James D. Morrow, *The Logic of Political Survival* (Cambridge, MA: MIT Press, 2005).

41. Sean Gailmard, "Accountability and Principal Agent Theory," in *Oxford Handbook of Public Accountability* (Oxford, 2014).

42. Rachel Augustine Potter, "Slow-Rolling, Fast-Tracking, and the Pace of Bureaucratic Decisions in Rulemaking," *The Journal of Politics* 79, no. 3 (July 2017): 841–55.

43. Frank R. Baumgartner, Christian Breunig, Christopher Green-Pedersen, Bryan D. Jones, Peter B. Mortensen, Michiel Nutemans, and Stefaan Walgrave. "Punctuated Equilibrium in Comparative Perpective," *American Journal of Political Science* 53, no. 3 (2009): 603–20.

44. Doner and Schneider, "The Middle Income Trap."

Chapter 1

The Theory of the Enabling Condition

The theory of the "enabling condition" states that governments require favorable political conditions to carry out major intensive growth policy initiatives. The theory defines those conditions in terms of a strong central leadership, weak elite opposition, and a cohesive public. The theory explains that this configuration best permits central leaders to compel recalcitrant elites to implement policies they might otherwise oppose. However, this configuration is extremely difficult to achieve, and its realization is often fragile and short-lived.

This chapter will explain the theory. It will clarify the type of major economic policy initiative that is the focus of this book. It will then review the three groups of political actors and how their interactions shape prospects for policy implementation. The chapter will also review the set of cases that will be analyzed in subsequent chapters.

MAJOR ECONOMIC POLICY INITIATIVES

The theory aims to explain the political challenge associated with the implementation of contentious economic policy initiatives. Why economic policy? The most compelling reason is the one cited by many governments themselves: Successful economic performance is essential for the legitimacy of many modern states. Less astute leaders often arrive at a similar point when other forms of legitimacy, such as ideology, have been exhausted. Economic activity generates the resources with which governments can address many issues. For authoritarian regimes, gains from economic income fund the autocrat's standard of living and those of his cronies. It also pays for the security apparatus that suppresses opposition and the clientelist policies that can keep the public quiescent.

Another reason to focus on economic policy is related to the study of contemporary China. Chinese leaders under Xi have affirmed the importance of economic development as a basis of political legitimacy.[1] Although autocrats have historically pursued many different forms of political legitimacy, this book will examine single-party authoritarian regimes that prioritized development. A common feature of all the cases selected for analysis in this book, therefore, is the stated intent of the relevant autocrats to improve economic growth as a means of keeping the ruling party in power.

How much of a political challenge an economic initiative might pose depends on the situation. Not all economic policies carry the same political risks. Some may provide a modest boost in wealth with little disruption to the status quo, while others may promise larger gains but at the risk of severe dislocation. In his analysis of policy implementation in developing countries, Peter Cleaves, a professor at the University of Texas, observed that policy implementation tends to be easier for initiatives that feature simple technical features, incremental change, and clear, single-subject goals of short duration. By contrast, policy implementation tends to be more difficult when it entails complex issues, comprehensive change, and multiple, sometimes unclear goals of longer duration. He observed, "The more problematic the intrinsic features of the reform, the greater the amount of power that will be required for implementation."[2]

What I call "minor policy adjustments" are proposed measures that simply require adjustments in existing structures, mechanisms, and policy tools to achieve their goals. These do not require changes to the existing political or social structures of a society and pose no fundamental challenge to the nature of the economy. They are so minor, in fact, that frequently, top leaders do not get involved at all. Instead, they delegate the necessary decisions to relevant technicians and bureaucratic specialists. Examples include minor adjustments in monetary and fiscal policy. While these minor changes to economic policy may pose little danger to an autocrat's rule, they carry the disadvantage of offering only modest improvements to the economic situation. There is only so much a shift in interest rates can do, after all, to improve an economy burdened by obsolete, inefficient industries, rampant corruption, and crippling debt.

At the opposite end, major structural reforms could unlock dramatic economic gains. The possibility for gain may be greatest for countries hampered by gross inefficiencies, such as sclerotic industries, underutilized labor and capital, large working-age populations locked in low-productivity sectors like agriculture, and scarce capital squandered on non-productive uses. However, the political and social change required to realize this potential could prove profoundly destabilizing. At the most extreme end, a society may be so burdened by ossified political arrangements, obsolete technology, corrupt, predatory elites, and inefficient labor practices that an overhaul of the country's political and social system may be required. If radical enough, the changes could result in a social and political revolution. In their studies of the revolutions in France, China, Russia, and others, scholars Barrington Moore, Theda Skocpol, and Charles Tilley focused precisely on the nexus between economic imperatives and obsolete political structures as drivers of social upheaval.[3]

Between the two extremes lies a form of major economic policy change that promises to unlock growth, but only after enacting significant and potentially far-reaching political and social changes. This "major" form of policy requires changes in aspects of a country's political and government structures but does not require regime change. The changes, if implemented, could be compatible with the country's political system and might even strengthen it. For such major policy changes, there may be hundreds of actors, involving government agencies, companies, and nongovernmental groups. Implementation could take several years or more from the moment central leaders formulate a proposal. There may be overlapping efforts to address the same issue. Another complication is that major policy changes may entail disputes between different social groups. Such disputes might involve deeply held values, conflicting interests, and large amounts of money.[4] Scholars have documented the many ways that powerful interest groups can block the implementation of major policy initiatives.[5] The multisector changes thus may not be severe enough to trigger a social revolution, but they almost certainly entail some degree of political conflict, owing to the fact that beneficiaries of non-productive economic practices tend to resist initiatives that threaten their privileges and status.

Major economic policies may focus on extensive or intensive growth, but I will focus on those related to intensive growth. Such initiatives seek to upgrade the existing mode of economic activity into a more efficient and profitable mode. Another way to state it is that the proposed major policy initiatives, or major intensive growth initiatives, regard improvements to productivity as a primary goal.

Major intensive growth initiatives may feature multiple sectors, including potentially the government, industry, finance, the judicial system, and society. They may include some extensive growth measures but generally prioritize intensive growth. Implementation is expected to be especially contentious and may feature fierce political feuding. The scale and scope of the multisector policy initiatives outlined by Chinese leaders led by Xi Jinping at the Third Plenum of the 18th Party Congress in 2013 fit well within this category of "major" policy initiatives (table 1.1).

Table 1.1 Various Levels of Policy Changes to Improve Economic Performance

Level of Proposed Change	*Potential Political Disruption*	*Policy Changes Required*	*Potential Scale of Economic Gains*	*Method of Implementation*
Minor	Little to none	Economic	Modest	Technical adjustment of existing policies
Major	Significant	Economic, government, political, societal	Major	Central led overhaul of economy and governance while preserving basic political system
Revolutionary	Destabilizing	Economic, government, political, societal	Major	Radical restructuring of society, politics, and economy

Source: Author's definitions, Cleaves, Sautier, and Bunker.

Other examples of single party authoritarian regimes that pursued primarily intensive growth policies include the Doi Moi reforms in Vietnam in the 1980s and Deng Xiaoping's economic initiatives in China in the 1990s (chapter 2). It may be the case, of course, that central leaders underestimate the scale and scope of changes required. Indeed, if society's economic, political, and social structures are ossified enough, the distinction between "major" and "revolutionary" change may prove devastatingly illusory, as the Soviet Union's Mikhail Gorbachev painfully discovered (chapter 6).

THE POLITICAL ACTORS

The theory of the enabling condition focuses on the political interactions of three groups of actors: The central leadership, elites, and the public (table 1.2). The central leadership consists of the top decision-makers. In single party authoritarian regimes, this means the autocrat. But it also includes senior leaders and staff located in proximity to the autocrat who are responsible for overseeing the implementation of relevant policies. The central leadership provides the main impetus for the proposed major economic policy initiative.

Elites are the privileged political and economic individuals outside the central leadership whose income depends in part on the access provided by their position or connection to government offices. This includes the party and state officials at the provincial and local level governments who administer state-owned enterprises at both national and local levels, as well as the

Table 1.2 Political Actors and Role in Major Economics Policy Challenge

Political Actor	*Definition*	*Role in Major Economic Policy Implementation*
Central leadership	The top decision-maker, together with staff and allies in the central leadership organizations.	The central leadership develops the major policy initiative, provides direction, and oversees coordination.
Elites	The privileged individuals outside the central leadership who draw income in part through their association with the state.	Elites are responsible for policy implementation and may oppose policies that undermine their access to wealth and income.
Public	The individuals who do not belong to either of the previous two groups.	The public can provide or withhold political demand for economic change, and its involvement may be required for coordination.

Source: Definitions developed by author.

commercial entrepreneurs who depend on privileged access to state resources or permits.

The public consists of those individuals who do not belong to either the central leadership or the elites. The public can play an important role in providing or withholding support for the intensive growth initiative. The subsequent sections explain how the interactions of these political actors shape the prospects for successful policy implementation (see table 1.2).

THE IMPORTANCE OF A STRONG CENTRAL LEADERSHIP

Studies of policy processes have generally agreed on the importance of strong leadership for contentious policies. Where leadership is lacking, prospects dim considerably.[6] A study of post-Soviet Russia, for example, regarded the "strategic priority of reforms for the political leadership" as especially important for the implementation of policies.[7] Similarly, an analysis of Chinese officials who did not enforce centrally directed requirements to provide local social insurance to coal miners cited a lack of pressure from higher level authorities as a top factor.[8]

The theory of the "enabling condition" states that the central leadership must be *strong* enough to both deter coup attempts and to compel subordinate officials to support policies they might otherwise oppose. The strength of the central leadership depends on several key factors. First and foremost, the central leadership should have a firm grip on the nation's security forces. Control of the military and internal security forces is vital for two reasons. First, it denies elites the option of coopting the armed forces. Second, control of the military and security forces provides the central leadership with a credible threat of violence if elites continue to defy the central leadership. The threat of arrest and worse can motivate elites to carry out policies they personally oppose if they believe noncompliance will lead to even worse outcomes.

It is rare for any central leader to exercise total command, in the sense that every military and police unit perfectly obeys his commands. But a strong central leadership should exercise a dominant influence, with his authority respected and most of these organizations generally compliant. It is also rare for a central leader to be utterly devoid of authority among the security forces. Even the weakest autocrat can usually count on a palace guard. But a weak leader's control would be partial at best, retaining the loyalty of a small minority of security forces. In a situation featuring weak central leadership, large portions of the nation's security forces may operate autonomously or may be receptive to overtures by rival elites.

Control of a nation's security forces is not enough to ensure elites will carry out policies. As University of Washington professor Joel Migdal has pointed out, the appearance of a powerful state equipped with a well-armed military and ruthless security forces frequently belies state weakness in many developing countries. Real power often rests with influential regional powerholders who can defy the will of central governments with impunity. A fundamental struggle in developing countries (a category that includes most single party authoritarian states) often revolves around whether the authority of the central leadership or that of a regional power holder predominates over a given area. In a state featuring a fairly unified bureaucracy characterized by standardized rules, laws, and regulations nationwide, chances are better that the central leadership's directives will be obeyed. By contrast, in a situation in which the bureaucracy is fragmented and in which subnational or large parts of the national bureaucracy operate on rules, norms, and principles inconsistent with other parts of the government, policy implementation is likely to be more difficult. Such a fractured state facilitates noncompliance by elites, since they can easily exploit the conflicting rule sets to their advantage.

Thus, a key measure of the strength of the central leadership centers on the nature of its relationship with the various national-level ministries and subnational governments. To the extent the entire government adheres to common rules, norms, and standards, the central leadership's strength will be enhanced. Bureaucratic elites and their allies will find it more difficult to exploit bureaucratic tactics to evade accountability and defy directives. By contrast, in the case of weak central control over the government, the central leader's influence may extend partially to some aspects of sub-national governments. Much of the country's bureaucracies will appear to operate with little coordination and may routinely resist or ignore central directives.

A third measure of strength for the central leadership rests in the degree of discipline in the ruling political party. A defining feature of single party authoritarian political regimes is the dominant role played by a political party, often one characterized by adherence to some ideological identity. A Leninist-style political party penetrates and controls all parts of the government and many aspects of social and economic life. An autocrat who exerts a dominant influence in the political party is one whose authority is widely respected and who can expect compliance from most of the party's members. In this situation, there is general unity in the party and a fairly sturdy level of discipline and cohesion, with few branches acting autonomously or in contravention of the central leadership's will. By contrast, a weak central leadership will exert a partial and incomplete authority within the ruling party. In such a situation, much of the party organization may appear disorganized and chaotic, with unclear or contested authority, and with many branches operating semiautonomously. A chaotic political party lowers the cost of elite defiance of the central leadership's will.

In a single party authoritarian regime, it may seem that control of the government and the political party are one and the same thing. After all, the party controls the government. In some cases, the government may be so weak and dependent on the party that this may well be the case. But in more developed societies, such as those found in many middle-income countries, the strength of the party's vitality and discipline may be distinguished from the operation of the government bureaucracy. There are many examples, after all, in which a cohesive, unified government bureaucracy coexists with a ruling political party that experiences considerable internal turmoil or that has atrophied considerably. Indeed, one of the case studies examined in this chapter, that of KMT-led Taiwan in the 1970s (chapter 5), provides an example of a political party that experienced an erosion of its capacities even as the government bureaucracies became more firmly established. The converse of a strong party and a weak and poorly institutionalized government is also plausible, especially in the poorest countries that may have just established their independence, as happened in China in the years immediately following the CCP's ascent to power.

In short, a central leadership with a firm grip on the nation's security forces and that exercises fairly uniform authority across national ministries and subnational governments as well as the ruling party is best positioned to press elites to carry out policies that they may be tempted to resist. By contrast, weak central leadership makes it easier for elites to resist passively. If threatened, elites may also feel emboldened by the weakness of the central leadership to risk a coup or other violent countermeasures. However, evaluating this prospect through the lens of the central leadership's strength is inadequate. A more accurate assessment of the central leadership's prospects will depend, in turn, in part on the strength of the elite opposition.

THE IMPORTANCE OF WEAK ELITE OPPOSITION

Scholars have long noted the significance of elite dispositions for policy outcomes.[9] Massachusetts Institute for Technology professor Daron Acemoglu and James A. Robinson, an economist at the University of Chicago, pointed out that political elites often block beneficial economic and institutional change due to fears that such changes will cost them political power and future rents. Elites resist upgrading policies, in other words, not necessarily because their economic interests are adversely affected by proposed policies but because their political power and social status may be threatened.[10] Political scientists Ben Schneider and Richard Doner similarly noted the role of powerful interest groups and elites in determining policy outcomes. They described examples in which elites became "entrenched in their own traditional business strategies and in politics" and wielded power to "maintain institutions favorable to their existing businesses."[11] In his book, *Weak States, Strong Societies*, Joel Migdal observed that ambitions to carry out extensive economic and governance reforms have often foundered upon the resistance of powerful subnational actors such as tribal chiefs, local powerholders, or other subnational elites. For many developing countries, an apparently all powerful, intrusive state apparatus masks the reality of weakness. Real power rests with the strata of political and economic elites who mediate between the central government and the public.[12]

The theory of the enabling condition states that the relative strength of the elite opposition can directly affect both the prospects for successful policy implementation and the prospects for violence. A powerful and well-resourced elite may feel confident enough to passively resist the central leadership's directives, or they may peacefully neutralize such directives through measures such as lobbying or bribes. In extreme cases, they may even be tempted to try violent means, such as a coup, to assert their dominance over the central leadership. By contrast, a weak elite opposition may have little ability to defy the central leadership and a more palpable fear of the consequences of noncompliance.

Evaluating the strength of the elite opposition involves several considerations. First and foremost is the relative strength of the elite. This may be judged in part by their access to resources. An elite that controls a huge and disproportionate share of the nation's wealth is better positioned to defend its interests. With ample resources, elites can mobilize client supporters, bribe top-level officials, and perhaps recruit officials in the security forces or military. Ample resources could enable the elite to also fund political demonstrations, propaganda, and other activities to frustrate the central leadership's aims.

Elites can augment their power through cooperation. Collusion can extend vertically as well as horizontally. Horizontal collusion consists of cooperation between government, political, and economic elites at roughly the same level of government, primarily for the purpose of self-enrichment. Collusion differs from routine bureaucratic coordination in that collusion aims principally at self-enrichment and tends to distort the normal functioning of institutions. By contrast, normal bureaucratic cooperation and coordination tend to adhere to existing institutions and serve the interests of relevant bureaucracies and governments.

In vertical collusion, elites collaborate hierarchically for purposes of self-enrichment. Elites could, for example, recruit higher level patrons. As with horizontal collusion, vertical collusion differs from normal patron-client ties in that collusion tends to be corrosive to the political system, as a major purpose of such illicit collaboration is to evade law, discipline, and accountability for purposes of self-enrichment.[13] By contrast, the patron-client ties that appear in many countries may not fall into this characterization if they operate in a manner that affirms existing political institutions.

In vertical collusion, high-level patrons can protect their clients from discipline and provide privileged access or exceptions to the central leadership's policies. By contrast, highly differentiated elites with a low level of collusion could be more vulnerable to divide and conquer tactics in which the central leadership sets one group of elites against the others. A lack of vertical collusion also leaves lower-level officials more vulnerable to discipline and control from the central leadership.

The share of a nation's resources and the degree of collusion can provide a sense of the relative strength of the elites in a country. However, what counts for purposes of assessing prospects for successful policy implementation is whether the elites deploy their strength against the central leadership or not. The *disposition* of elites toward a proposed major policy initiative, therefore, matters a great deal to their potential *opposition*. Some economic initiatives to improve an economy's performance may require fewer concessions from elites and thus provoke little resistance. For example, a policy initiative that reallocates labor from the countryside to factories may be compatible with a high level of elite rent-seeking and corruption. China in the 1980s provides an example in which elites were generally disposed to support pro-market reforms from which they benefited disproportionately. By contrast, a case in which central leaders prioritize intensive growth policies in part by shutting down SOEs that provide a major source of rent for elites may result in more of a zero-sum standoff between the central leaders and elites.

The disposition of elites introduces an important risk that deserves emphasis. An apparent lack of opposition to the central leadership's upgrading agenda may miscommunicate the real danger. An elite that controls most of the nation's resources and features extensive collusion may offer "weak" resistance to the central leadership's growth strategy if the economy's prospects do not threaten their rent. But this apparent submissiveness will be an illusion. The elites are strong; it is merely their disposition that appears conciliatory. This possibility is illustrated in the case study of China during Deng Xiaoping's final years (chapter 2). Deng's initiatives to promote a socialist market economy enjoyed considerable support among subnational elites and their partners in the commercial sector due to the anticipated opportunities for self-enrichment. The central leadership regarded these elites as political allies in the struggle against a hardline faction within the central leadership. Moreover, Deng's growth strategy was compatible with a high level of elite corruption, which resulted in a low level of tension between the central leadership and subnational elites. But the increasing share of wealth and collusion that the elite experienced generated a powerful array of interest groups who would later flex their muscles when the central leadership changed course.

It is possible for the central leadership and elite opposition to both be "strong." A strong central leader could bolster his control of the nation's security forces and carry out measures to improve coordination among levels of government as well as party discipline. At the same time, elites who have amassed enormous resources and practiced a high level of collusion could decide to oppose the central leadership's policy initiatives. In such a situation, the central leadership could find itself in a stalemate with strong elite opposition. China under Xi Jinping from 2012 to 2022 provides an example of such a situation (chapter 4). To overcome strong elite opposition, the central leadership needs the help of the public.

THE IMPORTANCE OF PUBLIC COHESIVENESS

Researchers have long noted the importance of the public in the implementation of contentious policies.[14] Scholars have emphasized, for example, the importance of public demand for difficult and costly intensive growth policies that may not provide an obvious immediate benefit but can improve an economy's long-term prospects.[15] Doner and Schneider similarly noted that fragmentation within the business and labor sectors could undermine efforts by central leaders to build broad coalitions in favor of costly upgrading reforms. They observed that in middle-income countries, fragmentation is "both deeper than in most other cases and more consequential." Fragmentation means that firms and workers in different parts of the economy have "different strategies and therefore different interests regarding key upgrading reforms."[16] Renown political scientist Ken Jowitt's research on Leninist states highlighted how the Soviet Union's failure to politically integrate the populace resulted in a fatal weakening of Moscow's ability to implement needed economic reforms.[17]

An engaged public can help the central leadership by providing a strong demand signal for change. A politically mobilized public can signal its disapproval of elite misbehavior. Strong public support can also help the central leadership deter elites from risking coups or other violent actions.

Autocrats in charge of developing countries have unusual features that further underscore the need for public support and yet make efforts to access that support problematic. Their dependence on the elites to run the government bureaucracy leaves them highly vulnerable to manipulation by the same individuals. Moreover, a lack of independent institutions or powerful groups outside the party and state bureaucracy provides little ability to balance elites.

The central leadership's dependence on elites is compounded further by a general preference among autocracies to keep the public depoliticized. A citizenry disinterested in politics, after all, is less likely to question the ruling party's monopoly on power. And in autocracies within developing countries, the proximity of the local party boss to the public raises the likelihood that much of the public will be organized by clientelist ties and thus may hesitate to back the central leadership against the patrons who have the greatest ability to impact their lives. Attempts to politicize the public thus risk provoking a destabilizing process that could quickly escalate beyond the control of the autocrat. This is especially the case in volatile situations featuring widespread discontent over diminishing economic prospects, which is likely to be the case when embattled central leaders ponder the imperative of intensive growth policies.

The mobilization potential, or "cohesiveness," of the public provides a sense of the likelihood that the autocrat can successfully elicit the active support of the populace. Cohesiveness and fragmentation can occur economically, politically, or socially. Economic cohesiveness is the most important factor for assessing a country's potential implementation of intensive growth policies. Economic cohesiveness may be judged by the state of labor and business. A cohesive work force is one characterized by formal labor, that is, jobs that are taxed and in turn provide access to benefits in part from the central government. A work force characterized by formality has incentives to support agreements between government and business, such as those relevant to economic upgrading. Experts have highlighted how labor may be fragmented by informality, that is, labor that is not taxed or registered. A large informal sector impairs the central government's ability to mobilize popular support to carry out contentious policies for several reasons. For informal workers, the rules set by the central government matter little, since in their experience, formal laws and rules can be, and are, negotiated, bent, or violated. Moreover, informal workers learn that "who you know" matters more than the laws. This undermines efforts by the central government to rely on formal laws and rules to exert its influence over the populace. It also encourages workers to prioritize the patronage of local officials over the authority of a distant central government. An economy organized along the lines of informality could thus be expected to favor a dynamic of clientelism, which reinforces the power of local cadres and their associates and discourages the formation of strong public ties with central authorities.[18]

Fragmentation among businesses can similarly impair efforts by the central leadership to marshal support for its upgrading agenda. A cohesive business sector is one made of mostly domestic companies with strong linkages between upstream and downstream industries. By contrast, a fragmented business sector features many companies with few linkages with each other and may include a large foreign investor presence. Foreign companies generally have little interest in handing over their profits to pay for social welfare benefits or fund the host nation's efforts to upgrade its economy.[19]

Political cohesiveness occurs when the public has a readily available way to meaningfully participate in politics. While elections offer one way, there are other possibilities. Authoritarian leaders can carry out a range of political activities to marshal public support, intimidate political enemies, and involve the public in major policy initiatives. In China, Mao Zedong frequently used tactics such as the "mass line," in which cadres claimed to articulate the public's "true needs" by organizing and directing their political activities. By contrast, a politically fragmented populace is one that lacks meaningful ways to participate in the nation's politics. A fragmented society may be organized around principles of clientelism. Negative signs of fragmentation might also be seen in widespread anti-system behavior, such as sporadic violence, spontaneous protests, and other unsanctioned violent or mob behaviors.

Finally, social cohesiveness refers to the sense of solidarity among the public. Social cohesiveness can be related to class, ethnicity, religion, or culture. A low level of inequality can promote a sense of solidarity and shared identity among citizens. By contrast, high levels of inequality are likely to fuel bitterness and anger toward the state, as well as alienation and distrust toward society. A shared ethnic, religious, and/or cultural identity can facilitate solidarity and cohesiveness. By contrast, hostile polarization between competing ethnic, religious, or social groups can undermine efforts to build a common coalition in favor of change.

In sum, a public experiencing a high level of cohesiveness is likely to have strong economic cohesiveness but also robust political and social cohesiveness. A severely fragmented public will be economically fragmented and experience significant political and social fracture as well.

Paradoxically, a high level of cohesiveness does not guarantee that the public will support the central leadership if mobilized. For autocrats, the risks of mobilization can be substantial, which is why many prefer to keep the people demobilized. First, there is the risk that politically mobilized citizens may not support the central leadership but instead align with elites against the central leadership. This possibility confronted central leaders in Taiwan in the late 1970s (chapter 5). Political mobilization could also unleash long-held popular pressures that tear the country apart and initiate civil conflict. The disasters that befell the Soviet Union following the Glasnost reforms illustrate this danger (chapter 6).

Central leaders may thus urgently need the involvement of a mobilized public to help them achieve their goals, but they have sound reasons to dread doing so. A central leadership that lacks popular backing in its efforts to curtail the power of elites faces a high likelihood of failure, as the elites can manipulate their inherent political advantages to stymie policies they oppose. China's situation led by Hu Jintao (chapter 3) illustrates how a country's dependence on unsustainable growth models could lead to a feedback loop in which weak central leaders with weak ties to the public find themselves ever more dependent on powerful elites. Yet efforts to mobilize the public carry their own risks, as Gorbachev learned to his dismay (chapter 6).

HOW THE ENABLING CONDITION WORKS

The theory of the enabling condition states that central leaders require strong central leadership, weak elite opposition, and a cohesive public to successfully implement a major economic policy initiative designed in large part to improve intensive growth. The enabling condition allows the central leadership to compel elite compliance in a manner that minimizes the risk of political violence. A strong central leadership is better positioned to deter elite defiance and punish noncompliance. Weak elite opposition lowers the risk of political violence because elites are incentivized to choose compliance over resistance. A cohesive public providesa demand signal for change and a check on elite power. If the central leader can direct the public's involvement, then their support could pressure elites to carry out the assigned tasks and deter them from challenging the central leadership.

The public's role grows in importance according to the relative strength of the elite opposition. The more powerful the elite opposition, the more urgently the central leadership requires public support as a balancing influence. By contrast, a central leadership that confronts a weak elite opposition may not need to mobilize public support or may find a modest activation of political involvement sufficient to overcome his political adversaries. An example of this possibility is illustrated in the case study on China's experience under Deng Xiaoping in the 1990s (chapter 2).

Central leaders thus face a formidable challenge in shaping the political factors into an enabling condition. Countries embarking on economic upgrades rarely begin with an ideal situation and, in fact, are likely to face inauspicious political conditions. Elite actors in particular may have a strong incentive to perpetuate the status quo because it ensures central leaders cannot dominate them. Central leaders thus must find a way to change the value of political factors, but in a manner that minimizes the risk of political violence and overall instability.

Achievement of an enabling condition is not, however, a *sufficient* condition for successful policy implementation. Other factors play a role in determining whether the major policy initiative will achieve the intended goals. The policies must be well conceived and economically feasible, for example. However, the enabling condition is a *necessary* ingredient. Leaders who fail to achieve a favorable political situation as defined by this theory are unlikely to successfully implement major, intensive growth initiatives.

Timing is important. If the enabling condition has been achieved, then prospects are promising. If, by contrast, the central leadership begins the period of policy implementation with a less than ideal configuration, prospects are dimmer but not necessarily lost. The central leader has a window of time to shape the political factors to resemble those of the enabling condition. At the latest, success in building an enabling condition halfway through the projected implementation time frame offers the best prospects. This is because policy implementation is likely to be incomplete or erratic at best until the enabling condition is achieved.

Failure to achieve the enabling condition dooms policy implementation for two possible reasons. The first is that the central leader may back off his policy agenda in the face of stiff opposition. Compromise with elites can buy political stability, but at the cost of marginal to no improvement in the economic situation. The second possibility is that political conflict and instability halt policy implementation. Running roughshod over elite opposition could result in political violence, which in turn compels the central leader to abandon the policies and focus instead on restoring stability.

Any combination of the three political factors other than the enabling condition carries one or both of these risks. This point can be illustrated by analyzing in closer detail what these variations might entail. Table 1.3 lays out the possible combinations.

Table 1.3 Possible Starting Combinations of Political Factors and Predicted Outcomes

Central Leadership	*Elite Opposition*	*Public Cohesiveness*	*Predicted Outcome for Policy Implementation*	*Analysis and Example*
Strong	Strong	Cohesive	Failure	Risk of civil war as central leadership and elites mobilize support
Strong	Weak	Cohesive	Success	Enabling configuration (e.g., Taiwan case study, chapter 5)
Strong	Strong	Fragmented	Failure	Stalemate in struggle between central leadership, and elites (e.g., China case study under Xi Jinping, chapter 4)
Strong	Weak	Fragmented	Failure	Weak demand signal, low ability of public to help with policy coordination
Weak	Strong	Cohesive	Failure	Political mobilization of public could spiral out of control (e.g., Soviet Union case study, chapter 6)
Weak	Weak	Cohesive	Failure	Central leadership cleavages, society in transition, (China under Deng Xiaoping, chapter 2)
Weak	Strong	Fragmented	Failure	High risk of political conflict if central leadership tries to coerce elites (e.g., China under Hu Jintao, chapter 3)
Weak	Weak	Fragmented	Failure	Disintegrating or failed state

Source: Data summarized from preceding chapters.

In this table, there are two possible values for the first political factor, "central leadership:" "strong" or "weak." In the event of *weak* central leadership, *strong* elite opposition, and a *cohesive* public, the autocrat will be poorly positioned to overcome the elite opposition. The weakness of the central leadership makes it risky to carry out political mobilization. Due to their strength, elites are better positioned to exploit the mobilization potential of the public. The result is likely to be failed policy implementation and/or violence if the autocrat presses ahead. The case study of the Soviet Union under Gorbachev illustrates this possibility (chapter 6).

The combination of *weak* central leadership, *weak* elite opposition, and a *cohesive* public is relatively unusual for a single-party, authoritarian state, although the case of China in 1991 begins with this configuration (chapter 2). This suggests a situation of intense feuding or conflict involving central leaders. If this combination persists through the halfway point of the implementation period, prospects for successful policy implementation would dim, as the government would be poorly positioned to carry out long-term plans due to gridlock. Of course, Deng overcame this unpromising situation to build the enabling configuration.

The combination of *weak* central leadership, *weak* elite opposition, and a *fragmented* society suggests an even more chaotic society, perhaps one headed toward disintegration. A combination featuring *weak* central leadership, *strong* elite opposition, and a *fragmented* public would suggest dim prospects for successful policy implementation due to the ability of elites to defy the central leadership with little cost. The case of China under Hu Jintao illustrates this possibility (chapter 3).

There are also possible variations featuring a "strong" leadership beyond that of the enabling configuration, but each of these entails risks of either policy failure or destabilizing conflict. If the *strong* leadership faces *strong* elite opposition and a *cohesive* public, there is a high political risk that both the central leadership and elites will mobilize the public against each other as part of the central leadership's effort to compel elites to comply with a broad range of policies, including economics. The result could be severe political conflict or civil war. Another combination could be *strong* central leadership, *strong* elite opposition, and a f*ragmented* public. In this case, the autocrat would be unable to overcome elite resistance by itself. The fragmented state of the public would leave the central leadership little hope of mobilizing public support. The result is likely to be a stalemate between the central leadership and the elite opposition and disappointing policy implementation. The case of China under Xi Jinping analyzed in this study provides an example of such a situation (chapter 4). Another possibility could be *strong* central leadership, *weak* elite opposition, and a *fragmented* public. This combination favors the successful implementation of at least some policies. The main drawback is that the fragmented state of the public would probably result in a weak demand signal for the upgrading policies. As a result, the elite opposition need not be very strong to frustrate many of the policies. The outcome could be uneven or failed implementation of relevant policies.[20]

In sum, of all the possible combinations of the three political factors, the configuration represented by the "enabling combination" offers the most promising prospects for successful policy implementation. Subsequent chapters will illustrate these points in more detail.

Achieving the enabling condition is difficult, but even in the best cases, success is likely to be short-lived. Inevitably, the value of the different political factors changes. In fact, successful implementation of major economic upgrading policies may contribute directly to the dissolution of the enabling condition and the onset of a more problematic configuration. In the case of China in the 1990s, for example, the country experienced significant gains in productivity after successful implementation of the "socialist market" initiatives advocated by Deng Xiaoping. However, the improvements came at the cost of deepening public fragmentation, as tens of millions of SOE workers lost their jobs and moved into a rapidly expanding informal sector. The same policies also provided incredible opportunities for elites to enrich themselves, which increased their strength. It also contributed to a weakening of party discipline and of the central leadership's power relative to subnational governments (chapter 2).

Even if the central leadership successfully implements the major policy initiative, he must anticipate how to manage the effects of its imminent dissolution. The evolution to a suboptimal configuration of the political factors may be tolerable so long as the newly implemented growth strategy remains in place. However, inevitably, the possibilities of existing modes of growth will be exhausted. When that moment arrives, the central leadership will once again face a compelling incentive to rebuild the enabling conditions to carry out a new set of upgrading policies.

POLITICAL STRATEGIES

If the central leadership confronts a configuration that is anything other than the enabling condition, he might try to change it through political strategies. *Political strategies* consist of actions taken to strengthen the central leadership, overcome elite opposition, or improve the mobilization potential of the people. The advantage of political strategies is that the central leadership can control them. The disadvantage is that in general, the effect tends to be modest, owing to the inherent constraints posed by each strategy. The constraints stem from the fact that each of the political strategies carries risks of political destabilization or of impairing the implementation of policy.

To bolster the strength of the central leadership, for example, the central leader can amass power in the hands of his allies or his own person. He might purge rivals and remove officials deemed insufficiently loyal. He may direct measures to bolster his personal control over security forces. The leader could assign loyalists control of the propaganda apparatus and direct a cult of personality campaign. The main risk of this strategy, however, is that it could appear to many elites as highly threatening. The elites may in turn be motivated to take preventive measures to preserve their lives, perhaps through a coup. Domestic or international audiences may regard the changes as illegitimate or excessive. This may reduce the willingness of the public to support the central leadership.

To weaken elite opposition, a central leadership might rely on coercion. This could entail both legal and extra-legal measures to remove, detain, or intimidate powerful elites. Naturally, the elites are likely to regard such measures as threatening and might be willing to risk violence to protect themselves. In desperate situations, they might consider coups, civil war, or assassination. To minimize the risk of political opposition and violence, the central leadership needs to firmly control the security forces.

Central leaders might try to enhance the potential for public mobilization through political liberalization. This involves loosening government control, usually by permitting greater media and individual political liberties, reducing repression, and encouraging the public to form social and civic groups to advocate for their own interests. In a society featuring elites too weak to exploit such a situation and a public that is highly cohesive, the strategy might result in a favorable potential for public mobilization. However, in situations featuring a powerful elite opposition and a fragmented public, the results of liberalization are likely to prove disappointing. This is because in such situations, a loosening of central control could merely strengthen subnational elites, who carry out a counter-mobilization of their clientelist networks against the central leadership.

Another strategy might be for central leaders to overcome strong elite opposition through administrative measures such as training, education, personnel promotion, and management practices. They might also try personnel shuffling, the appointment of loyalists, and other measures aimed at displacing the most die-hard opponents and coopting the rest. The advantage of this strategy is that the central leadership does not involve the public. Thus, a high degree of public fragmentation does not pose an obstacle. Another advantage is that this method minimizes the risks of political violence because it is far less threatening to elites. However, the disadvantage is that its success depends on the voluntary compliance of elites. Elites can simply feign compliance while refusing to carry them out in practice. This also carries a systemic risk. The central leadership's stated ambitions may raise public expectations that elite non-compliance completely undercuts, resulting in a serious and growing gap between the central leadership's stated policy goals and the reality of anemic implementation. The case of Hu Jintao's efforts to oversee major policy change in 2004 illustrates this peril (chapter 3). As his experience showed, a political strategy that focuses exclusively on converting elites offers poor prospects for the implementation of intensive growth policies.

Mass mobilization is another strategy. Here, the central leadership directs efforts to involve the public by applying pressure on cadres and elites. In authoritarian societies, this may involve "struggle sessions" led by grassroots cadres and party officials, demonstrations, rallies, and other political activities. The advantage here is that the public can add significant pressure on elites to comply with the central leadership's directives. The principal risk, however, is that a politicized public can easily spin out of control. Demands could escalate or even be turned against the central government, especially if elites are powerful enough to capture some of the party bureaucracy, such as the security forces and ideological apparatus, or if the public feels greater solidarity with elites than it does with the central leadership. Moreover, situations featuring powerful elites often include publics that have become deeply fragmented. The dependence of many citizens on clientelist relations with powerful elite patrons can render political mobilization extremely risky or simply ineffective.

Central leaders can employ more than one strategy at once, of course. In fact, political strategies to shape an enabling condition are more likely to be effective when combined than if employed alone. Employing multiple strategies at the same time could also allow a central leader to shape multiple factors at the same time.

Finally, political strategies to change the value of political factors may be affected by pressures unrelated to the pursuit of large-scale economic change. External pressures may drive leaders to pursue strategies that undermine prospects for successful policy change but nevertheless appear necessary for reasons of political survival. For example, the Soviet Union experienced severe pressure to generate economic revenue to fund its war in Afghanistan. Yet the war also strengthened the hand of the defense ministry, which refused to carry out reforms to reduce the overall burden of defense spending. The war indirectly strengthened the power of military elites and undercut Mikhail Gorbachev's efforts to curtail defense spending (chapter 6).

THE ROLE OF IDEOLOGY AND THE CENTRAL LEADER'S PERSONALITY

The theory of the enabling condition argues that the structure of political factors plays a crucial role in determining the prospects for successful policy implementation and the risks of political conflict. However, the value of these political factors does not determine the result. The role of ideology and identities also plays an important mediating role, especially in the single-party authoritarian regimes that are the focus of the study. The political strategies and tactics available to the central leadership are strongly shaped by their own ideology and the identities of involved groups. Highly ideological regimes may be better positioned to carry out a mass mobilization, as Mao Zedong did, but the same ideological commitments are also likely to lead to catastrophic policies. In pro-market regimes, the weakening of ideological commitment can avoid disastrous economic policies but also weaken the central leadership's ability to mobilize public support. How the central leadership defines its ideology also informs the priority it may place on placating versus attacking elites or in courting popular opinion. It's also possible in some cases that elites may advance their own ideology and identity, or ones may emerge among the public that prove to have more salience and appeal to the public than officially sanctioned ones. The case of Taiwan (chapter 5) provides an example in which identities and ideologies emerged among the public that lacked sanction by the KMT authorities.

The individual personality of the central ruler matters a great deal as well. In some cases, the personality of the top leader may shape available political strategies. Even if he possessed sufficient clout, a cautious leader averse to violence or conflict may prefer administrative methods to persuade recalcitrant elites, as Hu preferred (chapter 3). A more confident and shrewder leader in the same position, by contrast, might adopt more coercive measures, as Xi did (chapter 4).

CASE STUDY OVERVIEW

All five cases selected for this study's comparative analysis consist of a single-party authoritarian regime that sought to carry out a major economic upgrading initiative but achieved dissimilar results. Three of the cases involve the People's Republic of China. The fact that these cases involve the same country with the same political system offers some of the benefits of a controlled comparison. Of course, the controls are inexact since China's situation inevitably changes as time marches forward. However, a time series comparison does allow the possibility of analyzing variation in cases in which many factors remain consistent. In addition to the three cases involving China, two international cases examine Taiwan and the Soviet Union.

In each case, the ruling party featured a "Leninist" type of ruling party, in which the ruling party aspired to penetrate and control all government bureaucracies and principal social and economic organizations. In practice, the extent of control varied. The parties in each case also espoused an ideology as the basis for political discipline and organization. Again, the rigor of the ideology varied. Most of the cases I have selected consisted of communist parties, but one case (Taiwan) involved a noncommunist party that upheld a vaguely nationalist ideology yet shared some aspects of Leninist political organization.

The cases selected span specific periods in the history of each country. In each case, the senior leadership declared some ambition to carry out a major, multi-sector policy initiative designed to improve the country's economic performance. A common aspect of all these cases is that they all share, to varying degrees, the goal of improving productivity. However, the degree to which each policy initiative prioritized productivity over other goals varied. Moreover, the cases selected involved varying mixes of inclusive and extensive growth measures, which further complicates direct comparisons. In the case of Taiwan in 1974, for example, the government outlined an ambitious policy to improve the country's economic prospects by both improving productivity through intensive growth measures and by upgrading the country's infrastructure, which consisted primarily of major capital investments (i.e., extensive growth measures). By contrast, the case of the Soviet Union in 1985 featured a restructuring initiative that prioritized intensive growth policies, mainly because extensive methods had long been exhausted. In the cases of China under Hu Jintao and Xi Jinping, the government prioritized measures to improve intensive growth yet also maintained extensive growth methods to maintain employment and ensure growth targets.

Each case involved analysis over a period of roughly six years. Some initiatives may have required more than six years to fully realize the policy goals, and some less, but the nature of the proposed policy initiatives suggests that sufficient results should be apparent in each case to permit at least a preliminary evaluation after six years. In cases where the results prove disappointing, the reason should be primarily due to difficulties in the implementation process itself, not to a lack of adequate time to permit policy change or to flaws in the policy's design.

The beginning of the time span is roughly correlated with the start of an effort by the top leadership to carry out the designated major policy initiative. However, in some cases, the timing was adjusted to permit a closer analysis of key political developments that illuminate dynamics relevant to the theory of the enabling condition. In particular, I backed up the start of the analysis of the case of China in the 1990s to show how China arrived at the "enabling condition" in the years leading up to the implementation of relevant policies.

This chapter has provided an overview of the theory of the "enabling condition" and has sought to explain what this entails and why it is a necessary condition for autocrats seeking to upgrade the performance of their economies. This chapter has reviewed the general approach of comparative case study employed in the rest of the book. The following case studies and comparative analysis illustrate how the enabling condition proved necessary for successful policy implementation and how its absence contributed to the failure of major policy implementation efforts.

NOTES

1. *China Daily*, "Full Text of Xi Jinping's Report at 19th Party Congress," November 4, 2017. As of February 20, 2022: Full text of Xi Jinping's report at 19th CPC National Congress - China - Chinadaily.com.cn.

2. Peter Cleaves, "Implementation Amidst Scarcity and Apathy: Political Power and Policy Design," in *Politics and Policy Implementation in the Third World*, ed. Merilee Grindle (Princeton, NJ: Princeton University Press, 1980), 289.

3. Barrington Moore, *Social Origins of Dictatorship and Democracy* (New York: Beacon Press, 1993); Theda Skocpol, *States and Social Revolution: A Comparative Analysis of France, Russia, and China* (Cambridge, MA: Cambridge University Press, 2015); Charles Tilly, *Coercion, Capital, and European States, A.D. 990-1990* (New York: Wiley-Blackwell, 1992).

4. Paul Saultier, *Theories of the Policy Process* (New York: Westview Press, 2007), 3.

5. Stephen Bunker, "Policy Implementation in an Authoritarian State: The Case of Brazil," *Latin American Research Review* 18, no. 1 (1983): 33–58.

6. Saultier, *Theories of the Policy Process*, 16.

7. Vladimir Gel'man and Andrey Starodubtsev, "Opportunities and Constraints of Authoritarian Modernisation: Russian Policy Reforms in the 2000s," *Europe-Asia Studies* 68, no. 1 (2016): 97–117.

8. Jiajian Chen and Qiongwen Zhang, "Fluctuating Policy Implementation and Problems in Grassroots Governance," *The Journal of Chinese Sociology* 3, no. 7 (2016): 1–19.

9. Doner and Schneider, "The Middle Income Trap," 640.

10. Acemoglu and Robinson, *Why Nations Fail*.

11. Doner and Schneider, "The Middle Income Trap," 635.

12. Joel Migdal, *Weak States and Strong Societies* (Princeton, NJ: Princeton University Press, 1988).

13. Errol D'Souza, "Collusion in Government and Corruption," *The Journal of Interdisciplinary Economics* 21 (2009): 17–33.

14. Baumgartner et al., "Punctuated Equilibrium in Comparative Perpective."
15. Doner and Schneider, "The Middle Income Trap."
16. Ibid., 620.
17. Ken Jowitt, *New World Disorder: The Leninist Extinction* (Berkeley, CA: University of California Press, 1992).
18. Matt Ferchen, "Informality in China and Latin America: Comparisons and Interactions," *Carnegie-Tsinghua Center for Global Policy*, October 1, 2012.
19. Doner and Schneider, "The Middle Income Trap."
20. Melina Hernandez, "Democracy and Labor Market Outsides: The Political Consequences of Economic Informality" (Dissertation, Duke University, 2015).

Chapter 2

China 1991–1997

Deng Xiaoping's Triumph and a Toxic Political Legacy

This chapter examines the political interactions accompanying China's effort to improve the country's economic performance during the years 1991–1997. Conservative central leaders preferred a more cautious approach in the aftermath of the Tiananmen Square massacre, and Deng Xiaoping's proposed reforms appeared to have stalled in 1991. However, Deng outmaneuvered his foes, consolidated his grip on the military and party, and cultivated widespread latent support among sub-national elites and the public. By 1993, the central leadership under Deng achieved a favorable political situation resembling the "enabling condition." This political success facilitated the implementation of pro-market reforms over the ensuing years.

However, despite the triumph, Deng's success came at a heavy cost. The favorable political conditions that Deng achieved by 1993 began to disintegrate almost immediately. By 1997, Deng's policies had dramatically improved the country's economic performance, but it also directly contributed to the long-term weakening of central power, the strengthening of elites, and the fragmentation of the public. These features would pose an irritating but manageable problem so long as the country followed Deng's growth policies. However, when the country had exhausted its economic potential, central leaders would labor to overcome the disadvantages of their situation. Ironically, one of the most lasting legacies of the economic miracle from the late 1990s would be a toxic political landscape that severely constrained efforts by subsequent leaders to achieve their own economic successes.

BACKGROUND

In 1991, China's leadership remained deeply divided as it grappled with the fallout from an array of political and economic setbacks. Politically, the country was still reeling from the Tiananmen Square massacre in 1989. The domestic and international furor led supreme leader Deng Xiaoping to resign key leadership posts and also resulted in the downfall of his protégé Zhao Ziyang, a leading advocate of liberalizing reforms. Moreover, the CCP was shaken by the collapse of communist rule in East Europe and the disintegration of the Soviet Union.

Economically, the economic gains unleashed by de-collectivization and market-friendly reforms beginning around 1979 had ebbed. Amid slowing growth rates, the state-owned enterprise (SOE) sector proved an enormous burden, with losses accumulating rapidly and nonperforming loans accounting for 20 percent of outstanding loans.[1] But pressure to curtail costs encountered resistance from officials worried about the potentially massive losses in jobs and income among the urban populations.[2] Another problem centered on the state's two-tiered pricing system, which permitted officials to profit through arbitrage, spurring a public outcry. In 1988, senior leaders agreed on the need to transition to a market-based pricing system. However, authorities reversed course when a relaxation of price controls led to surging inflation.[3]

Senior leaders disagreed on the way forward. Deng Xiaoping remained the undisputed top leader, but the ailing 87-year-old's influence had suffered a blow from Tiananmen Square. When he fell sick in 1991, hardliners launched a political attack on "bourgeois liberalism" and "peaceful evolution" that criticized pro-reform politicians allied with Deng Xiaoping. In late 1991, it appeared hardliners had gained the upper hand. They rebuffed Deng's efforts to advance a robust market-friendly reform agenda into the Eighth Five-Year Plan, prescribed tighter political control, and pursued a more cautious economic agenda.[4] Beijing maintained relatively modest economic growth targets from 5 percent to 6 percent annually, a sharp reduction from the rapid growth rate of 11.2 percent that China experienced as late as 1988. They also opted to sharply limit the growth of the country's money supply and prioritize balancing the national budget.[5] Observers at the time anticipated a slowdown in the pace of pro-market policy changes.[6]

Deng Xiaoping rejected this prescription as too cautious. He argued that the party's best hopes of avoiding the fate of the Soviet Union lay in accelerating economic growth and thereby delivering concrete improvements in the standard of living for Chinese citizens. Accordingly, he urged a program of accelerated reform aimed at supercharging the economy. At the top of his list, he sought to roll back price controls and allow the market to set prices for many goods. He also recommended reducing the burden imposed by the state sector by privatizing large numbers of the SOEs. If implemented, these reforms could be expected to significantly improve the economy's performance. A World Bank memo published in 1992 regarded China's prospects as "extremely bright" if pro-market reforms were adopted. The report noted that the export sector had become the "strongest area of performance" and recommended measures to encourage its growth. At the same time, it urged authorities to rein in state credit, downsize the SOEs, and reform the fiscal and financial sectors to control deficits.[7] Deng's allies promoted similar policies in the lead-up to the Seventh Plenum in 1991, but they were defeated by conservatives who favored a more cautious path.

Developments Related to the Central Leadership

The debate over the way forward took place within the context of a country experiencing signs of internal disintegration. The problem of a weak central government owed to developments in the 1980s, when China decentralized economic policy and governance responsibilities to enable faster growth.[8] Although the central government maintained political control primarily through its management of personnel appointments, governments at the provincial level and below bore primary responsibility for coordinating relevant policies, providing public services, and making and enforcing laws within their jurisdictions.[9] By 1991, China had become one of the most fiscally decentralized countries in the world. Subnational governments accounted for about 70 percent of the government's budget, which exceeded that of large federal governments, including those of the United States (46 percent) and Russia (38 percent).[10]

While encouraging flexible decision-making to realize rapid economic growth, central authorities in the early 1990s betrayed anxiety about the increasing autonomy of the provinces. Symptomatic of the problem was the fact that wealthier provinces defied Beijing's demands to transfer resources to poorer provinces. In the face of such intransigence, the central government conceded and modified its demands. According to Richard Baum, a professor at the University of California, Los Angeles, this "retreat by Beijing in the face of provincial resistance was almost without precedent."[11] Interprovincial inequality accordingly began to grow around 1990, when coastal provinces experienced faster growth than inland areas.[12] Despite Beijing's desire to reduce regional inequalities, richer provinces transferred a far smaller part of their income to poorer regions than had been the case in previous years. In 1993, for example, Guangdong transferred only 0.4 percent of its GDP, and the poor inland provinces received very little in remittances. Beijing's acceptance of the trend marked a sharp contrast with earlier periods, when it compelled richer provinces to transfer over a far larger share of their income. For example, over the period 1978–1980, Shanghai turned over half of its provincial GDP, while the poor provinces received subsidies as large as 20–25 percent of their GDP.[13]

The central government also encountered resistance to its directives regarding subnational market protections. The domestic market had grown fragmented through the 1980s as local officials erected regulatory barriers to protect local markets and revenue sources. Protectionist measures included roadblocks, the seizure of cargo, locally initiated taxes, commercial surcharges, and licensing fees. By 1989, observers concluded that Beijing had lost much of its regulatory authority over the country.[14] To curb these centrifugal tendencies, the Central Committee enacted a series of regulations to tighten control of personnel appointments, such as one in 1990 that required local officials to transfer to a new position if they remained in one position for ten years.[15] However, such measures had little impact on the overall structural trends.

Not only did the central government face resistance from subnational governments, but the CCP central leadership experienced serious problems with internal discipline and cohesion as well. Fragmentation occurred through rival factions and a general breakdown in discipline. The CCP in the 1980s and 1990s featured competing networks of factions that contended for supremacy. Although Deng based much of his power in central organizations in Beijing, he maintained a strong patronage network throughout the country. For example, Deng's experiments with the household responsibility system began in provinces where he had the strongest supporters, including Guangdong, Guangxi, Guizhou, and Henan. Deng's supporters replaced conservative local leaders with their own allies through the 1980s. They also promoted provincial supporters such as Zhao Ziyang and Wan Li to Beijing, from where they could direct nation-wide policies.[16]

A principal source of opposition stemmed from the heart of the central leadership. Chen Yun, widely regarded as the second most powerful leader in China after Deng Xiaoping, served as the chair of the Central Advisory Commission, the most powerful decision-making body in the CCP at that time. Although a key architect of the reform and opening-up policies initiated in 1978, Chen grew progressively disenchanted with the pro-market reforms through the 1980s. In addition to policy differences, Chen resented Deng's tendency to make decisions unilaterally and without consulting his colleagues.[17]

These factional divisions prevented the party leadership from arriving at a consensus on major policy decisions, including personnel and national development plans, as shown in the deadlocked Seventh Plenum, the diluted Eighth Five-Year Plan, and the frequent deferral of major personnel and other decisions beginning in late 1989. When the Eighth Plenum finally met at the end of November 1991, the party leadership remained gridlocked. The most important decisions had to be put off until the Fourteenth Party Congress was scheduled for the following year.[18]

The divisions also reduced the coherence of the CCP's ideology and propaganda. Conservative hardliners controlled many of the party's news outlets, but their control was incomplete. Conservative propagandists failed to suppress pro-reform commentaries. Li Ruihuan, a Deng ally, continued to publish commentaries that championed Deng's ideas, frustrating the hardliner's efforts to dominate party propaganda outlets.[19]

In addition to formal challenges to his authority from rival factions, the CCP faced more general problems of rampant corruption and indiscipline. Polls indicated public anger over corruption and "economic crime" were among the leading causes of the Tiananmen Square protests. To conciliate an infuriated public, the central leadership launched an anticorruption drive in 1990 that lasted several years. By 1992, the CCP had expelled 156,000 party members and disciplined over 750,000 members.[20]

Control of the country's security forces appeared in dispute as well. Deng Xiaoping reportedly maintained a formidable power base within the military.[21] However, Deng lacked formal control of the PLA, having resigned from his post as chairman of the party's Central Military Commission in 1989. Although his protégé, Jiang Zemin, took over the post, Jiang had a small power base in the military and was regarded as a weak leader. Moreover, Jiang faced powerful rivals in the military in the form of the Yang brothers. Nor could Deng be sure of Jiang's loyalties. Aware of the fate of liberal reformers Hu Yaobang and Zhao Ziyang, Jiang Zemin appeared to distance himself from Deng's reform agenda throughout much of 1991. Jiang proved so cautious that Deng nearly replaced him.[22]

In sum, Deng started from a position of political *weakness* in late 1991. The central leadership lacked consensus on the imperative of pressing for major economic reform. Control of the military remained contested, and the central government experienced weak control over increasingly brazen and defiant subnational governments. The CCP suffered from a lack of unity and indiscipline as opposing factions vied for supremacy and the party experienced rampant corruption.

Developments Related to Elite Opposition

China's elites in the subnational governments and SOEs had experienced gradual gains in their income and wealth, but these remained relatively moderate, especially compared to the riches they would reap in the coming years. China's elites had a large share of the nation's income and wealth, but the share was slightly lower than that seen in rich democratic countries. From 1985 to 1990, the top 10 percent of Chinese income earners saw their share of income grow slowly from 30 percent to 31 percent. The top 10 percent of wealth owners had about 40 percent of the nation's wealth over the same period. By contrast, the top 10 percent of American income earners in 1990 had 38 percent of the share of national income, and the top 10 percent owned 64 percent of the nation's wealth.[23]

Although local-level officials wielded considerable power, collusion remained moderate. Party bosses controlled the courts, security forces, and other government-related institutions in their areas. Yet the political and economic elites remain distinct, in part because CCP rules in theory required the expelling of any members who became businessmen, as they would be capitalist "exploiters." In practice, many party members ignored the regulations and recruited private entrepreneurs into the party, but many officials respected this division by choosing to "jump in the sea" (*xia hai*) by leaving government jobs to pursue lucrative opportunities in the business sector.[24]

The power of subnational elites grew over this period, owing in part to several policy decisions made by Beijing. For example, the central leadership ended mass campaigns and popular "struggle" sessions against cadres as part of a general political demobilization. Although this improved political stability following the chaos and violence of the Mao era, it also reduced the accountability of cadres to the people.[25]

Changes in the performance evaluation system further insulated cadres from popular pressure. Introduced in the mid-1980s, the new system quantified objectives that had to be met. These standards incentivized cadres to ignore popular policies that could not be quantified into evaluation criteria, such as "respecting the rights of villagers."[26] In 1984, Deng also reformed personnel appointments to facilitate decentralization. He changed the policy of "two-level down management" to "one-level down management." Under this arrangement, cadres at each level of government gained full authority to appoint their subordinates. While designed to facilitate a more responsive government, in practice it spurred cadres to become extremely responsive to their immediate supervisors at the expense of other interests. It also empowered superiors to direct their underlings to carry out unpopular policies.[27]

In terms of the disposition of elites toward the central leadership's policies, there was considerable variation. Local and provincial officials aligned with Deng ignored the hardline positions of the conservative leaders in Beijing and pushed ahead with pro-market policies, such as creating enterprises and welcoming foreign investment. Areas aligned with the central leadership's hardliners may have slowed their pro-market activities or lacked opportunities to do so, as in the poorest landlocked areas. A divided leadership coincided with divided subnational elite as well.

In sum, the opposition posed by elites remained *weak*. The share of income and wealth owned by the top 10 percent had increased but remained moderate, indicating limited access to resources that could be used to counter Deng. Collusion between elites in the party, government, and economy had grown but remained somewhat constrained by CCP rules restricting entrepreneurs from membership. Divisions among subnational elites mirrored the divided central leadership. But overall, elite opposition to Deng's vision was weak. Many of the sub-national elites favored the changes Deng advocated due to their hopes of self-enrichment.

Developments Related to Public Cohesiveness

The public experienced a relatively high level of economic and social cohesiveness but remained politically fragmented at the start of the 1990s. On the one hand, the non-rural workforce experienced a high degree of formal employment, extensive social welfare benefits, and a relatively small informal sector. On the other hand, the national labor and consumer markets experienced growing fragmentation as local officials erected regulatory barriers against one another. The urban SOEs offered relatively generous social welfare benefits. The dominance of the SOE was clearly in retreat, however. By 1991, the share of China's state sector in the national economy had shrunk from 78 percent in 1978 to 53 percent. The country's phenomenal growth was largely powered by the privatization of the state sector, the most important of which was township and village enterprises (TVE). By the early 1990s, TVEs accounted for about four-fifths of the output of the non-state sector. Moreover, TVEs had substantially higher productivity growth rates than the state sector.[28]

In terms of social cohesion, inequality had grown but not yet reached the extreme levels of subsequent years. The Gini coefficient in 1990 was 0.35, below the 0.40 level identified by the IMF as politically destabilizing.[29] While all income groups experienced gains, inequality grew, with the bottom 50 percent of income earners experiencing a decline from 25 percent to 22 percent of national income from 1985 to 1990.[30] Disparities between provinces increased in the 1990s, reversing a downward trend since 1978.[31] The rise in regional inequality was partially offset by the rising cost of living in urban areas. The ratio of urban to rural disposable income actually declined from 2.5 times in 1978 to 2.2 times in 1990.[32]

Politically, the public remained demobilized, yet central leaders solicited their support. Indeed, the hardliners continued to advocate for the public to remain engaged in politics and counter liberalizing influences, although their proposals generally received a lukewarm reception.[33] Deng Xiaoping and his allies also cultivated broad political support. But they generally preferred to avoid revisiting the destructive political conflicts of the Mao era by keeping the public demobilized. Aware of the fact that the party's legitimacy had been severely damaged by the political fights, Deng and his supporters sought to strengthen the party's legitimacy through its ability to deliver economic goods. Accordingly, they downplayed ideological issues by blurring the distinctions between socialist and capitalist techniques. They also sought to suppress debate on this topic. The political demobilization reduced turmoil, but it also reduced the accountability of cadres to the people. In the eyes of many villagers, the abandonment of rectification campaigns encouraged cadres to trample the rights of the people with impunity.[34]

Political participation was limited to passive support, with no direct means for people to select their leaders or determine policies. Nor did the CCP tolerate competing political groups. The repressive political environment left little opportunity for new social groups to form. There was a near total absence of autonomous social forces such as churches, newspapers, unions, or commercial associations after authorities cracked down on the few nascent entities that did appear.[35] However, the solicitation of public support, the lack of competing social groups and identities that could claim the loyalty of the people, and the persistence of generous social welfare benefits from the SOEs provided the CCP provided some degree of cohesiveness that suggested a still substantial potential for mobilization, a potential the competing leadership groups paid tribute to through their efforts to elicit support. One important exception concerned the restive minority populations in minority-dominated provinces. The collapse of the Soviet Union coincided with a surge in unrest and violence in the ethnic minority provinces of Tibet and Xinjiang, with the late 1980s and early 1990s experiencing some of the worst violence in years.[36]

In sum, Chinese society in this period experienced relative *cohesiveness* owing to the fact that SOEs employed most non-rural people and provided generous social welfare benefits. The state economy was dominated by domestic industries with linkages, at least within provinces. There was relatively moderate, but growing, social and regional inequality as well. The CCP adhered to formal demobilization in favor of pragmatic policies to develop the economy, but leaders actively solicited popular support. Although the people had no opportunities to directly impact political leaders or choose policies, Deng's pragmatic reforms enjoyed broad popular backing, suggesting considerable potential for political mobilization. A lack of competing social groups and identities aided moderate social cohesiveness as well.

Deng and his allies in the central leadership, who sought to enact major, multi-sector policy change, faced some promising conditions but also key challenges. Deng faced a relatively weak elite opposition and some potential for mobilizing the public's support. Moreover, the weakness of the elites suggested Deng did not require a substantial involvement of the people in politics. The principal challenge Deng faced was the weaknesses related to the central leadership, owing to severe divisions and Deng's lack of formal control. To build the "enabling condition," Deng and his allies needed to gain control of the security forces, strengthen control over the CCP, and bolster the central government's control over subnational governments.

INTERVENING DEVELOPMENTS, 1992–1994

In the years 1992–1994, Deng and his allies carried out a variety of political actions to consolidate his power and weaken elite opposition. Deng also benefited from developments that together resulted in favorable political conditions for the enactment of the pro-growth major multi-sector policies.

Developments Related to the Central Leadership

Deng rallied from a position of weakness to strengthen his grip on the central leadership. Frustrated by the intransigence of his political opponents in the central government, Deng embarked on what would be widely regarded as a political masterstroke. From January to February 1992, Deng undertook a tour of southern China, visiting Shenzhen, Zhuhai, Guangzhou, and Shanghai. Throughout the tour, Deng promoted his market-friendly policies while upholding a more conservative political message that emphasized the importance of maintaining political order and controlling corruption. He also frequently criticized his leftist opponents in Beijing.[37]

Initially, Deng's journey did not receive media attention from central propaganda outlets, reflecting the influence of conservatives. However, provincial papers in Shanghai and other southern cities provided extensive coverage. The enthusiastic reports showed that Deng and his pro-reform message resonated broadly with the public. Other party papers followed suit. Deng skillfully solicited the latent popular support that he enjoyed across the country. Everywhere he went, crowds cheered and greeted him, and the public displays of support resulted in considerable political pressure on the conservatives. By the end of February, the conservative editors of *People's Daily* had yielded and endorsed Deng's southern initiative. Deng's supporters further exploited the popularity of the "supreme leader" to build political support for his policy agenda. Supporters argued in the media that an attack on the reforms equaled an attack on Deng's person.[38] By midsummer of 1992, Deng's allies had consolidated control of the party propaganda apparatus with the resignation of several hardliner editors and propaganda officials.[39] Meanwhile, the mood among top leaders began to shift. In March 1992, Jiang

Zemin expressed his self-criticism to the Politburo and pledged to support Deng's policy agenda.[40]

The 14th Party Congress held in late 1992 marked a major victory for Deng. The report issued by the Congress outlined measures to strengthen the "socialist market economy," in part by transforming the state-owned sector. It called for the rapid development of a market system, and it endorsed fiscal reforms in the tax system. Further consolidating his influence, Deng abolished the Central Advisory Commission at the 14th Party Congress.[41] Deng consolidated his control of the military in this period as well. He carried out an extensive purge of the military, removing the powerful Yang brothers and sidelining about half of the entire PLA's generals who may have supported the brothers.[42]

In the wake of these political moves, hardliners saw their support dwindle to a trickle. In late 1993, People's Congresses in a number of provinces and municipalities voted to oust incumbent officials who were backed by the party establishment.[43] The purges and resignations of conservative party elders and their supporters ended organized political resistance to Deng's authority by 1993.

Deng and his protégé, Jiang Zemin, pushed through the long-sought market-friendly policies. The central leadership's approval of the "Decision on Issues Concerning the Establishment of a Socialist Market Economic Structure" in November 1993 abolished the planning system altogether and set a goal of establishing a modern market system based on international best practices. The decision called for the creation of market-supporting institutions, including a centralized money system and the beginnings of a social safety net. It set a rule-based approach to revenue transfers between the central and provincial governments based on a fixed formula. It also directed the transformation of SOEs into "modern enterprises" with clearer property rights and responsibilities.[44]

Although Deng made substantial progress in consolidating control over the party and the military, the central government's control over the provinces remained weak through this period. Fiscal decentralization reached its peak in 1993, during which time the subnational fiscal revenue to national fiscal revenue ratio reached 78 percent.[45] However, Deng and his supporters regarded the provincial leaders, especially in the coastal regions, as important allies. These elites had demonstrated that lucrative profits and economic growth could be realized if the Dengist agenda could be implemented. Reflecting the political alliance between Deng and the coastal provinces, Deng promoted many provincial leaders to the Politburo at the 14th Party Congress.

Beneath the surface, however, tensions grew between central and subnational leaders. In 1993, the central government issued a circular that denounced local cadres that seized property and levied illegal fees. Official media also noted numerous reports of malfeasance, with CCP General Secretary Jiang Zemin personally denouncing "local emperors."[46] The following year, the Chinese leadership also began to reassert its authority over the subnational governments. The most important efforts centered on taxation and central banking reform. The 1994 fiscal reform pushed fiscal spending responsibilities to lower levels while granting the central government a larger share of tax revenues. The central government's revenue as a share of GDP stopped declining and started to recover.[47] The recentralization of revenues upward and devolution of expenditures downward helped strengthen central government control of the provinces, as the increasing fiscal dependence of local governments on higher levels weakened their independence and rendered them more vulnerable to punitive measures from the central leadership. Central edicts carried more weight than they did the old fiscal system.[48]

Jiang took several steps to consolidate his power in the military and the party. He promoted a cadre of loyal generals in the PLA and placed key supporters in the central committee and other government organizations. In a calculated bid to boost his own—and the CCP's—flagging credibility, in the summer of 1993, Jiang pledged to intensify the crackdown on economic crime and corruption, particularly at the upper levels of the party, government, and army.[49] It took several years, but Jiang emerged as the core of the party leadership.[50]

In sum, Deng and his protégé Jiang made considerable gains in consolidating their control over the government, security forces, and CCP. The gains proved sufficient to enable a *strong* central leadership to overcome organized political opposition to the Dengist policy agenda, facilitating successful implementation. Despite the successes, however, structural weaknesses persisted, such as the relative autonomy of the provinces and ongoing corruption in the CCP.

Developments Related to Elite Opposition

Rivals in Beijing posed the greatest opposition to Deng's authority. However, despite incessant propaganda, support among the rank and file for such hardline positions remained soft. For example, after the Tiananmen Square Massacre, party conservatives tried to carry out a "party rectification" campaign to boost enthusiasm for more hardline views, but the effort reportedly fizzled. Similarly, hardliners struggled to identify and punish active supporters of the democracy movement. The effort yielded meager results owing to widespread open sympathy toward the student movement in April and May 1989 among party members as well as a "tacit conspiracy of silence" among leading cadres in many cities.[51] Moreover, although Deng faced firm opposition from the party's top leadership, he still maintained a strong patronage network, including in many of the provinces as well as in the military. Deng's economic reforms also appeared to enjoy strong support among the rural populace, which comprised 75 percent of the population, as well as in the major urban areas of prosperous coastal provinces.[52]

Outside of Beijing, the strength of subnational elites increased over this period, but this was partially masked by the continued convergence of interests with the central leadership. The proportion of income owned by the top 10 percent of the population increased further, from 31 percent to 34 percent. The top 10 percent owned about 40 percent of the nation's wealth, a slight increase from 1991.[53]

Collusion between elites for purposes of self-enrichment grew substantially over the period, owing principally to the privatization of SOEs. From 1991 to 1993, economic crime and corruption grew not merely in frequency but also in magnitude. According to reports, the PLA engaged in rampant smuggling of crude oil, cars, consumer goods, construction materials, and many other items to the tune of billions of dollars.[54] In 1993, Jiang Zemin was forced to acknowledge openly that "corruption is a virus that has infected the party's healthy body. If we just ignore this phenomenon, it will bring down our party and our system."[55]

Local officials continued to erect numerous internal trade barriers to protect local industries. Studies by western economists noted a decrease in domestic trade flows from the 1980s through the 1990s. Interprovincial trade relative to total trade decreased significantly from 1987 through 1992. According to one study, the disintegration of the Chinese domestic market owed principally to political reasons, namely the desire of local officials to maximize growth, employment, and their incomes through protectionist measures and administrative monopolies.[56]

Despite the misbehavior of local cadres and their role in distorting the domestic market, the central leadership and subnational elites generally shared an interest in carrying out market-friendly reforms that supercharged economic growth, elevated incomes for all people, improved the economy's productivity, and provided ample opportunities for elite self-enrichment.

In sum, elite opposition remained *weak*. Opposition to Deng's policy agenda was mostly concentrated among a handful of leaders in Beijing, which Deng and his allies successfully outmaneuvered. Outside Beijing, many party cadres favored Deng's economic program. While the share of wealth and income increased and collusion intensified, subnational elites found that their interests largely converged with those of Beijing and thus had little incentive to oppose the implementation of policies from which they benefited enormously.

Developments Related to Public Cohesiveness

The problem of internal fragmentation was exacerbated by the country's integration into the global economy. China's development as a hub of global production provided the impetus for extraordinary GDP growth rates, but it also accelerated centrifugal forces as provinces oriented their economies toward foreign customers and suppliers. As the country's export sector boomed, for example, China experienced a decrease in interprovincial trade. According to a study by the World Bank, as of the early 1990s, internal trade as a percentage of GDP among the Chinese provinces was 22 percent, which was lower than the then European Community's 28 percent and the 27 percent among the republics of the former Soviet Union.[57]

This period saw an increase in regional inequality due to disparities in the ability of coastal and inland regions to export and reductions in interprovincial transfers. Social inequality increased as well, as the SOEs began to shed workers. However, the workforce retained a degree of cohesiveness due to the fact that most employers were domestic firms. In this period, foreign-invested enterprises only comprised about 5 percent of companies, with TVEs still playing a major role in the export sector. There were a few private firms at this point as well.[58] However, foreign direct investment began to increase significantly after Deng's southern trip in 1992, with total investment nearly tripling from US$4.6 billion in 1991 to US$11.3 billion in 1992.[59]

Politically, the party continued to discourage the sort of mass mobilizations and campaigns that pervaded the Maoist era, but competing factions did solicit public support for their agendas. Media coverage of enthusiastic crowds during Deng's trip encouraged the public to demonstrate support for Deng. Similarly, hardliners in Beijing repeatedly tried to revive interest in more orthodox socialist politics, albeit with little success.

In terms of loyalties and identities to social groups, the public faced a period of transition. While the CCP retained a dominant presence, its abandonment of Marxist ideology and focus on rapid growth policies eroded public support for communist ideas. The enthusiastic crowds that greeted Deng revealed that he retained considerable personal influence. However, other party leaders did not receive such popular acclaim. The hardliners failed to stir public enthusiasm for their orthodox socialist ideals. Nor did Jiang Zemin draw crowds the way Deng could. Moreover, the party's downsizing of the SOE workforce hinted at a rupture in the economic links that once bound many workers to the party's ideology and identity.

Not surprisingly, observers began at this time to detect signs of an increasingly pluralistic society as disillusioned individuals began to explore other identities and social groups. In 1992, Harvard University professor Tony Saich described a growing pluralism in society as well as increasing social and economic inequality, which he suspected could further strain the sense of solidarity that the CCP had long tried to cultivate. However, during this period, such social forces had just begun to be unleashed, with little indication that any competitor groups had any substantial followings.[60]

In sum, the public experienced a fading sense of *cohesiveness* as both Deng and his hardliner opponents cultivated passive public support in their struggle for mastery. However, this brief moment of public political involvement also coincided with an increase in national fragmentation as regional and social inequality intensified and the workforce began to experience major reductions in force. The business sector remained dominated by TVEs and a still substantial SOE sector, but the foreign-invested sector began to take off.

During this period, China achieved the "enabling condition" outlined in this theory. The central leadership regained unity behind Deng's agenda as organized political opposition in Beijing collapsed. The elites in the provinces, localities, and SOEs had grown wealthy under the earlier reforms and stood to gain further from the proposed reforms. The power of the wealthy provinces in particular proved formidable, but key reforms allowed the central leadership to regain some of its leverage over subnational governments. Corruption and collusion grew to alarming proportions during this period, but the elites experienced relatively low levels of friction with the central leadership because Deng viewed the conservative opposition as a greater threat. By contrast, he regarded the provincial leaders as political allies and cultivated their support. Thus, although the elites grew powerful during this period, they had little incentive to oppose Deng's reform agenda. Deng also elicited public support in his struggle with hardline opponents through the Southern Tour. Thus, the efforts by Deng and his allies to mobilize public opinion provided a brief moment in which the public played an important role in impacting national politics.

INTERVENING DEVELOPMENTS, 1995–1997

The period from 1995 through 1997 saw continued successful implementation of the pro-market policy agenda, even as Deng passed away in 1997. Jiang Zemin consolidated his position as Deng's successor and continued the recentralization of power. The country's integration into the global economy vastly expanded opportunities for profitable trade. Local cadres exploited this opportunity, however, by colluding more closely with businesses, developers, and regulators to protect local industries and lure foreign investors. As a result, the country experienced a deepening of internal segmentation and a widening of regional and social inequality. The populace experienced a new level of fragmentation, opening opportunities for competing social groups, including religious and ethnic groups, to claim the loyalty of disillusioned citizens.

Developments Related to the Central Leadership

While recentralizing power, Beijing continued to carry out reforms designed to curb the autonomy of provinces. In 1995, China passed legislation that granted the central bank the authority to determine monetary policy. The law and associated regulations substantially reduced the influence of local governments on monetary policy and credit allocation decisions. As a result, the overall budget constraints of the local governments became much harder in the 1990s compared to the 1980s.[61]

Politically, Jiang strengthened his control over the military and internal security forces with additional purges, the promotion of supporters, and hefty defense budget increases. By 1997, most observers agreed that he had consolidated control.[62] Jiang also strengthened his position in the party and government. He placed his supporters in key central government ministries, and propaganda organs compliantly promoted his ideological authority. However, although Jiang prevailed over the clearly defined rival factions of the type that struggled against Deng, he still faced problems of corruption and a lack of discipline. David Shambaugh observed of China at the time, "Corruption is rampant inside and outside the party and is a major source of resentment among the citizenry." He noted pessimistically that "despite widespread arrests and executions, law enforcement authorities appear to be losing the fight" against corruption. He added that "in many cases, police and customs officials are themselves deeply involved in corruption and smuggling rings." Despite party rectification campaigns and anticorruption arrests, the problem appeared to fester without abatement.[63]

In sum, the central leadership remained *strong*. It continued to reap the benefits of recentralizing reforms and a stronger grip on the nation's finances. Jiang consolidated his authority over the CCP and the military and oversaw what would prove to be a largely successful effort to withdraw the military from commercial activity. Party indiscipline and corruption remained pervasive, but Jiang appeared to have successfully controlled rival factions.

Developments Related to Elite Opposition

In this period, the organized opposition in Beijing disintegrated. Subnational elites saw their fortunes and positions remain steady. The share of national income in the top 10 percent remained at around 34 percent. Their share of wealth increased significantly, from around 40 percent in 1994 to about

48 percent in 1998, however, as cadres exploited their political access for gain.[64]

Although reduced in number, the SOEs continued to profit from collusive arrangements between enterprise leaders, regulators, and party bosses.[65] However, the privatization of SOEs opened major opportunities for enrichment and profitable collusion. Before the transition, political elites had control of public firms but no property rights. Privatization, however, created unprecedented opportunities for them to monetize their access to public property.[66] The mixing of government and business encouraged corruption and market interference, including regional protectionism, backroom dealing, mistreatment of nonlocal trading partners, and out-of-control bank lending practices. Many of these problems were exacerbated by a judiciary that was frequently corrupted and captured by regional elites.[67]

Despite the central leadership's recentralization efforts, the effects of economic decentralization had also strengthened the power of the subnational elites. Once local government cadres became businessmen and capitalists, they gained new resources to resist demands by the central government.[68] Symptomatic of the growing clout of wealthy local cadres, Chinese officials and commentators stepped up their criticism of "localism" and "provincial protectionism" during this time.[69]

Yet, although the elites grew wealthier and tensions increased, their position regarding the central leadership generally remained mostly congruent. Jiang Zemin prioritized economic growth and encouraged local cadres to oversee rapid development. So long as the local officials maintained high GDP growth rates, Beijing tolerated considerable corruption and malfeasance by local officials, with only token efforts to crack down. Symptomatic of the central leadership's support for the elite was the adoption of a "strike hard" crackdown to deal with popular protests regarding cuts in services and local malfeasance. Central authorities backed law enforcement in cracking down on anyone who criticized local authorities. Official media tended to downplay the discussion of malfeasance by local officials and blamed individual malefactors for crime and acts that disturbed social stability. One typical commentary in the party journal *Seeking Truth* explained that the crackdown was essential to "ensuring social stability and ensuring a stable environment for development."[70]

In sum, elite *opposition* remained *weak*. Subnational elites skillfully exploited China's deepening integration into the global economy and the dismantling of the SOEs in this period to gain a larger share of income and wealth and to grow even more powerful. However, the congruence of interests between elites and the central leadership meant that these elites did not oppose the growth agenda led by Deng and Jiang. The situation masked an increasingly potent elite that would pose a serious political problem when Beijing inevitably changed its growth strategy.

Developments Related to Public Cohesiveness

The 1994 fiscal reform may have bolstered the central leadership's power over the provinces, but it exacerbated problems of social fragmentation. As a result of revenue recentralization and the devolution of fiscal responsibilities, local governments fell into debt. Many local governments in poorer western regions provided fewer and lower quality public services and passed along a higher proportion of the costs to their constituents. Other local governments developed extra-budgetary and off-budget resources in the form of illegal fees and charges, over which local officials faced virtually no oversight. Illegal fees became the main source of extra-budgetary funds at the local level, and these ranged from surcharges on household utility bills and infrastructure maintenance to surcharges for hospital services and schools. The proliferation of these illegal fees at the local level became a source of intense public resentment.[71]

China's workforce also experienced substantial fragmentation owing to the downsizing of the state sector, which resulted in a loss of social welfare benefits for much of the urban work force. Privatization of small-sized SOEs began to emerge on a large scale in 1995, when the central government promoted downsizing under the slogan of "grasping the large and releasing the small." From 1995 through 2003, the number of SOEs declined from 118,000 to 34,000, and the labor force fell by 44 million.[72] About ten million workers from SOEs and urban collectives were laid off each year between 1996 and 1998. Although it improved productivity by reducing costly obligations for the state, the downsizing left many workers without social welfare benefits.[73]

Indeed, the restructuring of SOEs and downsizing of the workforce resulted in an explosion in the informal sector in the 1990s.[74] The business sector became more fragmented as well, as the number of foreign companies setting up factories in China surged, increasing tenfold between 1990 and 1994, when it reached US$34 billion.[75] Foreign businesses that relocated to China generally had little interest in paying into expensive social welfare schemes or supporting domestic upgrading strategies, the expense of which might undercut the economic rationale for relocating to China. Moreover, local officials lacked an incentive to pressure foreign employers into funding such initiatives due to the intense competition among provincial leaders for foreign investment.[76]

Chinese leaders had sought to replace a social welfare system tied to SOEs with benefits that could be available to all workers, but this effort made little progress. In 1993, the central government enacted reforms to create a basic social welfare system that featured "pay-as-you-go" programs paid by employers and local governments and individual "fully funded" programs. But as of 1996, China had not established a unified national program. Instead, provincial and municipal governments became responsible for implementing their own local programs. After several years of effort, pensions remained seriously underfunded and only covered a fraction of eligible workers.[77] As jobs became less secure and benefits vanished, social inequality surged. The Gini coefficient increased above 0.40. Regional inequality increased as well. The fiscal and tax recentralization reforms of 1994 proved to have only a modest effect on reducing regional inequality.[78]

Politically, the populace experienced deepening fragmentation with the passing of the revolutionary giant Deng. Authorities did not offer any new avenues for popular participation in politics but instead continued to encourage the people to focus on increasing their incomes through work. However, the problem of popular disaffection from the party began to alarm CCP officials. Party thinkers introduced a form of moralizing indoctrination to combat what they regarded as a spreading amorality, political drift, and lawlessness. Reflecting this top-down response to social disintegration, a commentary published in 2001 called for "vigorously promoting the basic moral standards of 'loving one's country and observing laws, understanding etiquette and honesty, promoting unity and goodwill, improving oneself through diligence and thrift, dedicating oneself to work, and making sacrifices.'"[79]

With the lingering effects of Mao's assault on traditional beliefs and religion, coupled with the widespread insecurity generated by the SOE downsizing as well as the dismantling of the official ideology's traditional vision of solidarity, China's social scene experienced a new level of pluralization. A hint of the depth of public alienation from the CCP appeared in the emergence of competing social groups that claimed the allegiance of growing numbers of disaffected Chinese, such as Falungong, a revitalized Christianity, and other religious groups. Citizens began to form nongovernmental organizations (NGO) to serve a variety of humanitarian and business purposes as well, with the number climbing to 180,000 in 1995. Dismayed by the rapid spread of these groups, authorities initiated a crackdown, especially on groups like Falungong that proved capable of drawing large numbers of adherents independent of CCP control.[80] In the late 1990s, the Chinese government launched a campaign to "rectify" and "regularize" existing NGOs by requiring all NGOs to register at the Ministry or Department of Civil Affairs and shutting down others.[81]

The intensified repression did little to heal a social fabric that was irrevocably torn from a dismantled social welfare system, underfunded government services, pervasive official corruption, and deepening job insecurity. The growing appeal of groups such as Falungong only underscored the depths of bitterness many had begun to feel in such a situation. Managing this discontent through stepped-up repression may have been tolerable enough for a central leadership committed to a grow-at-all-costs economic strategy, as was the case in the late 1990s, but it would also open a major vulnerability when Beijing needed robust public support for new growth strategies in the future.

In sum, the public grew *fragmented* during this period. The dismantling of SOEs and migration from rural areas resulted in a massive explosion of the informal labor sector. In addition, the government failed to build a substantial national social welfare system, and foreign companies expanded their share of the economy. The party continued to keep the populace politically demobilized and instead encouraged a focus on increasing incomes. Increasing insecurity, yawning inequality, and popular disenchantment with a CCP plagued by rampant corruption opened opportunities for competing social groups and identities.

At the close of the selected period, the most striking development was the fragmentation of the public. The weakness of elite opposition to the central leadership's pro-growth agenda masked the reality of their growing strength. The combination of an increasingly powerful elite and a fragmented public posed a long-term danger to the central leadership when the potential of the rapid growth model inevitably exhausted itself, leaving an unfavorable political environment for the launch of a more contentious, intensive growth strategy.

CONCLUSION

Under Deng Xiaoping's leadership, China succeeded in dismantling the planned economy and establishing a socialist market economy. Successful policy implementation generated the impressive economic growth that Deng's allies hoped for. By 1996, the government had expanded market mechanisms to 93 percent of retail activity, up from 53 percent in 1990. The government had restructured 25 percent of the nation's 87,000 SOEs in 1998, and restructuring continued apace into the 2000s. The state sector declined dramatically, with companies shedding 60 percent of the workforce.[82] Productivity growth surged 5 percent from 1991 to 1996. The policies turbocharged the economy, with GDP growth soaring 12 percent from 1991 to 1997.[83] The living standard of ordinary Chinese people improved significantly. The number of people living in absolute poverty was substantially reduced from over 250 million in 1978 to less than 100 million in this period. By the end of 1997, reform enjoyed broad popularity because so many people benefited from it.[84]

The policy initiative was largely, but not completely, successful. Banking and financial reforms lagged. Despite the large amount of capital infusion into the four state banks in 1999, the status of the banking and financial system by the end of 1998 was perhaps even more fragile than that in 1994. This was primarily due to delays in reforming SOEs and state banks. The inadequate SOE reform meant that the nonperforming loan problem became worse and worse.[85] The state's economic dominance preserved systemic economic inefficiency as local elites continued to exploit scarce resources for gain. The World Bank estimated that almost a third of investment decisions made between 1991 and 2000 were misguided.[86]

When carrying out the policy initiatives, Chinese leaders carried out a minimal level of coercion against opposing elites. The principal reason was the weakness of his opposition. Deng's rivals consisted primarily of a handful of ideological hardliners in the central leadership and their supporters. Efforts by these conservatives to rally popular support fizzled, underscoring the weakness of their position. Deng toppled them through a media campaign, and after 1993, hardliner opposition vanished. Neither did the subnational elites pose much opposition. Deng's policy agenda largely converged with their interests and that of much of the public. Subnational officials saw lucrative opportunities in the policies Deng advocated. But others could see opportunity as well, such as the migrant and rural workers who desperately sought to flee crushing poverty for a chance at better-paying jobs.

The period did see a major increase in the repression of the populace. Through the 1990s, the central government found its interests best served by backing the elites against the public, as seen in the central leadership's endorsement of the "hard strike" campaign that blamed crime and unrest on citizens while largely absolving local officials. When they proved insufficient for the task of repression, cadres began to order armed police and other security forces to enforce order and suppress popular protests. Yet a deepening reliance on repression to control popular anger and frustration at local cadres risked alienating the people further.

Throughout the six-year period, Deng retained a major advantage in that the policies he advocated corresponded with trends well underway. Ultimately, Deng and his allies prevailed primarily because their policy prescription simply reflected what was already happening in the Chinese economy. Despite the hardline rhetoric coming out of Beijing, the program of economic austerity imposed in late has reached its limits. Subnational governments had recognized the potential of pro-market reforms and were busily carrying them out across many provinces, even as Deng and his opponents feuded.[87]

Despite the success, the improvements to the nation's economic performance carried a steep political cost. The central leadership's position regarding subnational governments and party discipline continued to deteriorate. Despite the fiscal and financial recentralization measures of 1994 and 1995, provincial governments continued to resist central authority. Party discipline eroded further as well. Deng's passing left an energized ruling party riven by corruption and ideological incoherence. The disappearance of cohesive factions underscored the dissolution of ideological-based groupings and the emergence of new elite networks that competed over the rights to loot state assets and manipulate the party-state apparatus for self-enrichment. Corruption remained pervasive, and abuses of authority eroded the public's trust.

Another cost lay in the deepening fragmentation of the people. Perhaps the biggest losers of the market-friendly reforms were the tens of millions of SOE workers who lost their jobs and social welfare benefits, as well as local citizens who felt the brunt of cutbacks in local services due to the recentralization reforms of the mid-1990s. The jobs that replaced formal state jobs mainly consisted of far more precarious jobs in the informal sector. The enterprise sector experienced significant change as well, as a larger number of foreign-invested enterprises, often set up as joint companies with local industries, entered in search of low-cost manufacturing.

The national market's fragmentation worsened over the 1990s as well, as interprovincial trade declined as a share of overall trade while provincial trade with foreign partners soared. In addition to economic fragmentation, the populace experienced political fragmentation as they lacked opportunities for political participation. Central leaders after Deng did not invest the effort that the revolutionary generations did in cultivating popular support for the CCP's ideology and agenda. Instead, authorities urged the people to focus on improving their incomes through work. Worsening inequality eroded further the relevance of the CCP as a party ostensibly dedicated to the solidarity of the people, but which in practice seemed more focused on enriching elites. The diminishing ability of the CCP to shape the social identity and culture of the people opened a yawning gap that competing groups exploited. Minority regions saw a resurgence of protest and agitation, and new religious and other NGOs began to attract supporters.

The country's economic success depended on its integration into the global market, but the political costs of this strategy deserve mention as well. China entered the global economy with a mostly decentralized economy and weak central control, which Beijing mainly exercised by controlling personnel appointments. The lack of nationally consistent rules, laws, and regulations encouraged subnational governments to erect internal market barriers to protect local industries. This ironically deepened the central leadership's dependence on local elites to sustain growth since the local elites directly managed the drivers of growth and served as the vital middlemen between foreign employers and the labor force. The subnational elites also competed in a "race to the bottom," which exacerbated problems of public fragmentation as local officials stepped up repression to control public protests regarding worker mistreatment, sharpening inequality, ecological despoilation, official malfeasance, and corruption.

In short, the phenomenal economic success that China enjoyed depended on unusually favorable political conditions, which Deng had largely achieved by 1993. However, a situation featuring a strong central leadership, a weak elite opposition, and a cohesive public began to dissipate almost as soon as Deng had secured it. A principal driver of this undoing owed to the success of the policies that Beijing pursued. Unlocking productivity and supercharging economic growth required, as Deng planned, the dismantling of the state sector and a deepening of the country's integration into the global economy. The benefits were clear and the profits impressive, but the corrosive effect on the country's politics would prove exceedingly durable and far-reaching. In subsequent years, an increasingly powerful subnational elite began to colonize and subvert the central government itself, extending their reach into the military and security forces. With its most important ally, the public, fragmented and demoralized, the central leadership would find itself with dwindling hopes of ever repeating Deng's astonishing success.

NOTES

1. Yingyi Qian and Jinglian Wu, "China's Transition to a Market Economy: How Far Across the River?," Working Paper No. 69, Stanford Center for International Development, August, 2000, 9.
2. Ezra Vogel, *Deng Xiaoping and the Transformation of China* (Cambridge, MA: Belknap Press, 2011), 600.
3. Zhao Dingxin, *The Power of Tiananmen: State-Society Relations and the 1989 Beijing Student Movement* (Chicago, IL: University of Chicago Press, 2001), 127.
4. Tony Saich, "The Fourteenth Party Congress: A Program for Authoritarian Rule," *The China Quarterly* 132 (December 1992): 1138.
5. Richard Baum, *Burying Mao: Chinese Politics in the Age of Deng Xiaoping* (Princeton, NJ: Princeton University Press, 1996), 303.
6. Saich, "The Fourteenth Party Congress," 1137.
7. *World Bank*, "China: Country Economic Memorandum," Report No. 10111-CHA, June 19, 1992.
8. Chunni Shen, Jing Jin, and Heng fun Zou, "Fiscal Decentralization in China: History, Impact, Challenges and Next Steps," *Annals of Economics and Finance* 13, no. 1 (2012): 1–51.
9. Zheng Yongnian, "Power to Dominate, Not to Change: How China's Central-Local Relations Constrain Its Reform," EAI Working Paper 153, July 2009.
10. Chenggang Xu, "The Fundamental Institutions of China's Reforms and Development," *Journal of Economic Literature* 49, no. 4 (December 2011): 1076–151.
11. Baum, *Burying Mao*, 300.
12. Tianlun Jian, Jeffrey D. Sachs, and Andrew M. Warner, "Trends in Regional Inequality," NBER Working Paper No. 5412, January 1996.
13. Shen, Jin, and Zou, "Fiscal Decentralization in China."
14. Pak K. Lee, "Local Economic Protectionism in China's Economic Reform," *Development Policy Review* 16 (1998): 281–303.

15. Qingjie Zeng, "Control, Discretion and Bargaining: the Politics of Provincial Leader Rotation in China," *China Political Science Review* 1 (2016): 623–44.

16. Hongbin Cai and Daniel Treisman, "Did Government Decentralization Cause China's Economic Miracle?," *World Politics* 58, no. 4 (July 2006): 505–35.

17. Baum, *Burying Mao*, 340.

18. Ibid., 338.

19. Ibid., 320.

20. Ibid., 318.

21. David Schambaugh, "Deng Xiaoping: The Politician," *The China Quarterly* 135 (September 1993): 457–90.

22. Joseph Fewsmith and Andrew Nathan, "Authoritarian Resilience Revisited: Joseph Fewsmith with Response from Andrew J. Nathan," *Journal of Contemporary China* 28, no. 116 (2019): 167–79.

23. World Inequality Database, "World Inequality Report 2018," 2018. As of November 4, 2020, https://wir2018.wid.world/executive-summary.html.

24. Joseph Fewsmith, "The Sixteenth National Party Congress: The Succession That Didn't Happen," *China Quarterly* 173 (March 2003): 1–16.

25. Kevin J. O'Brien and Lianjiang Li, "Selective Policy Implementation in Rural China," *Comparative Politics* 31, no. 2 (1999): 167–86.

26. Ibid., 173–76.

27. Ibid., 171.

28. Xu, "The Fundamental Institutions of China's Reforms and Development."

29. Terry Secular, "The Challenge of High Inequality in China," *World Bank, Inequality in Focus* 2, no. 2 (August 2013). As of November 5, 2020, https://www.worldbank.org/content/dam/Worldbank/document/Poverty%20documents/Inequality-In-Focus-0813.pdf.

30. World Inequality Database, "World Inequality Report 2018."

31. Thomas Gries and Maargarethe Redlin, "China's Provincial Disparities and the Determinants of Provincial Inequality," *Journal of Chinese Economic and Business Studies* 7, no. 2 (2009): 259–81.

32. Sonali Jain-Chandra, Niny Khor, Rui Mano, Johanna Schauer, Philippe Wingender, and Juzhong Zhuang, "Inequality in China: Trends, Drivers, and Policy Remedies," IMF Working Paper, WP/18/127, 2018.

33. Saich, "The Fourteenth Party Congress," 1144.

34. O'Brien and Li, "Selective Policy Implementation in Rural China," 172.

35. Adrian Chan, "In Search of a Civil Society in China," *Journal of Contemporary Asia* 27, no. 2 (2007): 242–51.

36. Baum, *Burying Mao*, 324.

37. Ibid., 325.

38. Saich, "The Fourteenth Party Congress," 1154.

39. Baum, *Burying Mao*, 356.

40. Saich, "The Fourteenth Party Congress," 1151.

41. Zheng Yongnian, "China in 2012: Troubled Elite, Frustrated Society," *Asian Survey* 53, no. 1 (January 2013): 162–75.

42. Lena Sun, "Deng Completes Major Army Purge," *Washington Post*, February 12, 1993.

43. Baum, *Burying Mao*, 372.
44. Qian and Wu, "China's Transition to a Market Economy."
45. Xu, "The Fundamental Institutions of China's Reforms and Development."
46. O'Brien and Li, "Selective Policy Implementation in Rural China," 177.
47. Qian and Wu, "China's Transition to a Market Economy," 14.
48. Shen, Jin, and Zou, "Fiscal Decentralization in China," 1–51.
49. Baum, *Burying Mao*, 355.
50. Fewsmith and Nathan, "Authoritarian Resilience Revisited," 172.
51. Baum, *Burying Mao*, 316.
52. Ibid., 308.
53. World Inequality Database, "World Inequality Report 2018."
54. James Mulvenon, "To Get Rich is Unprofessional," *China Leadership Monitor*, No. 6, June 2003.
55. Baum, *Burying Mao*, 343.
56. Sandra Poncet, "Measuring Chinese Domestic and International Integration," *China Economic Review* 14 (2003): 17.
57. Zheng Yongnian, "Power to Dominate, Not to Change."
58. Qian and Wu, "China's Transition to a Market Economy."
59. Nicholas Lardy, "The Role of Foreign Trade and Investment in China's Economic Transformation," *The China Quarterly* 144 (1995): 1065–82.
60. Saich, "The Fourteenth Party Congress," 1158.
61. Qian and Wu, "China's Transition to a Market Economy."
62. You Ji, "Jiang Zemin's Command of the Military," *The China Journal* 45 (January 2001): 131–38.
63. David Schambaugh, "China's Fragile Future," *World Policy Journal* 11, no. 3 (Fall 1994): 41–45.
64. World Inequality Database, "World Inequality Report 2018."
65. Carlos Wing-Hung Lo and Shui-Yan Tang, "Institutional Reform, Economic Changes, and Local Environmental Management in China: The Case of Guangdong Province," *Environmental Politics* 15, no. 2 (2006): 190–210.
66. Duoduo Xu and Xiaogang Wu, "From Political Power to Personal Wealth: Privatization, Elite Opportunity, and Social Stratification in Post-Reform China," Hong Kong University Working Paper, 2017.
67. Michael C. Davis, "The Case for Chinese Federalism," *Journal of Democracy* 10, no. 2 (1999): 124–37.
68. Ka Ho Mok and Xiao Fang Wu, "Dual Decentralization in China's Transitional Economy: Welfare Regionalism and Policy Implications for Central-Local Relationship," *Policy and Society* 32, no. 1 (2017): 61–75.
69. Shi Kaifeng and Luo Shijian, "Oppose Local Protectionism" [*Fandub Defang Boushey*], Outlook [*Liaowang*] 12 (March 22, 1999): 1.
70. *Seeking Truth* [Qiushi], "'Strike Hard' Campaign is Strategic, Popular Move Aimed at Safeguarding Development" [Yanda Yundong Shi Zhanlue Xingde, Shou Huanyingde Judong Zhizai Weuhu Fazhan] 8 (April 16, 2001): 3–4.
71. Shen, Jin, and Zou, "Fiscal Decentralization in China."

72. Ligang Song, "State Owned Enterprise Reform in China: Past, Present and Prospects," in *China's Forty Years of Reform and Development 1978-2018*, ed. Ross Garnaut, Ligang Song, and Cai Fang (Canberra: Australia National University, 2018).

73. Qian and Wu, "China's Transition to a Market Economy."

74. Qian Jiwei, "Why Informal Workers are Opting Out of China's Welfare System," *Sixth Tone*, October 9, 2019.

75. Lardy, "The Role of Foreign Trade and Investment in China's Economic Transformation."

76. Qian Jiwei, "Why Informal Workers are Opting Out of China's Welfare System."

77. Qian and Wu, "China's Transition to a Market Economy."

78. Yang Song, "Rising Chinese Regional Income Inequality: The Role of Fiscal Decentralization," *China Economic Review* 27 (2013): 294–309.

79. *Xinhua*, "Implementation Outline on Building Ethics among Citizens" [Gongmin Daode Jianshe Sheshi Gangyao], October 24, 2001.

80. Vicky Xiuzhong Xu and Bang Xiao, "Falungong: Two Decades After a Deadly Ban, Adherents Still Face Pressure in Australia," *ABC News*, April 20, 2018.

81. Zhang Ye, "China's Emerging Civil Society," Brookings Institute Working Paper, June 2003.

82. *China Labor Bulletin*, "Reform of State-Owned Enterprises in China," December 19, 2007. As of January 31, 2020, https://clb.org.hk/en/content/reform-state-owned-enterprises-china#part1_3.

83. World Inequality Database, "World Inequality Report 2018."

84. Qian and Wu, "China's Transition to a Market Economy."

85. Ibid.

86. Minxin Pei, "The Dark Side of China's Rise," *Foreign Policy*, October 20, 2009.

87. Saich, "The Fourteenth Party Congress," 1138.

Chapter 3

China 2004–2010

Hu Jintao: Professionalization Fails to Convert Opposing Elites

Facing the prospects of a slowing economy and mounting externality costs, Chinese President Hu Jintao pursued a new growth model characterized by higher productivity and balanced development. He advocated for a "scientific" form of development characterized by a greater reliance on consumption, reductions in government debt, improvements in advanced technology to elevate productivity, and a stronger social welfare system.

However, Hu inherited political and structural disadvantages that augured ill for such efforts. A central dilemma that confronted Hu was that successful implementation of the proposed policies required a downgrade in the income and privileges of the same elites charged with implementing those policies. If Hu pressed too hard on the elites to carry out the new policies, they might resist, perhaps violently. However, if Hu accommodated their interests, he would buy near-term stability at the cost of a deterioration in the country's long-term prospects.

Additional factors exacerbated the dilemma. The central government remained weak relative to subnational governments, which routinely ignored or circumvented central directives that threatened their interests. Hu's military inexperience and lack of a constituency among the PLA rendered his control of the security forces uncertain. The CCP's atrophy intensified after the death of popular revolutionary hero Deng Xiaoping. By the early 2000s, the party was plagued with rampant corruption and ideological demoralization.

The elite opposition had grown stronger too, especially once Hu put forth his intensive growth agenda. In the 1990s, Deng wrestled with a relatively well-defined, but feeble, hardliner faction that collapsed once he marshalled popular support. Hu, by contrast, faced a more diffuse, entrenched, and wealthy network of elites whose main opposition to central power stemmed not from ideological principles but from self-interest. No amount of theoretical argument was likely to persuade these individuals to adopt policies that undercut their livelihoods.

Moreover, the public had become deeply fragmented, leaving the central leadership without a strong political ally at a moment in which it was urgently needed. In part due to the country's thorough integration into the global economy, the urban workforce became dominated by informality. The business sector featured a large foreign investor presence, which had little interest in funding either the country's social safety net or upgrading its economic competitiveness. In addition, social inequality rose to extreme levels, and the social welfare system remained threadbare, straining an already faltering tie between the public and the CCP. New social groups began to claim the allegiance of disenchanted citizens, alarming the state. These trends further eroded an already low potential for public mobilization. In short, Hu faced a daunting political situation as he contemplated carrying out a contentious set of major, multi-sector-intensive growth policies.

Hu also faced competing priorities that complicated the pursuit of intensive growth. Improving the quality of governance stood as a top priority, as the leadership hoped to ease public resentment over issues of local malfeasance by elevating the competence and professionalism of the nation's public servants. Strengthening the governing capacity of officials also promised to potentially help achieve Hu's goals of economic upgrading. With proper training and motivation, officials might voluntarily carry out difficult and contentious intensive growth policies, including those that cost them lucrative rents. If his strategy succeeded, Hu Jintao would have overseen the implementation of difficult, intensive growth strategies in a manner that bolstered CCP legitimacy and avoided debilitating intra-elite conflict.

Consistent with this approach, central leaders reframed the party's identity as one defined by "governance" and implemented a rigorous program of education, training, professional development, and moral exhortation. To facilitate accountability and compliance, central leaders also oversaw an overhaul of the government's administration. Hu advanced the standardization of processes, procedures, and norms. The changes helped make party procedures and decision-making more transparent, rigorous, and amenable to supervision, at least to leaders within the party. Given the low quality of education and professional ability of Chinese officials at the start of Hu's tenure, these measures were sorely needed.

At the same time, Hu made tentative efforts to improve the cohesiveness of the public. Since he had little ability to reverse economic fragmentation, he sought instead to bolster political cohesiveness by tentatively promoting nationalist sentiment, suppressing rival groups that might claim the loyalty of citizens, and reinvigorating the party's ideology.

Hu's efforts made some progress in raising the professional and educational level of the cadre corps. Central leaders also succeeded in avoiding a debilitating conflict with elites. But Hu failed to implement the intensive growth policies needed to put the economy on a sustainable footing. To be sure, the economy's growth continued to surge, and the leadership oversaw incremental progress in its efforts to reduce severe regional imbalances and improve social services. But the high growth rates obscured the desultory reality of a deepening dependence on obsolete, extensive growth policies. The effort to build a more productive, efficient economy failed.

Hu's political strategies played an important role in the disappointing outcomes. The central leadership's approach failed to break the power of the elite opposition or remedy its frayed ties with a fragmented public. In its efforts to compel subordination from the same elites upon whom it depended, the central leadership found itself easily outmaneuvered. Subnational elites coopted the central leadership's institution-building processes and procedures to maintain the illusion of compliance with policies that they thwarted in practice.

BACKGROUND

In the early 2000s, China's economy remained in the midst of a remarkable decades-long expansion. From 1979 to 2004, the country's real GDP grew at an average of 9.4 percent.[1] The rapid growth lifted as many as 400 million Chinese out of poverty, and per capita income increased tenfold from US$158 in 1978 to US$1,508 in 2004.[2] Economists attributed much of China's phenomenal success to two sources: Large-scale capital investment and rapid productivity gains. China's large reservoir of capital is owed in part to policies of financial repression and government policies that directed the reinvestment of profits from SOEs.[3] With one of the world's highest savings rates, China used its access to a vast pool of capital to fund investment-driven growth. The volume of foreign direct investment (FDI) also soared starting in the late 1990s as China deepened its involvement in global production following its accession to the World Trade Organization in 2000.

However, China also benefited from major productivity gains. In particular, China in the 1980s and 1990s reallocated poorly employed labor to more productive uses, especially in sectors that were formerly heavily controlled by the central government, such as agriculture, trade, and services. The rise of nonstate enterprises further aided productivity, as these tended to be more efficient than SOEs. Local and provincial governments operated various enterprises according to market principles with little interference from the central government.[4] China also benefited from large inflows of FDI, which brought new technologies and more efficient labor practices. One IMF study concluded that labor productivity in foreign-invested enterprises (FIE) exceeded that of their non-FIE counterparts by a factor of 9:1. FIEs began to play a dominant role in the economy. In 2004, the FIE sector contributed half of China's exports and perhaps as much as 40 percent of its GDP growth.[5] Chinese manufacturers and exporters also experienced efficiency gains through integration into the global economy. In 2000, China's accession to the WTO expanded access to overseas markets.[6] Trade surged accordingly. In 2004 alone, China's exports increased 35.4 percent to US$593.36 billion, while imports increased 36 percent to US$561.38 billion.[7] That year, China surpassed Japan to become the world's third-largest trading economy after the United States and Germany.[8]

Yet the period of extraordinary economic growth and rapid productivity gains was nearing its end. By 2004, China's productivity rates began to decline as it exhausted the growth potential of structural reforms from the previous two decades. The gains from the mass reallocation of labor from low-productivity agriculture to higher productivity manufacturing began to recede when migration slowed. The market liberalization and privatization initiatives advanced by Deng in the 1990s had also largely run their course.[9]

Future growth would depend on finding ways to unleash productivity by tackling a suboptimal financial system and dismantling state enterprises in a number of protected sectors. The state sector remained a prime target due to its massive size and low productivity. Although SOEs accounted for one-third of industrial production, over half failed to generate a profit and had to be supported by politically directed bank loans. Indeed, half of the loans from state-owned banks went to money-losing SOEs.[10]

Chinese leaders also faced mounting pressure to address the mounting costs of "externalities" imposed by a growth model premised on low-cost labor, repression, and lax environmental regulations. The decades of rapid growth may have raised income levels, but they also spawned yawning inequality, choking environmental pollution, and pervasive official malfeasance.[11] Years of underfunded government services exacerbated public anger as local governments resorted to illegal fees and exploitive practices to make up revenue shortfalls or simply failed to provide services. In the late 1990s, mass the protest increased in volume and severity.[12] Left unaddressed, these problems threatened the CCP's grip on power.

The nature of the economic challenge thus invariably entailed confronting directly the role of powerful interest groups and officials in sustaining inefficient and politically damaging practices. Chinese officials and scholars recognized the severity of the challenge. A typical Chinese commentary, publishing in the party journal *Outlook*, observed in 2004 that "noneconomic factors are increasingly restricting our ability to achieve economic reforms."

The article explained that economic reforms "increasingly touch noneconomic fields such as politics, the sources of political power, and the methods of the party's leadership."[13] Lu Zhongyuan, a researcher at the State Council, similarly lamented that the situation in the preceding decades, in which "all of society benefits" from reforms, had turned into a situation in which "only some people can benefit while some suffer from reforms." The crux of the issue, he observed, lay in the "reallocation of interests, readjustment of social status, and the splitting-up of social groups." He predicted that the implementation of reforms to improve the country's economic prospects would generate "new conflicts one after another."[14]

These scholarly observations appeared to reflect thinking among the country's leaders. At the Third Plenum of the 16th Party Congress, the central leadership under Hu outlined its policy agenda to improve the country's economic prospects, a task his officials viewed as inseparable from renovating an outdated and dilapidated governance structure. Hu pledged to deliver "people-centered" governance under the guidance of a "scientific development concept." He called for policies that assured the quality and safety of consumer goods, such as food, higher quality social welfare services, technological innovation, and sustainable development. This agenda reflected a view among top Chinese leaders that the country needed to move beyond its dependence on inefficient and wasteful legacy growth models toward a more balanced, sustainable, and technologically advanced economy that provides incentives for talented professionals, knowledge workers, and entrepreneurs to work hard, innovate, and generate new business.[15]

In a speech in 2003, Premier Wen Jiabao acknowledged that improving the country's economic performance depended on improvements to the government's ability to "comprehensively perform its functions." He endorsed economic regulation but added, "It is necessary to pay greater attention to the government's functions of social management and public services." He called for "coordinated development between the economy and the society, between the urban areas and the rural areas, between the eastern region and the western region, and between human beings and nature."[16]

Developments Related to the Central Leadership

To carry out an ambitious policy agenda, Hu's administration would have to overcome severe political disadvantages that he had inherited from his predecessor, Jiang Zemin. These included persistent central government weakness, potent elite opposition, and severe public fragmentation.

Jiang oversaw a number of recentralizing fiscal and budgetary reforms in the mid to late 1990s aimed at consolidating the central leadership's regulatory authority in policy areas such as the environment, product safety, labor, and land.[17] However, these efforts only yielded partial and unsatisfactory results. On the one hand, the recentralization efforts, in some cases, succeeded in constraining powerful, wealthy provinces. On the other hand, the same provinces usually remained strong enough to resist many of the central government's demands. Moreover, the poorer provinces lacked the resources to carry out the policies directed by the central leadership. As a result, many of the central leadership-directed policies experienced uneven and suboptimal implementation.[18]

China's integration into the global economy exacerbated the problem of internal fragmentation and provincial resistance to central authority. Large influxes of FDI coincided with a continued decline in inter-provincial trade as a share of total trade from the 1990s through 2002. Over the same period, both intra-provincial and international trade climbed.[19] The infusion of foreign capital resulted in a flourishing labor-intensive processing industry in the rapidly developing southeastern coastal provinces. These industries attracted migrant labor from the inland regions but generated only limited linkages and weak spillovers. Coastal cities benefited, but inland provinces fell further behind.[20] The wealthy provinces continued to resist decrees that impinged on their economic interests. For example, after prohibiting regional protectionism in 1982 and 1990, the State Council issued another regulation in 2001. None of the decrees reversed the fragmenting internal market.[21] And despite repeated injunctions by the central government, local cadres continued to avoid enforcing labor, environmental, and other regulations. They also continued to maintain lucrative monopolies that increased GDP and profits but distorted prices and wasted resources. A 2005 World Bank study noted that despite incremental progress in expanding linkages between wealthy provinces, the fragmentation of capital markets in particular had worsened over time, resulting in "large misallocations across industries."[22] Chinese scholars warned that central control had become dangerously fragile. An article in the party journal *Outlook* published in 2005 criticized provinces as having become "increasingly independent." The article observed that the "relationship between central and local governments has changed from the previous subordinating relationship between administrative organizations to a negotiating relationship between economic entities."[23]

Hu also inherited a weakening central grip on the party. Hu presided over a CCP that had become enervated by years of rapid growth and ideological incoherence. In pivoting to support market-friendly reforms, the CCP's ideology and "Marxist" identity seemed increasingly irrelevant and detached from reality. Echoing a view common among the China-watching community of the time, Misra Kaipana observed that the CCP's ideology had degenerated into a "post-Marxist patchwork doctrine" characterized by "intellectual fuzziness, inconsistency, and eclecticism."[24] Party discipline appeared weak, with widespread reports of corruption, demoralization, and official malfeasance.[25]

Curbing the independence of the provinces and restoring party discipline under such conditions posed a formidable political challenge to any leader, even a strong and confident one. Yet the new president, Hu Jintao, faced serious political and structural impediments. Hu, a technocratic engineer, lacked the revolutionary credentials and personal charisma of Deng Xiaoping. He also faced a strong political challenge within the party from his predecessor, Jiang Zemin, who eagerly sought to protect his networks of clients. A prolonged transfer of power from 2002 to 2004 underscored the weakness of Hu's position. It took two years after he had ascended to the post of General Secretary before Hu finally appeared to have gained an upper hand over Jiang, but behind the scenes maneuvering by rivals would continue to plague a leader widely perceived to be weak.[26]

Despite his personal liabilities and the resistance posed by Jiang's networks, Hu had formally consolidated his position as the nation's top ruler by early 2004. In terms of controlling the security forces, Hu at last gained the position of the Central Military Commission (CMC) chair in 2003 and quickly promoted supportive generals to higher level positions while retiring those suspected of loyalty to Jiang. He also oversaw major changes to the military's organization in 2004 and defense budgets. These measures appeared to strengthen the military's loyalty, although how much remained unclear, given the weakness of his client base.[27]

In sum, the central leadership experienced serious *weakness*. Hu Jintao formally gained the top offices in the government, party, and military by 2004, but in reality, his grip was tenuous and incomplete. The party remained riven with corruption and demoralization, the central government continued to face resistance to its authority from provinces, and Hu's nascent ties to the military rendered his control suspect.

Developments Related to Elite Opposition

The resistance of subnational governments to central authority stemmed in large part from the power of cadres to marshal their considerable resources. Reaping gains from years of rapid growth, the elite share of income and wealth soared. The top 10 percent of income earners increased their share of national income to 45 percent in 2004, up from about 35 percent a decade earlier. The share of wealth increased dramatically as well, from 40 percent in 1994 to over 50 percent a decade later.[28]

Elites also operated in a more collusive manner, horizontally across political and commercial domains and vertically through the highest reaches of government. To be sure, China's political elites have long exploited their positions for self-gain. In the 1980s and 1990s, for example, they launched careers in business in part by manipulating their government and party connections. But in the 2000s, newly arising business elites showed growing interest in getting involved in politics, in part to expand opportunities for profit. The expansion of party membership to business professionals as part of Jiang Zemin's Three Represents ideology, formalized at the 16th Party Congress in 2002, merely consolidated a tightening network of interlocking political and business elites.[29]

The collusion between the central government and sub-national elites through the 1990s and early 2000s reflected a common interest in maintaining rapid economic growth. However, the cooperation frayed over time as elite power grew. Local society became increasingly dominated by the interlocking political-economic elite, who prioritized self-enrichment. Local cadre faced few constraints and strong incentives to carry out harsh and sometimes illegal measures, such as excessive taxes and land seizures, to offset inadequate revenues and line their own pockets. The local elites also provoked public anger by remaining generally closed to newcomers and by relying on corruption and nepotism to maintain their privileged positions.[30]

The new elites also consolidated their position in a more subtle, insidious way that made controlling them difficult. In the 1990s, Deng faced a fairly well-defined factional opposition whose vocal criticisms belied their organizational weakness. The opposition to Deng melted away under his skillful political maneuvering, in part by mobilizing latent public support. But Hu faced a more diffuse, well-resourced, entrenched elite that controlled large segments of the same party state apparatus that he sought to lead.[31] These new elites prioritized the protection of their lucrative interests over compliance with central directives. The strong position held by these elites could be seen in the fact that they saw little need to publicly defy the party's ideological pronouncements. On the contrary, these elites found it far more effective to simply feign compliance while undermining Beijing's intentions through the manipulation of bureaucratic processes. Despite the appearance of unity and cohesion, elite networks continued to protect their interests, evade accountability, and undermine central directives.[32]

Thus, although the central leadership largely backed the local elites during the 1990s, when both profited from rapid growth, their interests diverged in the 2000s. Beijing directed more efforts to alleviate public anger and end wasteful and unproductive practices, but elites opposed these measures since they entailed a reduction in their profits and privileges. Accordingly, elites simply ignored or otherwise circumvented the central directives. As but one example, local officials ignored Beijing's orders to stabilize soaring real estate prices. They feigned compliance, but in reality, they disguised the price increases and continued to secure profitable deals from developers.[33]

Chinese scholars harshly criticized the frequency with which local cadres refused to carry out their assigned duties. Scholar Chen Zewei blasted the "common phenomena" of "failure to abide by the law, lax enforcement of law, and impunity for violation of law" among sub-national officials. He accused "some public officials" of "abusing their power, engaging in corruption, and knowingly violating the law."[34] Other scholars highlighted the problem of extensive collusion between government officials and commercial actors. One expert observed that the "root of the problem" lies in the fact that local governments "ally themselves to groups seeking profits" and create "interrelated self-interest-oriented groups." He argued that such groups posed "strong resistance that impedes reform."[35]

In sum, the elite opposition was *strong* in this period. The elites accrued a disproportionate share of national income and wealth. An interlocking elite between government officials and entrepreneurs developed. The elites also stepped up collaboration vertically to more effectively protect their privileges in an atmosphere of growing antagonism with the central government.

Developments Related to Public Cohesiveness

Hu Jintao also inherited a country that had sustained severe social fragmentation. Inequality reached new heights in the 2000s. The Gini coefficient remained above 0.40, a level identified by the World Bank as destabilizing.[36] Although the people enjoyed rising incomes, their social welfare needs remained largely unmet outside of the shrinking state sector. Chinese scholars acknowledged that reducing the SOE sector meant that the country urgently needed to make progress toward building a national social welfare system, but neither had advanced very far by the early 2000s. One Chinese economist observed that without the construction of a robust social welfare system, "there is no channel to release the social burden that accompanies the state-owned enterprise reform."[37] The services the local governments provided varied widely by province, reflecting the country's internal polarization. For example, by 2005, China's richest province (Shanghai) had more than eight times the per capita spending on its citizens of the poorest province (Anhui).[38]

As of 2003, Chinese citizens had few opportunities for political participation. The fragmentation and weak links between the public and the party raised fears that competing organizations could grow in the vacuum. The brutal repression of Falungong, household Christian churches, and other autonomous groups continued. In the wake of "color revolutions" across

Eastern Europe and the Middle East, Chinese authorities grew suspicious of "underground organizations" as well as NGOs. Hu Jintao urged vigilance about these organizations and the Foreign Ministry established an office to more closely monitor foreign NGOs.[39]

The mobilization of the public against elites had long been a staple of communist politics, but developments since the 1990s had rendered this option less viable at a moment when central leaders urgently needed it. Chinese officials recognized the imperative of strengthening the central government's ties with the people. They also acknowledged the need to expand opportunities for popular political participation, in part to hold local officials accountable. Yet fears of losing control led them to adopt largely symbolic and ultimately ineffective measures. For example, to help bridge the gap between the people and the central government, authorities promoted ideals and values drawn from traditions outside of Marxism. Officials promoted, for example, Confucius and other classical thinkers who espoused harmony between rulers and ruled.[40] Officials also cultivated nationalist fervor, as they did when Japan's prime minister visited its military shrines in Yasukuni in 2005.[41] However, officials continued to manage patriotic sentiment carefully, aware that it presented a double-edged sword that could threaten CCP rule if mishandled.[42] A few experts, such as Beijing University scholar Yu Keping, recommended the adoption of democratic practices to strengthen ties between the people and the central government.[43] Many more scholars advocated measures to at least improve the transparency of decision-making and expand information disclosure as a way to bolster public trust in the government.[44] These recommendations went unheeded.

The public was deeply *fragmented* at the start of this period. China's deepening integration into the global economy fueled a surging informal sector. FIE drove a larger share of economic growth, and a politically disconnected populace experienced worsening insecurity and inadequate social services. Inequality reached destabilizing levels, and desperate people began to seek support in groups and communities outside CCP control.

The political situation in 2004 appeared unfavorable, with the values of the three political factors the complete inverse of the "enabling condition." A *weak* central leadership facing a *strong* elite opposition alone provided grounds for pessimism, but prospects dimmed further in light of the severe *fragmentation* of the public. To shape the values closer to those of the "enabling condition," China's central leadership would need to find a way to strengthen central power, restore discipline and cohesion to the CCP, ensure tight control of security forces, weaken the power of elites, and enhance the cohesiveness of the public—all without provoking destabilizing political conflict.

INTERVENING DEVELOPMENTS, 2005–2007

To cope with the simultaneous issues of inadequate governance capacity, central government weakness, disarray in the CCP, entrenched recalcitrant elites, and popular fragmentation, central leaders under Hu carried out a governance strategy that built on Jiang's cooptation of business elites. They sought to remake the CCP and government into modern, competent, rational bureaucratic actors capable of governing an increasingly wealthy, modern, pluralistic society—an ambition well captured in the decision to abandon the CCP's old identity as a "revolutionary party" in favor of that of a "governing party." As part of the new paradigm shift, the CCP no longer claimed to merely represent the "revolutionary forces" of proletarian workers and peasants but instead sought to represent the whole nation. In practice, the central leadership consolidated its base of power among the country's political and economic elites. At the same time, the central leaders sought to transform these elites from cadres who narrowly defended their interests, often to the detriment of the nation's welfare, into professional technocrats who realized their enlightened self-interests through the implementation of policies set by the central leadership.[45]

The central leadership outlined a governance agenda with many noneconomic goals, such as improving the quality of government services. But its governance agenda also aimed to facilitate intensive growth policies. Chinese leaders directed efforts to institutionalize and regularize party processes and procedures and promote the professional development of the cadre corps through training, education, and exhortation. It sought, in short, to transform noncompliant, corrupt, and inept cadres into educated, competent, highly professional officials capable of effectively administering the country. If successfully implemented, the central leadership would have achieved their goals of strengthening party discipline, improving governance, and energizing the economy's performance, all in a manner that avoided intra-elite conflict and avoided politically involving the public. This technocratic vision likely appealed to central leaders eager to avoid repeating the destructive political conflicts of the pre-reform period. It also well suited the conflict-averse personality of Hu Jintao.

In subsequent years, the central government undertook a number of initiatives consistent with the new governance agenda. Authorities offered incentives for official compliance, for example, by easing up on the anticorruption drive. According to political scientist Minxin Pei, the rate of prosecution declined by almost half between 1995 and 2006. Pei noted little evidence that the decline was due to a reduction in real corruption.[46] More likely, it reflected a political decision to encourage cadres to comply with Hu's new policy agenda.

Starting around 2001 and lasting through the decade, the party also issued numerous regulations, rules, and laws that detailed standardized procedures for decision-making, recruitment, promotion, retirement, and discipline.[47] In 2004, for example, the Central Committee promulgated a set of regulations on "inner-party supervision" that aimed to institutionalize many procedures and improve the accountability and discipline of party cadres.[48] Many western scholars noted the striking emphasis on the standardization of procedures, policies, and processes. Portland State University professor Bruce Gilley regarded Hu Jintao's governing style as one of "proceduralism." He concluded that the main point of Hu's approach was to improve the quality of decision-making with more transparent and rigorous procedures.[49] The CCP also reinvigorated traditional methods of enhancing discipline and building consensus in favor of Hu's policy agenda. In 2003, Hu initiated a series of political campaigns, the most important of which was the "Campaign to Maintain the Advanced Nature of the Party." The campaign aimed to strengthen the party's cohesion and leadership and purge ineffective members. At the close of the 18-month campaign in July 2006, Chinese media reported that nearly 3 million heads of party organizations received intensive training, and 44,738 members were expelled from the CCP.[50]

The CCP also invested considerable effort into its professional development. Central leaders directed more training and education in hopes of building a more competent and professional cadre corps. Authorities also revamped recruitment, evaluation, and promotion criteria and procedures to incentivize compliance with central edicts and encourage responsible governance.[51] Beginning in the early 2000s, local cadres began to be evaluated according to a broad set of indicators, spanning economic, social, and political domains.[52] However, the revised assessment criteria had little effect, in part, because indicators for social welfare measures proved difficult to quantify, required long-term commitments, and competed with the more easily quantified economic indicators that played a decisive role in the promotion or demotion of the officials. Accordingly, the central leadership under Hu tried numerous times to revise evaluation criteria to include noneconomic indicators as part of its "scientific development" approach to development. These efforts met with only incrementally better results, however.[53]

The political measures were not entirely futile. The introduction of long-overdue education and professional training requirements, procedural regulations, and promotion criteria helped improve the competence of the cadre corps. However, these measures by themselves failed to persuade elites to abandon their rent-seeking behavior. Nor did Hu develop an effective means of compelling obedience. As he would learn in the following years, institutions, rules, and regulations do not enforce themselves. Any hope that elites could be persuaded to voluntarily surrender their own substantial income and privileges was bound to be disappointed. At the end of the day, the elites were free to publicly affirm their compliance with central orders while, in practice, withholding compliance. In short, Hu's ambitions for economic upgrading were fatally undermined by his own governance strategy.

The same decision also carried important implications for the central leadership's relationship with the public. The central leadership's decision to base its political support on the nation's political and economic elites weakened an already badly frayed relationship with the public. This would make it even more difficult for the central leadership to mobilize the people to support its intensive growth agenda, the failure of which in turn merely deepened the central leadership's dependence on elites.

Developments Related to the Central Leadership

During this period, the central leadership led by Hu Jintao focused on improving the central government's authority over the provinces, bolstering national unity, and strengthening political discipline and control over the party. In terms of the central leadership's relations with the provinces, Beijing continued efforts to reduce internal fragmentation through large-scale transfers. After promulgating a "Go West" policy in 2000, the central government transferred US$50 billion to the western provinces from 2000 to 2005, accounting for 52 percent of their provincial budgets.[54] China also provided incentives for foreign investors to move to those regions. Development accelerated, but the overwhelming majority of investment continued to focus on the coastal provinces.[55] As a result of the investment stimulus, GDP growth accelerated in the western provinces, although through 2006 the gap between coastal and inland provinces experienced little change.[56] Indeed, studies remain inconclusive as to the effectiveness of the "Go West" affiliated programs in reducing intra-regional inequality.[57]

Beijing also revived efforts to crack down on the autonomy of provinces. The central leadership targeted, in particular, the pernicious protectionist and monopolistic practices that left the domestic market fragmented and wasted resources through redundant and inefficient practices. In 2007, the central leadership passed yet another law outlawing administrative monopolies.[58] An article in a CCP journal, *Seeking Truth*, explained the reason for the law, denouncing unnamed local officials for "abusing their administrative power to eliminate or restrict competition" and "maintaining regional blockades."[59] However, the enforcement powers that came with the law proved so weak that the law's passage scarcely reduced the practices.[60]

Hu's efforts to consolidate his control of the security forces continued apace. The security forces continued to experience generous budget increases, and Hu promoted more generals who might support his authority.

Western analysts of the time noted the military's increasing acceptance of meritocratic criteria and norms for retirement. No signs of overt opposition to Hu's rule appeared. However, absent any crises that might test his control, it was difficult to judge the extent of Hu's control, given his doubtful power base in the military.[61]

Hu also experienced mixed progress in consolidating his position within the CCP. On the one hand, the 17th Party Congress held in 2007 confirmed Hu Jintao's ideological authority and endorsed his policy agenda of balanced, sustainable growth. Inscribing Hu's signature concept of the "scientific development" into the party's guiding ideology added to his authority. On the other hand, the central leadership deemphasized Hu's personal authority as part of a broader trend of collective decision-making and institutionalizing power. This trend invited rival elites to exploit collective decision-making arrangements to block and frustrate policies that might cost them dearly. Underscoring this point, efforts to tighten discipline in the party yielded disappointing results. Despite government pledges, the crackdown on corruption in 2008 yielded meager results, and corruption did not appreciably diminish.[62]

Under Hu, the central leadership stepped up measures to strengthen rules, regulations, and professional training. One notable development was the annual provincial and ministerial leaders training session, which began around 2003 and in itself underscored the power held by subnational elites and their counterparts in the central ministries. The annual training session typically featured a speech by the general secretary and served as a venue to socialize and exhort elites to carry out work assigned by the central leadership.[63] The Central Committee also continued to issue regulations and detailed procedures on issues such as performance evaluations, decision-making, and discipline, as well as cadre rotational policies.[64] Hu also directed efforts to systematize the ideology and render it more coherent and useful for purposes of governance. In 2005, China established a new Research Academy on Marxism.[65] Over 500 experts and scholars took part in a multiyear effort to systematize the party's guiding ideology, which they completed in 2006.[66]

These efforts yielded modest results, but far less than what the central leaders required. The expansion of training and education requirements, the weeding out of poorly qualified and inept cadres, and the standardization of many procedures and norms noticeably increased the meritocratic qualifications of party officials. It also facilitated the differentiation of functions among the bureaucracy and rendered some political processes more transparent, stable, and predictable. Western observers noticed improvements in the resilience and effectiveness of the CCP rule. Andrew Nathan cited these features when he coined the phrase "resilient authoritarianism" to explain the CCP's unusual organizational strength and success in avoiding the grim fate of its Soviet counterparts.[67] However, the effects of the changes could be easily overstated. While these developments may have improved educational qualifications and made some improvements in governance, they did not provide a compelling incentive for officials to abandon lucrative but inefficient and unproductive practices. Nor did the measures stop their illegal and abusive behavior toward the public. The systematization of the party's ideology may have rendered it more coherent and useful for party theorists, but it did not do much to reinvigorate popular enthusiasm for the CCP.[68]

In short, the central leadership remained *weak*. Hu made gains in consolidating his personal network in the security forces, but the central leadership made little progress in asserting its control over the provinces, party officials, and the military.

Developments Related to Elite Opposition

During this period, the power of elites began to stabilize at a high level. The share of national income increased for the top 10 percent and leveled off at around 43 percent over this period, owing in part to the effects of policies that prioritized more equitable growth. Structural transformations may have also had an impact, such as a shrinking rural labor force, which caused wages to grow more rapidly than output.[69] However, the share of wealth held by the top 10 percent increased from around 51 percent in 2004 to 56 percent three years later, which showed that the elite continued to successfully exploit their positions for gain.[70]

Problems of collusion between interlocking elites persisted. During this period, media attention focused on problems of weak enforcement of regulations, resulting in major scandals. Entrenched bribery and extensive patronage networks led officials to tolerate unsafe foods and shoddy products.[71] To maintain growth and maximize employment, cadres also maintained provincial trade barriers and administrative monopolies. The imperative to maintain clients and cronyistic incomes also encouraged cadres and their backers to value loyalty over competence for key positions and to continue practices that infuriated the masses, such as land sales and tolerance of ecological devastation by industry. Powerful SOEs and their political patrons also demanded banks prioritize lending to them, even as more productive private enterprises starved of capital. Scholars described a "shadow state" in which personalized rule, clientelistic bureaucratic behavior, and corruption served the needs of local party bosses and disregarded the needs of the public.[72]

By 2007, it had become apparent that the effort to bring the elites under the control of the central leadership through administrative and regulatory methods had failed. Noncompliance remained rampant, corruption and malfeasance continued apace, and many key policies remained unimplemented. This happened even though officials routinely participated in training sessions, approved plans to carry out central directives, and even penned articles that effusively praised the policies that they in practice ignored. Scholars bitterly criticized the cynical behavior they observed. Chen Zewei observed, "The relevant state laws and inner-party regulations have been promulgated, but they do not completely resolve the problem of lax implementation of and hindrance to the government orders." Chen blamed "ineffective implementation of policies" on "inadequate supervision."[73]

In sum, elite opposition remained *strong*. Chinese leaders made little headway in overcoming elite resistance. The elite share of wealth continued to grow, and the central leadership's efforts to socialize elites into compliance failed to weaken the collusive nature of elite power. Nor did efforts to professionalize the cadre corps succeed in persuading the same officials to abandon inefficient and counterproductive policies.

Developments Related to Public Cohesiveness

The challenge of disciplining and controlling an exceptionally wealthy and powerful elite under weak central leadership was formidable enough. But the challenge became even more daunting due to the fractured state of the public. At the moment when the central leadership needed, more than ever, a public who could be mobilized to support the central leadership, it faced a populace that had become extremely fragmented. Social inequality remained high, with the Gini coefficient reaching 0.49 in 2008, making China one of the most unequal societies in the world. The bottom 50 percent of income earners saw their share of national income fall to 15 percent from 20 percent a decade earlier.[74]

China's integration into the global economy aggravated the trend toward informal labor. Increasing globalization, as measured by international trade volume and foreign direct investment (FDI), correlated with an increase in the informal economy in China. The correlation was created largely by the subcontracting system typical of emerging economies at the time. In this system, manufacturing processes became decomposed into tasks and subtasks, which could in turn be subcontracted to small-scale firms and informal specialized factories to minimize costs. China experienced a rapid expansion of many informal factories or small workshops developed to satisfy the needs of the global subcontracting production system. This system became a critical ingredient in China's low labor cost and competitive advantage. Local governments tolerated the informal workforce to attract global capital.[75] Informal employment grew from 15,000 workers in 1978, when economic reforms began, to more than 168 million in 2006, representing over 60 percent of total urban employment.[76]

The evolution of the global economy presaged developments that drove China's economy in a direction sharply divergent from that of smaller Asian economies, such as Taiwan, South Korea, and Singapore. For one, the sheer size of the workforce rendered unlikely the possibility that China would ever reach the "Lewis turning point," in which all available surplus labor would be employed in a modern formal economy. Employment in the urban formal sector increased by only 20 million laborers after 30 years of marketizing reforms, from 95 million in 1978 to 114.9 million in 2006.[77] Throughout the 1990s and 2000s, China's workers received a shrinking piece of the expanding economic pie. Labor's share of the GDP declined from 53 percent in 1990 to 39.7 percent in 2007. This stood in stark contrast to most other countries, where labor's share of GDP usually ranged from 60 to 80 percent.[78]

As inequality increased and a lack of benefits became the norm for vast numbers of urban workers, authorities tried new strategies to elevate the living standards of the public. Over the past decade, the Ministry of Labor attempted several measures to expand social welfare policies among nonpublic enterprises. But these had all failed, in part due to the fragmentation of the enterprise sector. With FIE driving half of the country's GDP growth, local governments depended heavily on foreign enterprises to provide growth, jobs, and tax revenues. Competition from foreign companies incentivized local governments to waive requirements to provide benefits to workers. Moreover, workers distrusted the social welfare programs administrated by the state due to fears that corrupt cadres would simply steal their contributions.[79]

As the central leadership's dependence on elites deepened, the party's political links with the people decayed further. The central leadership became concerned that popular discontent could erupt over issues of inequality, official malfeasance, and other issues. To forestall such a situation, Hu directed moves in 2005 to tighten control of the internet, limit foreign involvement in the Chinese media, and more closely monitor the operation of both domestic and international nongovernmental organizations (NGOs). In June of 2005, all Chinese websites and bloggers were required to register their real names with authorities or risk being closed down by the end of the month. Later that year, the government issued new rules outlining tighter censorship of the internet.[80] The central leadership's inability to curtail the abuses by local elites led them to regard tight control of the media as essential for maintaining order. To justify crackdowns on the media and NGOs in 2004, for example, officials tended to cite the perils of unchecked rumors and a pervasive public distrust of the government. One scholar also noted that the inadequacy of the country's social safety net and persistent underfunding meant officials would be unlikely to fulfill many of the demands that might be raised by the citizens. He suggested permitting freer expression could simply result in worsening public fury and the erosion of the public's trust in the government.[81]

The government took halting steps to expand the accountability of officials to the public. Party officials announced in 2006 that elections would be held for the leaders of committees at the provincial, city, county, and township levels. The officials stated that the purpose of the elections was to help "realize the strategic goal of building a socialist, harmonious society." Although the public would not vote on the candidates directly, the article stated that, "opinion would be sought from different groups and that the public would have an opportunity to "air their views on the candidates."[82] But a few years later, Beijing reversed course due to fear that popular discontent might spread over reports that officials were gaming the procedures to stay in power.[83]

In another effort, central leaders outlined a set of policies to bolster the central leadership's ties with the masses. In 2005, officials promoted a slew of policies designed to address social welfare needs and restore stability under the moniker of a "socialist harmonious society." Scholars explained that this vision entailed a "society of consensus or unanimous agreement" in which the people and officials agreed on "detailed economic rules and policies" and relied on making decisions in a "scientific" and "democratic manner so that government policies will benefit as many people as possible."[84] Hu himself defined the idea as building a society serving "the fundamental interests of the people" and featuring "democracy, the rule of law, equity, justice, sincerity, amity, and vitality," while stressing that the regime must pay attention to social justice. What this implied was that social concerns such as income disparity, corruption, pollution, social stratification, and social unrest should be accorded importance on a par with economic growth in party theory and government policy. Yet with local governments responsible for 70–80 percent of social welfare spending, the weight of such statements depended on whether local cadres would choose to carry them out. And as before, few opted to carry out the policies. The persistent underfunding of local governments similarly resulted in a dearth of services, and frequent abuses of authority left the slogan mostly hollow for many citizens.

In short, public *fragmentation* intensified, in part due to the country's deepening integration into the global economy. Labor experienced informalization as local governments waived requirements to provide benefits amid an acute competition for foreign capital. And having allied closely with elites, the central government further diminished its ability to connect with the people. Accordingly, central authorities backed repression to control challenges to local officials, even as they tried with little success to strengthen ties with the populace.

The lack of change in political factors after three years provided grounds for pessimism. Little progress had been made in moving closer toward the enabling condition. Given the persistent weakness of the central government, the strength of the elite opposition, and the deep fragmentation of the public, the central government faced dwindling prospects for the successful implementation of its policies.

INTERVENING DEVELOPMENTS, 2008–2010

In this period, the central leadership's struggle to carry out its major, multisector policy initiative suffered a serious setback with the emergence of the global financial crisis. The crisis spurred major job losses and exacerbated popular unrest. To staunch the loss of jobs and stabilize society, the central leadership dramatically increased spending, primarily by SOEs. This strengthened the hand of elites and breathed new life into the inefficient state sector. Central leaders grew increasingly frustrated and embittered by the noncompliance of subnational elites, and the period ended with a general failure to oversee the desired economic transformation.

The central leadership's efforts to rein in the provinces resulted in a stalemate, despite some success in transferring resources to the western provinces. Hu's authority over the military proved weaker than it appeared after reports surfaced of widespread high-level corruption and defiance by generals toward disciplinary efforts. The central leadership made progress in improving the professionalism and competence of the cadre corps, but they failed to persuade cadres to quit their counterproductive policies.

Developments Related to the Central Leadership

In this period, the central government experienced little progress in its efforts to recentralize power and compel policy compliance among cadres.[85] Exasperated senior officials grew even more pointed in their criticisms. In a 2009 speech, Premier Wen Jiabao called for measures to break up provincial protections and curb the problems of regulatory noncompliance. Reflecting the lack of progress over the years, he highlighted persistent issues of "monopoly in industries and regional blockades" and the "production and sale of fake and shoddy commodities." Responding to the popular fury over mislabeled food and medicine, he pledged an "in-depth special campaign to improve the safety of food and medicine." Hinting at the broader structural problem that impeded progress, Wen denounced "malpractices in the political structure" that had "become the main constraining factor in the way of changing the pattern of economic development."[86] Party journals routinely lambasted cadres for not carrying out their duties. One typical article denounced "activities not in conformity with the party's nature and purpose." It stated that "policies and plans made by the party Central Committee have not been carried out seriously."[87] Western scholars similarly noted high levels of noncompliance among cadres, which some studies attributed to weak accountability mechanisms.[88]

Recognizing the problem, the Fifth Plenary Meeting of the 17th CPC Central Committee in 2010 called for changes in the management and monitoring of cadres.[89] Senior leaders and scholars associated with the Central Committee bemoaned the unresponsiveness and inadequacy of the existing government structure and called for major change. Citing Premier Wen Jiabao's speech on the same topic, one article in the party school journal *Study Times* stated, "Our failure in political structural reform will take away what we have gained from economic structural reform and make it impossible to attain our modernization goal." It warned that failure to make changes would "ultimately lead to the death of our cause."[90]

Party officials adopted a variety of measures to improve the accountability of cadres to the public. After years of new regulations, authorities issued new procedures for cadre selection and appointment to include steps such as "democratic recommendations, organizing inspections, standing committee considerations, decisions at standing committee meetings, and democratic evaluations." However, party officials grew dismayed to learn how cadres easily circumvented the measures while following them to the letter. An official in the CCP's Organization Department explained that "assorted problems crop up at every step, defeating the purpose behind the system's design." He gave an example, noting that "democratic recommendations" were supposed to enable peers in the party to nominate high-quality candidates. However, in practice, candidates manipulated the procedures to maintain their grip on power through lobbying and by selecting who could vote.[91] Similarly, in 2006, official media trumpeted a shift to "democratic" election of party committees at the local level. Three years later, however, the CCP judged the measure a failure and recentralized the process, with the provincial government assuming the powers of electing and appointing country party secretaries.[92] Western scholars concluded that the central government's focus on building up a law-based form of rule had made some progress but did not live up to high expectations. For example, the institution and law-building efforts had failed to "check abuses of power, unlawful actions, and reform-undermining behavior in the party-state."[93] Observers also noted that the provinces and areas that experienced the highest rates of growth often featured severe human rights violations.[94]

By the end of Hu's reign, evidence surfaced that suggested even his grip on the military and security forces had eroded to an alarming degree. Corruption in the PLA festered throughout both Jiang and Hu's tenure, especially among individuals involved with the lucrative logistics and personnel sectors. In 2006, reports emerged that former PLA Navy Deputy Commander

Vice-Admiral Wang Shouye siphoned off 160 million yuan when he was a General Logistics Department deputy director.[95] Even more shocking was the case of senior general Gu Junshan, who defied the military's disciplinary office when it investigated him for corruption. Hu Jintao reportedly had to personally intervene and direct the party's disciplinary office, the CCDI, to carry out the inquiry.[96]

In sum, the central leadership remained *weak*. Under Hu Jintao, Beijing had sought to strengthen its grip on subnational governments, improve party discipline, and build popular support for a broader agenda of economic and governance reform. But central authorities simply lacked the capacity to manage all the country's problems and had little choice but to rely on subnational elites, who in turn exploited the central leadership's dependence on them for advantage.[97] An example of the central leadership's ultimate backing for local cadres over the public can be seen in how officials who angered the people were generally treated. The Chinese press mentioned how, in many cases, cadres fired over "mass incidents" were "transferred to positions at the same or even higher levels." One scholar lamented that as long as cadres "do not make big blunders" and can "get the situation under control," they could continue to abuse the rights of locals.[98]

Developments Related to Elite Opposition

Although the elite share of income remained stable, with the top 10 percent earning about 43 percent of the nation's income, the share of wealth controlled by the country's elite continued to grow. By 2009, less than 1 percent of Chinese households controlled more than 60 percent of the country's wealth (by comparison, 5 percent of the households in the United States owned 60 percent of the wealth that year).[99] The elites who became the backbone of the regime consisted of party-state bureaucrats with extensive connections to developers, enterprises, and other powerful leaders. These collusive networks controlled lucrative government revenues and state assets.

The efforts to recentralize power also ironically increased the influence of special interests at higher levels of government. In the early 2010s, provinces and industrial and commercial associations set up "representative offices" in Beijing to cultivate good relations with key decision-makers in relevant bureaucracies. Businesses and governments at county levels quickly imitated this tactic in provincial capitals. Renown sinologist David Lampton concluded that lobbying for favorable exemptions to policy had grown routine across multiple levels of government, which further undermined the enforcement of central policy directives.[100]

The government's response to the global financial crisis exacerbated problems for the central government because it shifted large amounts of resources into the hands of elites. Chinese state media and independent international analysts agreed that the stimulus money flowed primarily into public sector construction and infrastructure projects. Such sectoral projects had become a major source of corruption among party-state cadres, providing many opportunities for them to pocket public funds.[101]

SOE reform efforts also experienced setbacks due to other effects of the stimulus response to the crisis. Government officials learned to use political and administrative means to merge enterprises in order to create giant monopolies to protect their interests. These patched-together SOEs lacked innovation, efficiency, and competitiveness since they relied primarily on administrative monopolies for profits.[102] Despite the central leadership's pledge to reduce the burdensome and inefficient sector, the value of SOE assets skyrocketed to US$3.17 trillion in 2009 from US$1.077 trillion in 2002.[103]

Other lucrative but illegal abuses flourished. A particularly vexing problem involved the illegal seizure and sale of land. The importance of land tax revenues grew in conjunction with China's booming housing market, going from less than 4 percent of tax revenues in 1999 to 20 percent in 2010. Local governments acquired massive amounts of land, often already occupied, and sold it to China's booming property developers. This resulted in the displacement of millions of people and became a key source of social tension. According to studies, fees from land sales reached 2.7 trillion RMB and were equivalent to 83 percent of budgetary tax revenues for local governments in 2010.[104]

The power of elites was most vividly shown in the astonishing rise of Bo Xilai. As CCP Secretary of Chongqing, Bo cultivated a leftist political style at odds with the more moderate image promoted by Beijing. Bo built a powerful clientelist network, cultivated powerful patrons with bribes and payoffs, and colluded with a corrupt police force and criminal elements to seize wealth from rich citizens. His downfall would come after Hu left power, but through 2010 Bo's political strategy appeared remarkably successful, earning him a position in the Politburo in 2007 and setting a disturbing precedent for what ambitious elites could achieve if sufficiently ruthless and determined.[105]

In sum, the power of the elites remained *strong*. Their collective strength reached new heights in this period. Corruption flourished, and the interlocking networks of elites grew even more robust, thanks in part to the political and administrative measures that tied the central leadership's fate ever more tightly to that of the elite. The military began to show disturbing signs of autonomy, rampant corruption, and a shocking disregard for discipline. The rise of Bo Xilai illustrated in a stunning manner just how strong elite networks had grown. Before his fall, Bo openly questioned the central leadership's authority and mobilized a massive clientelist network of supporters behind his bid for the highest echelons of state power.

Developments Related to Public Cohesiveness

In this period, the public experienced little improvement in its cohesiveness. Chinese scholars acknowledged the trends toward greater pluralization and fragmentation. They contrasted the situation in the past, when people "identified with the party emotionally," with a current situation in which the market economy has made "social interests more diversified and complicated," resulting in "many different interest groups." They noted that social values had become "polarized" and the public "splintered."[106] Chinese scholars and commentators warned that persistent inequality, inadequate social services, and problems of corruption could undermine confidence in the party.[107]

The central leadership made some progress in improving the social welfare of the poorest citizens. In 2008, the central government allowed farmers to trade their land-use rights and enacted a new labor law that outlawed inhumane working conditions. The government also continued investment and spending in the interior regions and increased rural access to education and medical care.[108] But public resentment over local malfeasance and corruption fueled a steady increase in unrest, protests, and mass demonstrations.[109] Labor unrest increased as well, with protests roiling some of the nation's key special economic zones.[110] In response, authorities vastly increased spending on internal security through the 2000s. By 2010, domestic security surpassed the nation's defense budget.[111]

In 2008, scholars began warning about the political implications of China's growing informal sector. As one scholar noted, China's social structure, far from taking on an "olive" shape featuring a large middle class, is in fact coming to "resemble more a flask shape." He explained that despite gains by elites, the work force was characterized by 250 million in the informal economy and 300 million peasants. The scholar warned that this feature would likely prove long lasting, with a small, high-income modern formal economy sitting atop a much larger base of low-income informal workers and peasants.[112] Other western scholars similarly concluded that China would likely continue to have a large agricultural workforce as well as a large pool of surplus labor for a long time to come.[113]

Analysts and scholars recognized that the party's links with the masses had atrophied considerably. In his 2009 speech, Wen Jiabao stated that "political structural reform "and the "establishment of a mechanism to supervise the exercise of power" offered the only way to control the ills of corruption and income inequality, which he identified as the top two grievances among the public.[114] Party officials began to step up training on how to more effectively involve the public in politics. Beginning around 2009, the Central Party School began holding research seminars on "The Party's Mass Work" for some leading cadres participating in the training. One party journal article acknowledged the "general view inside and outside the party that mass work has become more difficult." The scholar lamented how the "method of mass work that we used to rely on has gradually lost its effectiveness." He complained that "some people" are "creating chaos for reform, development, and stability." The article quoted an official of Jiangxi province's Yihuang County, who stated, "the people do not trust the government's story, even if the story is fair and reasonable." The official lamented that the "distance between the party and the masses is widening." The article also cited the views of Zhang Xixian, a professor at the Central Party School Party, who acknowledged that "traditional mass work is becoming less effective."[115]

Fragmentation spread in the ethnic minority regions as competing groups began to build loyalties among marginalized groups. Social turmoil climbed in July with riots in Xinjiang and in northeast China in 2008. The Uighur uprising in Xinjiang claimed 184 lives. Along with 2008's Tibetan rebellion, it further highlighted ethnic tensions. Liberal dissidents issued the "Charter '08" in December 2008, which proposed a constitutional democracy to replace the existing political institutions and remedy the problems created by the current Chinese model of development. The government responded with a crackdown.[116]

China experienced a dramatic growth in the number of NGOs, but most remained weak and under the control of local cadres.[117] Reflecting conflicting imperatives, authorities showed contradictory attitudes about NGOs. On the one hand, higher level authorities encouraged NGOs to "confront powerful authorities"—meaning local vested interests that resisted Beijing's demands. Yet at the same time, authorities worried that too much protest could prove destabilizing. A party brief known as Document Number 9, circulated to all government offices in 2013, also accused NGOs of cultivating "anti-China forces." The government subsequently stepped up its monitoring and control of NGOs.[118]

In sum, the *fragmentation* of society worsened as inequality grew, large numbers of the workforce remained vulnerable, and the appeal of competing religious, cultural, and political identities grew. The party's alliance with elites left it incapable of building meaningful ties with the public. Mass unrest signaled the extent of the public's disaffection. In response, the party doubled its reliance on repression, but this merely exacerbated the central leadership's lack of public support.

The Hu era was defined by the contradiction in the party's pursuit of a more procedural, depersonalized, and institutionalized form of rule and the reality of its deepening dependence on powerful subnational elites to govern China. Hu's political strategy of allying with the elite and improving the meritocratic quality of officials stabilized center-elite relations, but at the cost of diminishing the central leadership's leverage over the elites and eroding its already fragile links with the public. This may have been tolerable in running day-to-day policy-making, which depends on the governing elite to make incremental changes and manage the status quo. However, the defects of the political situation fatally undermined Hu's efforts to carry out more ambitious economic policy changes aimed at placing China's long-term growth trajectory on a sustainable footing.

CONCLUSION

At the end of the six-year period, China's economy continued to experience high growth rates, and the government oversaw substantial improvements in its overall meritocratic quality. Hu Jintao and Wen Jiabao made social justice issues central to their approach to governance and oversaw some progress in reducing extreme poverty, strengthening a threadbare social welfare system, and slowing the growing gap between regions.[119]

However, the central leaders under Hu Jintao failed to achieve some of their highest-priority policy goals related to putting the country's economy on a productive and sustainable basis. China's productivity continued to decline, especially after the global financial crisis. Productivity fell from an annual average of 3.5 percent in 2001–2007 to 1.5 percent in the decade since 2008. The Chinese government kept the economy afloat through massive infrastructure spending, much of it of dubious value. Large amounts of finance were channeled through unprofitable state-owned enterprises (SOEs), which soared in value. The debt-to-GDP ratio soared from 150 percent in the early 2000s to 200 percent by 2010.[120]

Hu Jintao appeared aware of the problems, and he proposed a solution. However, his years-long effort to enlist the cooperation of the country's elites in tackling the country's most urgent problems failed.[121] While the official media praised Hu's leadership, many people regarded his tenure as a "lost decade." The government had largely failed to address the sources of mass discontent, which grew unabated. By 2010, official media acknowledged the country had averaged 180,000 incidents of mass protest and unrest per year and subsequently stopped publishing data on the problem.[122]

Hu Jintao showed an aversion to conflict rooted in part in the technocrat's personality. But Hu's strategy also responded to severe political constraints. First and foremost, Hu inherited a political situation featuring a close alliance between subnational elites and the central leadership. This had been inaugurated under Deng, who eagerly cultivated the support of subnational officials to counter the hardliners who opposed market reforms. Jiang Zemin cemented this alliance with the ideological changes that welcomed business and professional elites into the party as part of the "Three Represents" ideology.

The decision to coopt these new elites reflected Beijing's recognition of the new locus of power in the socialist market economy.[123] But the tightening relationship between the central leadership and elites generated important consequences that constrained Hu's options. The central leadership's dependence on elites elevated the risks of antagonizing them and simultaneously weakened the central leadership's position. Provoking conflict with well-resourced elites could endanger both social stability and economic development. Moreover, the CCP's abandonment of class struggle and embrace of a pragmatic agenda shifted the locus of legitimacy to competent governance and economic growth, which strengthened the hand of elites since they were directly responsible for both.

The central leadership's relationship with the public, in particular workers, peasants, and other non-elites, frayed to the breaking point. Beijing's growth strategy relied on the agility of local officials to entice and accommodate foreign businesses and sought high profits in part by cutting social welfare benefits to the bone and stepping up repression. Local elites relied on low wages and a high tolerance for the externalities of rapid industrialization to gain a competitive advantage. When the public reacted angrily to these developments, Beijing backed a brutal repression that only aggravated its alienation from the public.

Hu thus entered office at a point at which the central leadership's relationship with the masses had reached a historical low point. These realities shaped his political strategy. Hu Jintao was perhaps the first top CCP leader to devise a political strategy to cope with powerful elites that did not include the public as an ally. Mao, of course, perfected mass mobilization as an instrument of political warfare against his enemies, including, at times, elites located in government bureaucracies. His successors, including Deng, routinely relied on mobilizing mass support to overcome political rivals and their elite backers. Jiang collaborated with most elites, and his economic growth policy permitted a high tolerance for official malfeasance, but he tried to replicate Deng's popularity with the masses with his own colorful—often bizarre—antics. But the party's deep alienation from the public over time limited the effectiveness of such tactics. Despite his performances, Jiang never gained the popularity and influence enjoyed by Deng Xiaoping. Thus, when Hu focused on "transforming" elites from opponents into compliant servants through education, training, and the implementation of standardized procedures and processes, he was responding as much to the impracticality of old tactics of building popular support as he was to the government's growing dependence on elites for legitimacy.

Hu's focus on professionalizing the CCP cadre and improving their overall capacity for governance through training, education, and the formalization of political processes addressed a dire need. The standardization of procedures, processes, and norms helped ensure a more durable CCP rule. However, as a strategy to compel elites to implement a contentious, intensive growth agenda, it was destined to fail. Hu and the central leadership had underestimated the power of the elites and their determination to resist policies that threatened their livelihoods, even as the elites acquiesced to many of the other procedural changes that they regarded as less threatening.

It is hard to see how Hu and his colleagues could have done otherwise, however. To bypass elites and try to politicize the public risked disaster since a resort to communist ideological mobilization would almost certainly have failed. There was no reason to believe the public would respond any more positively than it did when hardliners in Deng's day attempted to carry out a similar mobilization. Deng correctly discerned in the 1990s that most of the country was tired of hardline ideology and poverty. Years of increased living standards had only further weakened the appeal of orthodox communism.

By the end of his tenure, Hu and other top leaders recognized the futility of their strategy of elite transformation and concluded that only a top-down approach could overcome elite resistance and ensure needed reforms. Setting the stage for the evolution into a more brutal and violent stage of elite politics, the 18th Party Congress report reflected the growing consensus among central leaders that coercion of elites had become inevitable. The dry bureaucratic language of official documents called for a "top-down design" to "improve the mechanism for coordinating structural reforms and conduct major reforms in a holistic way according to the overall plan," language that largely escaped notice by foreign observers. Xi Jinping's ascent to power would more clearly reveal the meaning behind those words.[124]

NOTES

1. World Health Organization Social Development Department of the Development Research Center, "China Health Poverty and Economic Development," December 2005. As of November 9, 2020, https://www.who.int/macrohealth/action/CMH_China.pdf.

2. *World Bank*, "GDP Per Capita (current US$): China," 2020. As of January 2, 2021, https://data.worldbank.org/indicator/NY.GDP.PCAP.CD?locations=CN.

3. Nicholas Lardy, "Financial Repression in China," *Peterson Institute Policy Brief PB08-8*, September 2008.

4. Wayne M. Morrison, *China's Economic Conditions* (Congressional Research Service, January 12, 2006). As of November 5, 2020, https://fas.org/sgp/crs/row/IB98014.pdf.

5. John Whalley and Xian Xin, "China's FDI and Non-FDI Economies and the Sustainability of Future High Chinese Growth," National Bureau of Economic Research, Working Paper 12249, May 2006.

6. Thomas Rumbaugh and Nicolas Blancher, "China: International Trade and WTO Accession," IMF, Working Paper 04/36, 2004.

7. Ministry of Commerce, People's Republic of China, "Brief on China's Imports and Exports 2004," March 11, 2005. As of November 5, 2020: http://english.mofcom.gov.cn/article/statistic/ie/200503/20050300025384.shtml.

8. Aaron Amiti and Caroline Freund, "China's Export Boom," *Finance and Development* 44, no. 3 (2007): 38–41.

9. Norwegian Energy and Environment Consortium, "China's Productivity Imperative."

10. Morrison, *China's Economic Conditions*.

11. *Wall Street Journal*, "China Needs Fundamental Reform," June 30, 2015.

12. Shen, Jin, and Zou, "Fiscal Decentralization in China."

13. Wang Jianjun and Yang Lin, "Fight a Decisive Battle in Reform to Deal With a Complicated Situation in a Crucial Period" [Yingdui Gaigezhong de Juedingxing Zhandou, Yingdui Dui Guanjian Shiqi De Fuzaa Jumian], *Outlook* [Liaowang] 9 (March 1, 2004): 18–22.

14. Ibid.

15. Joseph Fewsmith, "The Third Plenary Session of the 16th Party Congress," *China Leadership Monitor*, No. 9, January 30, 2004.

16. *Xinhua*, "Wen Jiabao Emphasizes Deepening the Reform of the Administrative and Management Structure and Speeding up Changes in the Government's Functions in His Speech at a Study Class for Cadres at the Provincial Level of the National School of Administration" [Wen Jiabao Zai Guojia Xingzheng Xueyuan Shengji Ganbu Yanjiuban Jianghua Qiangdiao Shenhua Xingzheng Guanli Tizhi Gaige Jiakuai Shixian Zhengfu Zhineng Zhuanbian], September 15, 2003.

17. Zheng Yongnian, "Power to Dominate, Not to Change."

18. Ibid.

19. Anna Wong, "Measuring Trade Barriers: An Application to China's Domestic Trade," Job Market Paper, University of Chicago, 2012.

20. Jane Golley and Nicolaas Groenewold, "Domestic Market Integration and Inter-Regional Growth Spillovers," in *China: Linking Markets for Growth*, ed. Ross Garnau and Ligong Song (Canberra, AU: Australian National University Press, 2007).

21. Xu, "The Fundamental Institutions of China's Reforms and Development," 1150.

22. *World Bank*, "China: Integration of National Product and Factor Markets, Economic Benefits and Policy Recommendations," 2005-6. As of January 9, 2021, https://openknowledge.worldbank.org/handle/10986/8690.

23. Xiong Wenzhao, "Build Mechanisms for Virtuous Interactions" [Jianli Langxing Hudong De Jizhi], *Outloook* [Liaowang] 49 (December 2005): 22–26.

24. Kalpana Misra, *From Post Maoism to Post Marxism: The Erosion of Official Ideology in Deng's China* (New York: Routledge, 1998).

25. David Schambaugh, *China's Communist Party: Atrophy and Adaptation* (Washington, DC: Woodrow Wilson Press, 2008).

26. Joseph Fewsmith, *China Since Tiananmen: From Deng Xiaoping to Hu Jintao* (Cambridge: Cambridge University Press, 2008).

27. Joseph Kahn, "Hu Takes Military Reins, Completing Shift in China," *New York Times*, September 20, 2004.

28. World Inequality Database, "World Inequality Report 2018."

29. Joseph Fewsmith, "The Politics of Economic Liberalization: Are There Limits?" in *China's Rise and the Balance of Influence in Asia*, ed. William Keller and Thomas Rawski (Pittsburgh, PA: University of Pittsburgh Press, 2007), 82.

30. Ibid.

31. Cheng Li, "The Powerful Factions Among China's Rulers," *Brookings Institute*, November 5, 2012.

32. Bruce Gilley, "The 'End of Politics' in Beijing," *The China Journal* 51 (January 2004): 115–35.

33. Liu Hongbo, "The Practice of Regarding Oneself as an Exception Threatens Unimpeded Transmission of Government Decrees" [Jiang Ziji Shiwei Liewai De Zuofa Hui Zuai Zhengfu Faling De Wuzhangai Zhuanbo], *Outlook* [Liaowang], No, 39, September 25, 2006, 3.

34. Chen Zewei, "Development That Fails to Stress Overall Situation Is Not Scientific Development" [Buneng Qiangdiao Quanjun De Fazhan Bushi Kexue Fazhan], *Outlook* [Liaowang], October 22, 2007, 26–28.

35. Wang Jianjun, "'Hills of Interests' Are Biggest Resistance to Market Reform" [Liyi Zhi Shan Shi Shichang Gaige De Zuida Zuli], *Outlook* [Liaowang] 50 (December 11, 2006): 21–23.

36. *Financial Times*, "China Income Inequality Among World's Worst," January 14, 2016.

37. Wang and Lin, "Fight a Decisive Battle in Reform To Deal With a Complicated Situation in a Crucial Period."

38. Shen, Jin, and Zou, "Fiscal Decentralization in China."

39. Tony Saich, "China in 2005: Hu's in Charge," *Asian Survey* 46, no. 1 (January 2006): 37–48.

40. Richard McGregor, "Why Fast Changing China is Turning Back to Confucius," *Financial Times*, April 11, 2007.

41. *New York Times*, "Chinese Official Cuts Short Japan Trip to Protest Shrine Visit," May 24, 2005.

42. Suisheng Zhao, "Nationalism's Doubled Edged Sword," *Wilson Quarterly* 29, no. 4 (Autumn 2005): 76–82.

43. Yu Keping, *Democracy is a Good Thing: Essay on Politics, Society, and Culture in Contemporary China* (Washington, DC: Brookings Institute, 2008).

44. *Outlook* [Liaowang], "Overcome the Problems of Restraining Leadership Methods and Capacity" [Kefu Xianzhi Lingdao Fangfa He Nengli De Wenti] 36 (September 8, 2008): 40–41.

45. Heike Holbig, "Ideological Reform and Political Legitimacy in China: Challenges in the Post-Jiang Era," German Institute for Global and Area Studies, Working Paper. No. 18, 2006.

46. Minxin Pei, "Fighting Corruption: A Difficult Challenge for Chinese Leaders," in *China's Changing Political Landscape: Prospects for Democracy* (Washington, DC: Brookings Institute Press, 2008).

47. Timothy R. Heath, China's New Governing Party Paradigm: Political Renewal and the Pursuit of National Rejuvenation (Hampshire, UK: Ashgate Publishing, 2014): 24.

48. Zhao Hongzhu, "Propelling the Work of Inner-Party Supervision Into a New Stage" [Tuijin Dang Nei Jiandu Gongzuo Jinru Xin Jieduan], People's Daily [*Renmin Ribao*], February 4, 2018, 8.

49. Gilley, "The 'End of Politics' in Beijing."

50. Schambaugh, *China's Communist Party*.

51. Heath, *China's New Governing Party Paradigm*, 44.

52. Lo and Tang, "Institutional Reform, Economic Changes, and Local Environmental Management in China."

53. Zewei, "Development That Fails to Stress Overall Situation Is Not Scientific Development."

54. Zheng Lu and Xiang Deng, "China's Western Development Strategy: Policies, Effects, and Prospects," *Munich Personal RePec Archive*, December 1, 2011.

55. Ken Davies, "China Investment Policy: An Update," *OECD Investment Policy Review of China*, 2010.

56. Zheng and Xiang, "China's Western Development Strategy."

57. Felix Haifeng Liao and Yehua Dennis Wei, "Regional Inequality in China: Trends, Scales and Mechanisms," Working Paper No. 202, Territorial Cohesion for Development Program of Rimisp, 2016.

58. Yang Jingyu, "Accurately Understanding Several Issues Regarding the Anti-Monopoly Law" [Zhunque Lijie Fan Longduan Fa Ruogan Wenti] *Seeking Truth* [Qiushi], March 11, 2008.

59. Ibid.

60. Eleanor M. Fox, "An Anti-Monopoly Law for China: Scaling the Walls of Government Restraint," *Anti-Law Trust Journal* 75, no. 1 (2008): 173–94.

61. Li Cheng and Scott W. Harold, "China's New Military Elite," *China Security* 3, no. 4 (Autumn 2007): 62–89.

62. Andrew Wedeman, "Corruption in China: Crisis or Constant," in *China's Rise*, ed. Fred Bergeston (Peterson Institute, 2009).

63. Heath, *China's New Governing Party Paradigm*, 58.

64. Heath, *China's New Governing Party Paradigm*, 60.

65. Fewsmith, "The Politics of Economic Liberalization," 92.

66. Timothy R. Heath, "Xi's Mass Line: Realigning Party Politics to New Realities," *China Brief* 13, no. 16 (August 9, 2013): 50.

67. Andrew Nathan, "China's Changing of the Guard: Authoritarian Resilience," *Journal of Democracy* 14, no. 1 (2003): 6–17.

68. Schambaugh, *China's Communist Party*, 4.

69. Ravi Kanbur, Yue Wang, and Xiaobo Zhang, "The Great Chinese Inequality Turnaround," ECINEQ WP 2017-433, *Society for the Study of Economic Inequality*, April 2017.

70. World Inequality Database, "World Inequality Report 2018."

71. David Barboza, "Food Safety Crackdown in China," *New York Times*, June 28, 2007.

72. Graeme Smith, "Political Machinations in a Rural Country," *China Journal* 62 (July, 2009): 29–59.

73. Zewei, "Development That Fails to Stress Overall Situation Is Not Scientific Development."

74. *World Bank*, "The Challenge of High Inequality in China," August, 2013. As of January 9, 2021, http://www.worldbank.org/content/dam/Worldbank/document/Poverty%20documents/Inequality-In-Focus-0813.pdf.

75. Gengzhi Huang, Desheng Xue, and Bo Wang, "Integrating Theories on Informal Economies: An Examination of Causes of Urban Informal Economies," *Sustainability* 12 (2020): 1–16.

76. Sarah Swider, *Building China: Informal Work and the New Precariat* (Cornell, NY: Cornell University Press, 2015), 5.

77. Philip Huang, "China's Neglected Informal Economy," *Modern China* 35, no. 4 (July 2009): 426.

78. Swider, *Building China.*

79. Mok and Wu, "Dual Decentralization in China's Transitional Economy."

80. Saich, "China in 2005."

81. Chen Renze, "Why Has Credibility Decline?" [Wei Shenme Xinyu Xiajiang?], *People's Daily* [Renmin Ribao], September 8, 2011, 17.

82. *Xinhua*, "CPC Promoting Reform, Democracy in Local Leadership Elections," May 14, 2006.

83. Che Haigang, "Reform Towards the 'Direct Administration of Counties by Provinces' Advances in Depth" [Tuijin Sheng Fen Xian Zhixia Gaige], *Study Times* [Xuexi Shibao], August 3, 2009.

84. Jianjun, "'Hills of Interests' Are Biggest Resistance to Market Reform."

85. Zheng Yongnian, "Power to Dominate, Not to Change."

86. Hou Shaowen, "It Is the Will of the People to Push Forward the Political Structural Reform" [Tuijin Zhengzhi Tizhi Gaige Shi Renmin De Yuanyi], *Study Times* [Xuexi Shibao], September 13, 2010.

87. Qi Weiping, "Boosting the Party's Ability To Govern at the Grassroots Level as Viewed From the Characteristics of China's Political Party System" [Cong Zhongguo Zhengdang Zhidu De Tedian Kan Tigao Dangde Jiceng Zhizheng Nengli], *Study Times* [Xuexi Shibao], June 15, 2010.

88. Ting Gong and Alfred Wu, "Central Mandates in Flux: Local Noncompliance in China," *Publius* 42, no. 2 (2012): 313–33.

89. Fan Yugang, "Cultural Direction of Political Structural Reform" [Zhengzhi Tizhi Gaige De Wenhua Fangxiang], *Outlook* [Liaowang] 17 (April 25, 2011): 71.

90. Hou Shaowen, "It Is the Will of the People to Push Forward the Political Structural Reform."

91. *Outlook* [Liaowang], "Overcome the Problems of Restraining Leadership Methods and Capacity."

92. Che Haigang, "Reform Towards the 'Direct Administration of Counties by Provinces' Advances in Depth."

93. Jacques Delisle, "Legalization without Democratization in China Under Hu Jintao," in *China's Changing Political Landscape*, ed. Cheng Le (Washington, DC: Brookings Institute Press, 2008), 185–211.

94. Zheng Yongnian, "Power to Dominate, Not to Change."

95. Jonathan Watts, "Mistress Turns in Corrupt Chinese Vice Admiral," *The Guardian*, June 15, 2006.

96. John Garnaut, "Rotting from Within," *Foreign Policy,* April 16, 2012.

97. David Lampton, *Following the Leader: Ruling China, from Deng Xiaoping to Xi Jinping* (Berkeley, CA: University of CA Press, 2014).

98. Dong Ruifeng, "New Ordeals for the Ruling Party's Mass Work" [ZhiZheng Dang Qunzhong Gongzuo De Xin Kaoyan], *Outlook* [Liaowang], No. 44, November 1, 2010.

99. Pei, "The Dark Side of China's Rise."

100. Lampton, *Following the Leader.*

101. Jia Xijin and Zhao Yusi, "The Chinese Economic Stimulus Package and Its Impact on Envi- ronmental Protection Organizations," *Policy Forum Online,* 09-016A, February 26, 2009.

102. Zheng Yongnian, "Power to Dominate, Not to Change."

103. Wu Guoguang, "China in 2020: Dilemmas of 'Scientific Development'," *Asian Survey* 51, no. 1 (January 2011): 18–32.

104. Nicholas Borst, "The Link Between China's Property Market and Local Government Finances," China Economic Watch, Peterson Institute for International Economics website, October 18, 2011.

105. *Financial Times*, "Bo Xilai: Power, Death, and Politics," July 20, 2012.

106. Dong Ruifeng, "New Ordeals for the Ruling Party's Mass Work."

107. *Outlook* [Liaowang], "Pooling New Strength for Reform" [Huiju Gaige Xin Liliang] 3 (January 19, 2009): 32–33.

108. Cheng Chen, *The Return of Ideology* (Ann Arbor, MI: University of Michigan Press, 2016).

109. Li Jingtian, "Development and Justice are Distinctively Written on the Banne of Socialism with Chinese Characterstics" [Fazhan yu Zhengyi Bei Xianming De Xie Zai Zhongguo Tese Shehui Zhuyi Qizhi Shang], *Seeking Truth* [Qiushi], No. 13, July 1, 2011.

110. China Development Zones website [Zhongguo Kaifaqu Wang], September 19, 2010. As of January 5, 2021, http://www.cadz.org.cn/.

111. *Reuters*, "China's Domestic Security Spending Jumps Pass Army Budget," March 4, 2011.

112. Huang, "China's Neglected Informal Economy," 426.

113. Ibid., 428.

114. Hou Shaowen, "It Is the Will of the People to Push Forward the Political Structural Reform."

115. Dong Ruifeng, "New Ordeals for the Ruling Party's Mass Work."

116. Wu Guoguang, "China in 2009: Muddling Through Crises," *Asian Survey* 50, no. 1 (January 2010): 25–39.

117. He Zhengke, "Institutional Barriers of the Development of Civil Society in Current China," in *The Role of Civil Society Organizations in China and Germany*, ed. Klaus Segbers, Yu Keping, and Ole Jatschek (Berlin, Germany: Center for Global Politics, 2009).

118. *The Economist*, "Beneath the Glacier," April 12, 2014.

119. Fewsmith, "The Politics of Economic Liberalization."

120. Martin Raiser and Hoon Sahib Soh, "To Sustain Growth, China Can Learn from Previous Transitions to High Income," *Brookings Institute*, October 18, 2019.

121. Eve Cary and Cheng Li, "The Last Year of Hu's Leadership: Hu's to Blame?" *Brookings Institution*, December 20, 2011.

122. Manoranjan Mohanty, "Harmonious Society: Hu Jintao's Vision and the Chinese Party Congress," *Economic and Political Weekly* 47, no. 50 (December 15, 2012): 12–16.

123. Bruce Dickson, *Red Capitalists in China: The Party, Private Entrepreneurs, and Prospects for Political Change* (Cambridge: Cambridge University Press, 2003).

124. *Xinhua*, "Full Text of Hu Jintao's Report at 18th Party Congress," November 17, 2012.

Chapter 4

China 2013–2020

A Fragmented Public Impair Undermines Xi's Strategy to Dominate Elites

President Xi Jinping sought to reinvigorate Hu Jintao's effort to shift the country to a more efficient, sustainable, and balanced mode of economic growth. The intensive growth agenda announced at the Third Plenum of the 18th Party Congress resembled that proposed by Hu in the early 2000s in many ways: Both sought to rebalance the economy, improve productivity, reduce debt, control externality costs, and improve the social welfare system.

To achieve these goals, Xi took a starkly different approach from his predecessor. Xi centralized power, strengthened party discipline, revamped military command and control, and cracked down on elites. Xi also sought to bolster the cohesiveness of the public through a re-politicization focused on his personal authority, even as he stepped up repression of the populace. These measures helped strengthen the central leadership's position and slightly weaken the elites. However, Xi lacked viable ways of reversing the deep fragmentation of the people. Moreover, the sum of Xi's political strategies could not overcome the central leadership's ultimate dependence on elites to manage the country. Without the help of a mobilized populace, Chinese leaders found themselves in a stalemate with entrenched elites. Constrained by these realities, momentum toward the "enabling condition" stalled and with it the prospects for successful implementation of the intensive growth policies. Whether Xi can overcome these limitations could determine whether China realizes its growth potential and avoids stagnation, although prospects appear doubtful.

BACKGROUND

In the early 2000s, authorities under Hu Jintao promoted an ambitious economic upgrading policy that scored some modest successes but failed to ensure the economy's transition to a more productive, high-quality mode of growth.[1] In 2007, Premier Wen Jiabao described the growth as "unstable, unbalanced, uncoordinated, and unsustainable."[2] Beginning around the 2010s, the economy's anticipated deceleration began in earnest as rising wages rendered older industries less competitive, global markets became saturated, and the external costs of rapid industrialization yielded destabilizing levels of inequality, environmental despoliation, and corruption.[3] Adding to Beijing's woes, analysts warned that the compounding effects of mounting debt, low productivity, and demographic aging risked long-term economic stagnation.[4]

In addition, China in the 2010s began experiencing the same premature deindustrialization that has afflicted many other late-developing countries. Prior to the 1960s, successful industrializers often saw a dramatic increase in the share of the population employed in manufacturing, often above 25 percent. Taiwan's industrial sector, for example, peaked at over 30 percent of the workforce, the US share reached 25.6 percent, and West Germany's topped 35 percent. A high level of industrial employment and output mattered because of its correlation with higher per capita incomes since industry tends to be more productive than the agricultural or service sectors. Deindustrialization reduces a country's growth potential and lowers the possibilities for convergence with the income levels of advanced economies. Beginning in the 1960s, developing countries experienced declining levels of industrial employment and output as a share of the economy, owing to the effects of automation in manufacturing and global trade. China, too, reached its peak in 2013, when 19.3 percent of its workforce labored in manufacturing. Industry's share of the workforce and output has declined in both relative and absolute terms ever since.[5]

Deindustrialization compounded the structural weaknesses that left China's economy stuck at a low level of productivity. In 2019, China's labor productivity had only reached 30 percent of the most efficient economies over the past two decades.[6] Some of the reasons for low productivity can be attributed to politics. For example, the government expanded the inefficient SOE sector to support policy objectives following the global financial crisis, such as elevating employment. SOEs associated with local governments played the largest role in the enormous public works program that sustained China's growth in 2009 after the global financial crisis and again in 2012, when a smaller infrastructure-focused stimulus program was deployed. In many cases, local governments created new SOEs for these purposes, adding to the country's debt burden and exacerbating problems of low productivity.[7]

Chinese leaders recognized that the country's low level of productivity offered considerable potential for economic revitalization. However, realizing this potential required new policies. Western economists recommended measures to expand the role of consumption, increase the digital economy, move up the value chain, and improve energy efficiency.[8] Other common recommendations included overhauling a sclerotic state sector, reforming a massively indebted state banking system, and dismantling political controls over the market.[9] Chinese authorities under both Hu and Xi concurred with many such recommendations.[10] Echoing Hu's own policy agenda, the CCP leadership under Xi Jinping announced a major, multi-policy initiative at the 2013 Third Plenum of the 18th Party Congress. The Third Plenum published a programmatic "Decision" document that called for a fairer rule of law, technological innovation, reductions in corruption, reversals in environmental damage, restructured state industries, expanded social welfare benefits, and more efficient market institutions.[11]

Such changes would be demanding even under favorable political conditions, but Xi Jinping faced many of the same structural disadvantages as his predecessor. Continuing a theme that had grown pervasive in party writings during Hu's tenure, Chinese analysts in the 2010s regarded the task of government restructuring as inseparable from that of improving the economy's performance. A 2014 analysis published in the party journal *Economic Observer* stated, for example, that "the main obstacle to achieving the goal of economic reform is not in the economic field but in the government, and the fundamental thing is reform in the political and administrative field."[12] Echoing language from the Third Plenum, commentators affirmed the centrality of government and bureaucratic changes to an economic overhaul. One commentator in the party journal *Outlook* explained that "the most conspicuous problem in China's economic structure is excessive direct government intervention in resource allocation." It warned that "government collusion" had grown "serious," resulting in soaring debt and indifference to the wellbeing of the people. It also criticized unnamed central ministries for maintaining a rent-seeking "examination and approval setup" and "pursuing departmental interests." Among the problems cited, the article noted that "some officials even barter powers for cash and illegally pursue private profit," while others tolerated "cheap quality counterfeit products," which harmed the market and consumers.[13]

As vice president, Xi Jinping observed Hu Jintao's failures firsthand. Hu's lack of major progress meant that Xi Jinping entered office with the same unfavorable configuration of a weak central leadership, a powerful opposing elite, and a fragmented populace. But it also meant Xi would have the opportunity to attempt a different approach.

Developments Related to the Central Leadership

At the start of Xi's tenure, the central government faced routine noncompliance by subnational governments. Indeed, party officials became alarmed at the growing indiscipline and defiance of Beijing's authority. An example of the problem could be seen in the continued lack of progress in building an integrated domestic market. Through the early 2010s, intra-provincial trade as a share of total trade remained low. Vice Commerce Minister Jiang Zenwei lamented in a 2014 article that "due to reasons such as regional blockades and trade monopolies, the construction of a nationwide unified market continues to lag." He noted the "prominent problem of a splintered domestic market." Jiang observed that the proportion of inter-province trade had shown a "downward trend." He explained that the speed of domestic market integration had become "slower than that of international market development."[14]

Western studies similarly noted that in China, "localities often ignore or avoid compliance with central government regulations." One study by western scholars published in 2015 noted that China's unique development had resulted in a "fragmented policy structure, providing the institutional space, or regulatory autonomy, for noncompliance." Although Beijing frequently intervened in provincial affairs and exerted some level of control through the nomenklatura personnel system, disregard for central policy directives remained pervasive. The study noted that "even China's audit system, which checks that local agencies and firms are following central directives, allows for significant leeway in implementation, enforcement strategies, and outcomes."[15]

Hu Jintao's government had carried out a variety of recentralizing measures, but some had the ironic effect of aggravating problems of noncompliance. In 2003, for example, the National Development and Reform Commission gained broad administrative and planning power over the economy in hopes of reducing excess capacity, subsidies, and waste. The government shifted approvals for larger initiatives, such as the opening of a coal mine producing more than 500,000 tons, to authorities in Beijing. Similar standards were applied to a wide range of projects, from gas production and power plants to highways and tobacco production. But rather than discourage subnational governments and companies from pursuing unnecessary projects, it incentivized the same governments and enterprises to step up lobbying, bribing, and influence-peddling activities to gain approvals and exceptions. The number of firms with connections with the central government increased dramatically, with the proportion of firms connected with the national government having tripled between 1993 and 2012, whereas the proportion of firms connected with local governments increased only 30 percent.[16] A sign of the effectiveness of these lobbying efforts can be seen in the fact that the new restrictions had no impact on reducing the country's pervasive problem of excess capacity. In fact, the country experienced an expansion, not contraction, of excess capacity through the 2000s and early 2010s.[17]

Similarly, the policy of rotating local officials, in place since the late 1990s, sought to reduce the formation of local power bases but yielded unintended consequences as well. The policy partially disrupted the development of interlocking elites at the local level, but it also incentivized the formation of new linkages between economic and political actors at higher levels of government. Because national-level officials rotated less frequently, enterprising businessmen learned that connections formed with them could prove more stable and lucrative. They also learned that forming clientelist bonds with national-level officials carried a lower risk that their patrons would be targeted during anticorruption campaigns. Underscoring this point, western scholars documented a surge in national-level officials who served on the boards of provincial-based companies from the late 1990s through the mid-2010s.[18] These powerful patrons provided protection from central mandates and provided exceptions and privileged access to valuable state resources.

Xi began his tenure with an uncertain grasp of the security forces. To be sure, he had some experience in the military, having served briefly in a staff capacity. Moreover, he consolidated his formal leadership of the military faster than Hu did, gaining the CMC chairmanship at the same time as he ascended to the post of CCP General Secretary. But his grip on the military appeared uncertain.[19] Although Xi announced an anticorruption purge in late 2012, he had scarcely begun to move against the military in 2013. The arrests of high-profile generals such as Guo Boxiong and Xu Caihou would occur years later. News reports subsequently revealed that Xi had begun planning the downfall of Public Security Minister Zhou Yongkang as early as 2012, when Zhou retired, but only in late 2013 did authorities officially open a corruption probe.[20] In short, Xi's control of the country's security forces in his first year of office appeared tenuous.

Party discipline remained problematic as well. Authorities regarded corruption as spiraling dangerously out of control. At the 18th Party Congress held in 2012, Hu Jintao warned that corruption threatened the survival of the party.[21] Scholars and political analysts similarly warned of weakening party discipline. A typical article in the party journal *Outlook* noted that the "situation of failing to abide by party discipline still existed with some party cadres." The article denounced cadres who "turn a deaf ear to major policies and measures of the Central Committee about economic and social development" and "disobey orders and defy prohibitions." It stated that cadres showed "outward compliance but inward noncompliance."[22]

In sum, the central leadership in 2013 appeared *weak*. The central government continued to face problems of noncompliance by local governments, compounded by the migration of special interests to higher levels of government. Party discipline also proved problematic, with corruption threatening the CCP's legitimacy. Even Xi's control of the security forces appeared tenuous, as he had just entered office and had barely begun to assert his authority.

Developments Related to Elite Opposition

Data on wealth accumulation confirmed the impressions of an increasingly powerful and well-resourced elite. The share of national income for the richest 10 percent remained around 42 percent of national income in 2013. But the share of wealth owned by the top 10 percent increased dramatically from about 48 percent in 2002 to about 67 percent ten years later.[23] About two-thirds of household wealth in China consisted of real estate, with the remaining one-third in financial and business assets.[24]

By the early 2010s, central government-affiliated officials had identified the country's own elites as a principal obstacle to improving the country's economic performance. In 2012, a "China 2030" paper jointly published by the World Bank, China's Development Research Center of the State Council, and China's Finance Ministry concluded that the groups most likely to resist reform would be "vested interests," which the report identified as "those enterprises that enjoy partial or full monopoly in key markets as well as firms, groups, institutions, and individuals who obtain special privileges and benefits or enjoy preferential treatment from the current power structure and institutional setting." These groups "reap economic rents from distortions implicit in the current price, institutional, and administrative structures." The report warned that these interests were likely to be "very influential, powerful, resourceful, and resolute in protecting their interests." The report singled out in particular government officials in cooperation with partners in state enterprises, property developers, and the energy industry.[25]

Other experts similarly emphasized the hurdles posed by powerful and well-connected elites. An article in the party journal *Economic Observer* stated, "Vested interests have in fact already become the biggest obstacle and risk to China's reforms." It described such interest groups as "mainly dependent on the influence of public powers." The vested interests worked through cooperation with "offspring, spouses, relatives, or friends" to arbitrage public assets and get rich quickly. The article identified three forms of vested interests: The first consisted of "high-level vested interests represented by corrupt officials," the second consisted of "vested interests represented by monopoly sectors," and the third consisted of "vested interests represented by real estate and resource sectors." The article noted that these controlled "both power and resources" as well as a "considerable amount of China's wealth."[26]

Minxin Pei, a professor at Claremont McKenna College, has vividly described how these collusive networks operated. He explained that officials cashed in on their political power by setting up their immediate family members in business or finding partners in the private sector. As Pei noted, such cronyistic arrangements have proven incredibly lucrative. They created powerful parasitic patronage networks that accounted for a large portion of corruption cases tried by the government.[27] Xi Jinping's PhD advisor, Sun Liping, likely had these individuals in mind when he warned in 2012 that the biggest opponents of reform would consist of powerful political-economic elites.[28]

The strength of collusive networks of the rich and powerful was well illustrated in the case of Ling Jihua, who previously headed the United Front Work Department in the Central Committee and served as the director of the General Office of the Central Committee and chief advisor to Hu Jintao prior to his downfall. After his arrest for corruption, reports described extensive links between local government and local industries, especially coal, and between higher and lower-level party officials. Wealthy coal producers counted on ties with Ling, Zhou, and other top leaders to continue operations that central regulators sought to restrict.[29]

Collusion between local officials and individuals of an even more sordid character also grew. Starved of revenue to meet their governance obligations, local officials began to collude with criminals in some cases. Western scholars began to note evidence of "local mafia states," featuring collusion between Chinese officialdom and thuggish groups. These criminal groups forged ties with local authorities and controlled territories through three key mechanisms: Protection rackets, the purchase and selling of official positions, and the control of village elections for local people's congresses. One study noted that local governments had begun to "rely increasingly on third-party violence to execute routine tasks." The study also noted that since the 1990s, there has been "increasing collusion between the police and criminal gangs, resulting in the penetration of criminals into government institutions," a phenomenon well illustrated in the notorious Bo Xilai case, which featured police cooperation with criminals to rob and torture wealthy citizens.[30] But the phenomenon also appeared "throughout all administrative levels from village, township, to county- and provincial-level cities."[31]

In sum, elite *opposition* to the central leadership's intensive growth strategy remained *strong*. The country's elites had gained access to substantial resources, with their share of wealth reaching new heights and collusion extending both horizontally and upwards. The central leadership's agenda for improved economic performance depended in large part on curbing the powers and privileges of elites. Given the failures of Hu's nonconfrontational approach, a confrontation between central leaders and the elites appeared inevitable.

Developments Related to Public Cohesiveness

In the 2000s, the country experienced increasing underemployment, pervasive informality, a fragmented industrial sector, and an inadequate social safety net. The deindustrialization that began around 2013 exacerbated the fragmentation. Between 2012 and 2015, a total of 5.5 million workers lost their jobs in the secondary sector (industry and construction).[32] More job losses loomed as rising wages spurred many companies to expand automation and eliminate jobs. The restructuring of inefficient state-owned enterprises also threatened to both improve productivity and exacerbate job losses. The government estimated that up to six million workers could be made redundant through the process of restructuring unprofitable enterprises by 2019. Compounding the problem, a continued population shift from rural to urban areas increased the ranks of job seekers. In 2012, government plans envisioned that 60 million people would move from rural to urban areas by 2020.[33] Problems of underemployment extended beyond the industrial sector, however. Over this period, joblessness among the college-educated grew as well. In 2013, the government ordered schools, government agencies, and state-owned enterprises to hire more college graduates to help relieve joblessness.[34]

As the formal industrial workforce declined, China's informal sector ballooned. As of 2015, there were an estimated 260 million migrant workers concentrated in the cities, representing 25 percent of the population of Shanghai, 30 percent of Beijing, and 40 percent of Guangzhou.[35] According to some estimates, informality peaked at 60 percent of the non-rural work force around 2010 before declining to a low of 52 percent in 2012. However, in 2013, the informal sector began to climb again as the industrial sector began to shrink.[36]

Yet even as China's industrial sector declined, it remained highly fragmented, in part due to the country's economic strategy of serving as the hub for a processing trade largely managed by foreign manufacturers. China's manufacturers experienced a far lower level of linkages between upstream and downstream industries than had been the case in Asian "tiger" economies, a trend further exacerbated by the cellularization of provincial economies. Indeed, western economists characterized the country's industry as "significantly fragmented, even more so than Japan and Korea in earlier, comparable periods."[37]

Beijing had long recognized that the creation of a nation-wide social safety net could help offset the effects of the shrinking state sector, but progress remained slow. One nation-wide survey concluded that pension enrollment among informal sector workers remained below 47 percent. By contrast, 90 percent of formal sector workers had enrolled in the state pension scheme. The study noted that informal sector workers chose not to enroll in social insurance programs due to low benefit payouts and difficulties in accessing the benefits.[38] To reduce the dualization of the workforce, officials incrementally revised policies regarding the residency permit, or *hukou.* In China, a person's access to social welfare benefits is tied to the hukou, which poses a hurdle to migrant workers. Reforms in small and medium-sized cities featuring shrinking populations eased hukou restrictions, but urban amenities remained limited. Larger cities experimented with various point systems through which small numbers of rural people could qualify for urban *hukou*. But limited funding for social services severely constrained the extent of the *hukou* reforms.[39]

Politically, the state offered no substantive change in its lack of avenues for meaningful public participation. On the contrary, authorities maintained a tight grip on censorship. Repression of religious and other social groups that sought to operate with some autonomy from the state continued as well. Many western reporters noted a significant increase in the government's crackdown on dissidents and other critics of the government.[40] In 2013, a survey by western human rights group Freedom House judged China to be the third worst in the world in terms of civil liberties and the internet.[41]

Chinese scholars noted that despite the governments' call for social harmony, society appeared riven by conflictual relations. Chinese scholars have analyzed many of these types of social clashes. One expert summarized them as consisting of three types: Those between officials and the people; those between labor and capital; and those between the rich and the poor. The scholar warned that "either we vanquish vested interests or vested interests eventually swallow us." He concluded, "at the moment it is not easy to determine which will happen."[42]

In sum, the public's *fragmentation* appeared to be worsening at an already alarming level. The country's premature deindustrialization aggravated problems of informalization and severe segmentation of the industrial sector. The large informal workforce and increasing prominence of the low-paid service sector aggravated problems of inequality and reinforced the clientelist arrangements that dominated the local political scene.

Carrying over from the Hu Jintao era, the political situation did not favor policy implementation. To improve prospects, Xi would need to strengthen central power, weaken elite opposition, and strengthen the cohesiveness of the people. Particularly vexing for Xi would be the challenge of bolstering the cohesiveness of the public, given the trends of deindustrialization and the limited availability of funding for social welfare services. Some means other than economics would be required to deepen Xi's connection with the people if he hoped to mobilize public support.

INTERVENING DEVELOPMENTS, 2013–2015

This period saw the central leadership carry out a range of activities aimed at strengthening Xi's grip on power and bolstering the power of central authorities against subnational elites and their patrons in national-level government. As part of this approach, central leaders unleashed an extensive anticorruption campaign. To bolster the central leadership's political ties with the people and more sharply differentiate the central government from local elites, the party state promoted a cult of personality centered on Xi Jinping and demonized recalcitrant elites as "corrupt." Although the efforts yielded substantial gains in bolstering central power, the central leadership made more modest gains in weakening elite opposition and marshalling public support.

Developments Related to the Central Leadership

Xi Jinping took several key steps to consolidate his power within the government, party, and military. Building on decisions made by the central leadership under Hu Jintao, Xi proceeded with a "top-down," centralized approach to governing. Xi established new institutions and mechanisms to compel the government and party bureaucracy to comply with central directives. In 2013, President Xi established himself at the nexus of an array of elite supra-government small groups, the most important of which have been the National Security Commission and the Leading Small Group for Comprehensive Deepening of Reform.[43] These moves earned Xi the sobriquet "chairman of everything."[44]

Xi Jinping also launched an anti-graft campaign in late 2012 that allowed him to eliminate political opponents and accrue more power, as well as carry out the ostensible mission of tackling graft. While all preceding leaders launched anti-corruption campaigns, Xi's stood out for its scope and for his willingness to violate long-standing norms. For example, he arrested top officials, which broke the presumed inviolability of the most senior politicians. Beijing also issued regulations cracking down on the use of luxury items in formal functions and ostentatious signs of official privilege.[45] The purge provided political cover for Xi to impose stricter discipline on the government and party. For example, he singled out all kinds of cadre behavior that merited punishment, including ones that had long frustrated central authorities, such as noncompliance, feigned compliance, abuse of authority, and cronyism.[46] By 2015, the number of corruption cases had quadrupled from the number in 2013.[47] Party officials said the campaign had punished more than 1.5 million cadres by 2018.[48]

Xi also cemented his grip on the military with an extensive purge, including the removal and arrest of former CMC vice chairs Xu Caihou and Guo Boxiong. By 2015, the government had brought down 30 senior military leaders.[49] In addition to an extensive purge of the internal security forces following Zhou Yongkang's arrest and expulsion from the CCP, the government announced a major reorganization in 2015. Command and control of the People's Armed Police, the national paramilitary force responsible for domestic security, moved from a dual network involving both the State Council and the military to an exclusively military command, which Xi alone headed.[50] Organizational changes strengthened central oversight of the military while bolstering discipline and promoting military competence. For example, the separation of the PLA's operational command and administrative functions in 2015 helped improve efficiency *and* reduce the risks of delegating too much power to theater commanders.[51] Similarly, the creation of the National Security Commission in 2013 centralized decision-making regarding military affairs, improving prospects for coordination and reinforcing the military's subordination to central authorities.[52] In November 2015, authorities announced the creation of a new PLA Politics and Law Commission to monitor compliance with anti-graft provisions and other rules, mirroring a similar party organization that oversees legal and judicial issues in the state bureaucracy.[53]

Xi strengthened the party as an organization and sought to clarify the distinction between his authority and that of party elites, who often frustrated the central leadership's agenda. He did this in part by launching a "cult of personality" propaganda effort that personalized the party's authority and associated himself with popular measures, such as anticorruption. Chinese media launched numerous adulatory songs, cartoons, and books. Meanwhile, the official media provided fawning coverage of Xi's every move, and party theorists hailed Xi Jinping's thoughts in reverent tones.[54] Xi contrasted his authority with that of recalcitrant cadres, whom he demonized as "corrupt." Additionally, Xi tightened discipline within the party and bolstered the party's grip on the government and society. Central authorities announced a series of regulations, rules, and procedures aimed at institutionalizing party controls over the cadres. The new policies included disciplinary actions to promote austerity, curb lavish living, and punish wayward officials. According to official media, nearly 8,200 officials were punished for misusing public funds, 74,000 officials were punished for "bad work styles," and 63,000 officials were ordered to quit their parallel positions in enterprises to avoid a conflict of interest.[55] Xi also strengthened ideological indoctrination within the party and throughout society.[56]

With a more centralized government, Xi directed yet another effort to rein in subnational governments, with modest results. An example can be seen in his effort to reinvigorate a long-standing effort to break up regional protections and "build a unified and open market system." In 2013, the government issued a plan to revamp taxation rules for trans-regional business operators and address discriminatory pricing practices for rival provincial products and services.[57] However, the problems proved stubbornly persistent, leading Xi to renew his pledge to achieve the same goals in 2017.[58]

In sum, the central leadership became *strong* during this period. Xi Jinping consolidated his grip on power through widespread purges, an anticorruption drive, and a reorganization of central power, as well as stepped-up efforts to hold officials accountable. He achieved a strengthening of central power that had eluded his predecessor.

Developments Related to Elite Opposition

Despite the crackdown on official privilege and corruption, the share of national income earned by the top 10 percent of the population remained largely unchanged from 2012, earning about 41 percent of the nation's income in 2015. The share of wealth owned by the top 10 percent remained largely unchanged at 67 percent in 2015, suggesting that perhaps some of Xi's measures had at least slowed the pace of wealth accumulation among elites.[59] The problems of collusion between interlocking directorates at the local level appeared intact, despite the anti-graft measures. However, the arrest of several high-profile patrons of cronyistic networks may have hampered the vertical collusion between elites, although how much remains difficult to ascertain.

Tensions between elites and the central leadership deepened as Xi's government intensified its crackdown. Although officials refrained from criticizing Xi Jinping publicly, rumors regarding resentment and anger among the nation's elite grew plentiful.[60] Meanwhile, Chinese officials and scholars stepped up their criticism of elites, whom they described as obstacles to the central leadership's governance agenda. Xi Jinping obliquely referred to this issue when he explained that "structural contradictions had not been resolved" and that getting to the "root cause" of problems required "major surgery." More directly, he blasted unnamed officials for practicing "formalism, bureaucratism, hedonism, and extravagance."[61] Scholars offered more pointed comments. One analyst criticized the problem of "power above law" as the "main root" of the "distortion of the market economy structure, unfair social distribution, market disorder, and moral decline of our country."[62] One article warned that the corruption and obstructionist behavior on the part of certain cadres "posed a serious threat" to the CCP's "cohesiveness and effectiveness."[63]

The central leadership, in short, faced a growing danger of being captured by wealthy, powerful local politicians and their business clients, a danger well demonstrated in the revelation of several spectacular cases of high-level corruption that emerged during Xi's ascent to power. Most prominently, authorities arrested Minister of Public Security Zhou Yongkang, a member of the Politburo Standing Committee, in 2013 for corruption. Zhou had formed lucrative bonds as a patron for wealthy, powerful interests in the oil sector, law enforcement, and enterprises in the province of Sichuan, where he had previously served as governor. As he rose to the highest levels of national office, Zhou provided political cover for his clients and helped them deflect central directives while his family reaped billions of dollars from his patronage. His downfall was precipitated by the arrest of one of his clients, Bo Xilai, a local official who sought to emulate Zhou's example by ascending to the highest levels of national office after amassing vast wealth through cronyism, illegal seizures, and corruption.[64] Other top-level officials eventually arrested for corruption included former vice chairs of the Central Military Commission, Guo Boxiong and Xu Caihou, a sitting member of the CMC, Fang Fenghui, the vice chair of the Chinese People's Political Consultative Conference (CPPCC) Su Rong, and a former advisor to Hu Jintao and director of the Central Committee's United Front, Ling Jihua.[65] If central leaders could themselves be coopted by wealthy and powerful elite networks that permeated both the government and party, then the prospect of a unified central leadership overseeing the implementation of contentious policies seemed improbable, if not impossible.

In sum, elite *opposition* remained *strong*. Despite the anti-corruption drive, the elites saw little loss in their income or wealth. Their collusive networks likely persisted, although some may have been dismantled by the anticorruption probes. Tensions between the central leadership and elites stiffened.

Developments Related to Public Cohesiveness

Economically, the public's fragmentation continued apace. Deindustrialization began in earnest, and the informal sector resumed its expansion accordingly. The service sector flourished, but this offered bad news for authorities seeking to improve the country's productivity since service sector workers tend to be far less productive than industrial workers.[66] There were additional reasons to doubt that the service sector could provide the sort of powerful driver of growth that industry once did. A boom in financial services helped boost growth rates in 2015, but the boom ended in 2016. Growth accordingly fell afterwards.[67] Inequality began to creep upward again. The Gini coefficient declined from a high of 0.49 in 2008 due to a massive explosion of government spending following the global financial crisis, but it subsequently resumed an upward trend, reaching 0.46 in 2016.[68] FDI continued to play a role in the fragmentation of the domestic market. Scholars noted that competition for foreign investment led to a "race to the bottom" in terms of tolerance for pollution and malfeasance among provinces. One study found that central transfers made little difference in incentivizing revenue-starved cities to comply with central environmental and social welfare regulations.[69]

As efforts to provide a national social welfare system foundered, the government continued to rely on SOEs to provide jobs and social welfare benefits. SOEs also continued to serve as an instrument of labor policy, hiring workers who may not have been needed. These social policy goals compounded the problems of low productivity.[70] The economic performance of SOEs continued to deteriorate. By 2014, the gap in performance between state and non-state firms had widened to its largest extent yet.[71]

In this period, the government highlighted the potential of information technology as a potential driver of highly productive growth in the service sector. But despite the innovative power of Internet companies such as Alibaba, Tencent, or Xiaomi, their overall impact on the economy proved limited as they could only complement or replace existing businesses. For example, the e-industry grew 28.2 percent in the first six months of 2016, but the growth came at the expense of traditional retailers. Moreover, the service sector remained burdened by the dominance of state-owned enterprises. State monopolies and restrictions on foreign companies undermined competitive dynamics in key segments of the service industry. Crucial sectors such as transportation, banking, and telecommunications remained in the hands of state-owned enterprises. The government did not announce any plans to dismantle SOEs in the service sector.[72]

The CCP turned to politics to bring about a level of cohesiveness that eluded them in the economic domain. Party theorists underscored the urgency of mobilizing popular support to carry out proposed policies and warned that failure by the central leadership to gain the allegiance of the people could imperil CCP rule. One theorist stated, "Those who gain popularity among the people will gain power," and he noted that popular support is determined by the "increase or loss of benefits to the people."[73] Other party theorists lamented the party's inability to mobilize popular support. One article admitted, "It is absolutely not easy to pool the strength of the people." It noted that "people's ideological activities and value orientation have obviously become more independent, selective, changeable, and different." It noted that "various ideologies and cultures as well as diversified social interests," had "stimulated social vitality," but that this posed "unprecedentedly difficulty to unifying the thought and pool the strength of the people."[74]

Xi attempted to involve the people in politics by reviving political tactics such as the mass line. In the classic 1943 formulation from *Some Questions Concerning Leadership*, Mao explained that the aim of the "mass line" was to "take the scattered and unsystematic ideas of the masses," turn them into "concentrated and systematic ideas," and then "go to the masses and propagate and explain these ideas until the masses embrace them as their own." The party's interest in such tactics had faded considerably with its abandonment of Maoism in favor of pragmatic policies, but the need to curb the power of elites stimulated the central leadership's interest in reviving such practices. When the party launched the campaign in May 2013, Xi outlined objectives, including those of strengthening institutional controls over the cadres and increasing the public's role in politics. As explained by Xi at a Politburo study session, the "main point" of the mass line is for the party to "focus on working for the people" as well as for cadres to be "competent and incorruptible."[75]

Ironically, the CCP's efforts to revive the "mass line" failed to involve the masses, who remained uninterested in such campaigns. Instead, the party deployed the practice within its own ranks. The mass line campaign involved self-criticism sessions called "democratic meetings," in which cadres confessed their mistakes while supervisory teams composed of higher-level officials recorded the results.

Authorities leaned more heavily on nationalist propaganda and populist rhetoric to garner popular support for the central leadership. The promotion of a hardline nationalist policy proved politically popular, and Xi's government actively cultivated public support with a tough stand against the United States and other western governments on issues such as Taiwan, the South China Sea, and human rights, while avoiding military conflict, which would be unpopular.[76] Propaganda officials cultivated a populist "man of the people" image to differentiate Xi's authority from that of local elites, whom the public resented.[77] Central leaders revised much of the party's stale political terminology and propaganda methods to make them more accessible to the public. They promoted the vision of a "China Dream," for example, and distributed flashy videos that communicated images of national strength and prosperity.[78]

The central government also tried to rebuild its connections with citizens and increase societal cohesiveness through technology. In 2014, the government outlined its plan for a social credit system that aimed to extend financial credit scoring systems to other areas of government regulation, from contract enforcement to food safety, corruption, and environmental protection.[79] Chinese documents described the social credit system as a tool to reduce transaction costs and improve the public's trust in the government. Citizens could gain positive scores, for example, by downloading and reading speeches and texts by Xi Jinping.[80]

Yet the cult of personality propaganda, nationalist messaging, and partial rollout of the social credit system had only a modest effect on strengthening the cohesiveness of the people. Subnational elites simply had more power to directly impact the lives of citizens through their clientelist ties. Moreover, the public remained too fragmented to be of much help. Outside of potentially expressing passive support, the government did not provide a way for the public to participate meaningfully in politics. As criticism of Xi's centralizing and autocratic tendencies as well as CCP malfeasance increased, authorities stepped up arrests of critics, dissidents, and activists while extending censorship and media controls. According to a 2017 report by activist group Amnesty International, human rights in China reached their worst level since 1989 Tiananmen Square massacre.[81] The goal of political mobilization clashed with the goal of controlling unrest over persistent issues of local malfeasance, inadequate social services, and inequality.

In sum, society remained *fragmented.* Inequality continued to worsen as deindustrialization spurred job losses. Xi's efforts to build political cohesiveness behind his personal popularity and a more robust nationalism made some headway, but the people still lacked meaningful ways to participate in the political process.

Xi succeeded in strengthening the central government's position, but the central leadership's dependence on local elites to manage social stability and economic policy undercut efforts to bring them under control. Moreover, despite tentative efforts to involve the public politically, a deeply fragmented public left the central leadership without a crucial political ally. Three years after announcing the Third Plenum's major, multi-sector policy initiatives, China experienced only incremental change. Perhaps in part to buy time, the central government removed term limits, giving Xi greater scope and a longer time frame to press his policies. In the coming years, central leaders will continue to struggle to overcome elite opposition and build a cohesive public that can support their policy agenda.

Intervening Developments, 2016–2019

In this period, Xi continued to aggregate central power and intensify measures to bring the nation's elites to heel. He directed the dismantling of some collusive networks involving criminal elements. However, the lack of a cohesive public that could be mobilized to support the reform agenda continued to plague Xi's efforts. Without a strong public demand for change, the elites could subvert policies by manipulating their role as implementers to their advantage. The position of elites was strengthened by the reality that efforts to improve productivity would almost certainly entail downsizing a highly inefficient state sector, resulting in the loss of tens of millions of jobs and thereby exacerbating the problem of underemployment, a possibility that central leaders feared.

Developments Related to the Central Leadership

Building on preceding moves, Xi consolidated his grip with moves aimed at centralizing government power and elevating the party's role in governance. In March 2018, China issued a blueprint for government restructuring that extended the power of the CCP and merged government bureaucracies. The plan gave the Party's Propaganda Department control of censorship of film, news media, and publications and handed responsibility for overseas Chinese affairs and religious affairs to the Party's United Front Work Department. The blueprint upgraded the authority and status of key leading small groups for reform, cybersecurity, and finance.[82] China also established a new anti-graft agency, the National Supervisory Commission, which replaced the State Council's Ministry of Supervision and merged with the Party's Central Commission for Discipline Inspection (CCDI) to extend the reach of the anticorruption campaign.[83] The creation of the National Supervision Commission apparatus increased the CCP's coercive control over the Chinese state by extending the CCP's investigative and detention powers over non-CCP elements of China's bureaucracy.[84]

The "Plan of Deepening Reform of Party Institutions," adopted by the 19th Party Congress's Third Plenum in February and approved by the March session of the National People's Congress (NPC), laid out sixty reforms across the political system, including changes in the Party, in the NPC and the State Council, in state regulatory bodies, in the United Front's Chinese People's Political Consultative Conference, in police and military security forces, in mass organizations, and in local organizations. According to renown China expert Alice Miller, the institutional reforms mandated by the Third Plenum and the 2018 NPC session were the "most extensive in scope, if not in depth, of the entire post-Mao era."[85]

The anti-graft campaign continued. In a speech, Xi warned, "if the party is not managed forcefully and administered strictly and the outstanding contradictions and problems reported intensely by the people are not resolved promptly, then the foundation for our party's governance will falter and collapse."[86] By 2017, officials reported that more than 1 million Party members had been disciplined.[87]

The central government stepped up measures to ensure subnational governments complied with Beijing's directives. In August 2018, for example, Xinhua reported that China would conduct a series of "targeted inspections" to ensure proper implementation of central government policies. Xiao Jie, secretary-general of the State Council, said the inspections would focus on the way local governments implemented policies relating to priority issues such as poverty reduction, pollution control, the promotion of innovation, and the revitalization of the rural economy.[88]

In terms of the military, Xi made numerous high-profile visits to inspect the progress in the military's reorganization.[89] Anticorruption purges and arrests continued. In 2019, authorities issued new regulations designed to streamline command and control of the nation's sprawling array of internal security forces.[90] Overall, Xi's grip on the military and internal security forces appeared secure.

In March 2018, the National People's Congress, China's national legislature, voted unanimously to amend the constitution to remove presidential term limits.[91] The moves followed a portentous 19th Party Congress, at which the ruling party enshrined "Xi Jinping Thought" as its latest guide to action. No Chinese leader since Deng Xiaoping has had an eponymous ideology inscribed in the constitution while still in office.[92] The Sixth Plenum of the 18th Congress also designated Xi the "core" of the CCP Central Committee, an honorific title last used with Deng Xiaoping. Official propaganda continued to relentlessly cultivate images of Xi Jinping as a paternalistic leader that many compared to a "cult of personality."[93]

In sum, the central leadership remained *strong*. Xi had consolidated his position in the government, party, and among security forces through this period with additional measures. At the 19th Party Congress, Xi's attained the summit of authority throughout the party when the collective leadership designated Xi the "core" of the leadership.

Developments Related to Elite Opposition

> Senior officials maintained a critical stance toward elites who opposed the major, multi-sector policy agenda outlined at both the Third Plenum in 2013 and the 19th Party Congress in 2017. Authorities focused in particular on the threat posed by officials who misused their office for gain or collaborated with others to form factions. In a 2016 speech, Wang Qishan blasted party members and cadres for various types of misbehavior, including cronyism and excluding outsiders; forming cliques and factions; anonymously lodging a false accusation and creating rumors; buying popularity and buying votes; handing out official posts, making promises to grant special favor, and congratulating each other on their promotion; going one's own way and complying in appearance but opposing in heart; creating a situation in which the tail is too big to wag, and criticizing central authorities.[94]

Yet, despite five years of Xi's anticorruption drive, the power of elites appeared scarcely diminished. The share of income and wealth held by the top 10 percent remained unchanged from 2013.[95] A survey by Transparency International found the anti-graft campaign had made some progress and that corruption in China lagged that of India.[96] But the progress could be easily overstated. In 2017, China ranked seventy-seventh on Berlin-based nonprofit Transparency International's 180-country "Corruption Perceptions" scale, barely changing from when Xi took office.[97]

Elite collusion continued in opposition to the central leadership's directives. A 2014 working paper explained how crony capitalism operated in China. Municipal officials courted foreign firms, picked cronies, and then granted the joint companies local monopolies or near-monopolies in exchange for a partial ownership stake in the municipality itself. These favored firms enjoyed extraordinary privileges, monopoly rents, and access to the local party's patronage networks, while the municipalities used China's labyrinthine formal rules to seal out those firms' potential competitors. In return, the party officials gained monopoly profits while retaining enormous formal and informal control over the local economy.[98]

One area that the central government appeared to be making progress on concerned the problem of collusion between law enforcement and criminal gangs. In 2018, authorities announced a multiyear crackdown designed to end a pernicious practice that undermined public confidence in the government. By 2019, authorities claimed 79,000 individuals had been detained.[99] However, because authorities did not provide sufficient funding for services assigned to local governments, the temptation to resort to such expedients persisted.

In this period, the elite's opposition eased somewhat as Xi backed off the most demanding aspects of his policy agenda and instead sought to coopt some of the largest SOEs. Indeed, Xi's endorsement of an industrial policy that prominently featured champion SOEs suggested a recalibration of political strategy. It reflected, in part, the recognition that the central government ultimately depended on elites and that SOEs remained valuable tools for achieving social welfare goals, such as promoting employment and social stability. Nevertheless, the elites' wealth and lifestyles depended on the continuation of many policies the central leadership sought to end. The elites remained fundamentally opposed to the intensive growth policies proposed by the Third Plenum.

In sum, elite *opposition* remained *strong*. Despite the growing power of the central leadership and a prolonged crackdown on elites, the power of elites diminished only slightly. The elites remained fundamentally opposed to the central leadership's intensive growth agenda and relied on indirect methods to passively resist policy implementation.

Developments Related to Public Cohesiveness

The problems of economic fragmentation, yawning inequality, and political repression persisted through 2018. Economically, inequality remained high and continued to climb. Deindustrialization accelerated, the industrial sector shrank, the service sector grew, and informality continued to characterize the majority of jobs in the non-rural areas. Once Donald Trump became the US president, the US-China trade war intensified. Under such external pressures, Chinese leaders scaled back their plans to downsize SOEs and other industries.

In sum, the public remained deeply *fragmented*. Efforts to boost the cohesiveness of the public stalled due to inadequate funding of the social safety net. The use of nationalistic policies and cult-of-Xi politics may have boosted popular support for Xi, but persistent economic and social fragmentation, the pervasiveness of patron-client ties dominated by local elites, and the continuation of political repression left the public with low mobilization potential.

As of late 2019, China's top leadership found itself in a stalemate with the nation's elites. Xi Jinping's centralization of power could not overcome the formidable power of the nation's elites, and the severe fragmentation of the public constrained its ability to support Beijing. Although the central leadership's position reduced the dangers of coups and overthrows by elites, the political situation was unfavorable to the implementation of intensive growth policies.

CONCLUSION

Under Xi Jinping, China's central government made incremental progress in carrying out the major policy initiative designed to put the country's growth trajectory on a more productive and sustainable basis. The World Bank reported some progress in the country's economic rebalancing.[100] In a change from 2000 to 2014, when fixed investment was generally the largest source of China's GDP growth, in both 2015 and 2016, private consumption was the largest contributor to GDP growth.[101] The plan for reorganizing the government, released at the NPC, strengthened the central government's regulatory authority, which helped control some of the country's persistent financial, economic, and environmental abuses.[102] The legal and court systems experienced modest improvements as well. Plaintiffs reported that they began to receive fairer hearings in cases that did not touch on party rules.[103] China carried out these policy changes while remaining politically stable. Indeed, although many citizens resented local officials, Xi Jinping and the Chinese Communist Party enjoyed relatively high approval ratings, especially among the working and poorer classes.[104]

However, in many other respects, the implementation of major policy initiatives proved disappointing. Despite the measures to bolster central control, the government failed to carry out key reforms. Instead of dismantling a bloated state sector, for example, central leaders tolerated its expansion. They also proved reluctant to crack down on the unprofitable lending of local banks, fearing the destabilizing effects of large-scale job losses.[105] China's SOEs continued to suffer from low productivity. They experienced little improvement in profitability, and by 2019, about a third of SOEs remained unprofitable. Moreover, in some ways, the situation worsened, with SOEs growing more powerful and securing a larger share of credit while the more efficient private sector lacked credit.[106] From 2013 to 2019, for example, government-owned firms' share of new bank loans rose from 30 percent to 70 percent. The nation's debt-to-GDP ratio soared from 200 percent in 2010 to 260 percent in 2017. Meanwhile, the private sector share of output stagnated. Unfavorable structural shifts remained underway. The working-age population shrank, and investment grew to a massive 44 percent of GDP.[107] Given the highly inefficient economy, productivity grew at a relatively rapid rate of 1.5 percent from 2008 to 2018.[108] Analysts warned that if China did not boost productivity in the future, it would experience a sharp decline in economic growth.[109] China's already high level of income inequality appeared poised to rise.[110]

The implementation of the policy may have proved disappointing overall, but why did Xi risk political conflict with such coercive and repressive politics to achieve such modest gains? This analysis has suggested that the surprising politics undertaken by Xi reflected an effort to overcome the persistent weaknesses inherited from his predecessor. Central leaders from the time of Jiang Zemin onward faced a formidable elite who benefited enormously, both politically and financially, from the continuation of unsustainable policies. The massive transfer of resources to the state sector in the wake of the global financial crisis exacerbated the problems of central weakness and elite strength. Moreover, Xi inherited the central leadership's dependence on the same elites to provide political stability, employment, and GDP growth. This reality gave the elites a tremendous advantage against central leaders who sought to discipline them.

Moreover, the CCP's decision to align itself closely with all levels of government as a "governing party" deepened the central leadership's dependence on the elites and further diminished the CCP's faltering ties to the public. Other economic developments aggravated the trends. The mode of growth that powered China's rise depended on the administrative flexibility of officials, who could wave regulations and cut red tape to entice foreign investors. The same flexibility permitted officials to frustrate central efforts to discipline them, since the superior knowledge of how to sustain economic activity gave local officials an immense advantage over flummoxed central leaders who lacked the ability to redirect the economic activity.

The severe fragmentation of the public intensified following the country's premature deindustrialization starting around 2013. The popular understanding of China as the "world's factory" obscured the important ways in which China's industrial might differed from that of early industrializers such as the US, Japan, and even Taiwan. From the beginning, China's industrialization only reached a fraction of that experienced by early industrializers, and it petered out at a far earlier stage and at a lower income level. Moreover, unlike the early industrializers, Chinese factories lacked the sort of linkages and interconnections that enabled successful upgrading efforts among earlier industrializers. As of 2020, China remained a country defined primarily by a rural and informal workforce and with a fragmented industry consisting of a massive state sector and myriad subcontractors oriented largely to serving large foreign investors. The fragmentation of labor and businesses was compounded by the geographic cellularization of provincial economies and the general inadequacy of the social safety net. With the CCP increasingly detached from the day-to-day lives of the public and focused on managing elites, opportunities for competing social identities and groups emerged. Incapable of mobilizing popular support, authorities opted for repression as the best way to prevent the emergence of social groups that might challenge their rule.

Western critics have long focused on the possibilities of liberal democratic reformers as a principal challenge to CCP rule, an idea well captured in the popular coverage of the liberal critics whom authorities quashed. But the influence of liberalizing reformers may be overstated. While a handful of Chinese intellectuals might have found the concept of liberalizing political reform appealing, its salience among the public is less clear. The severe fragmentation of the public and the dominance of local society by elites raise doubts about how much liberalizing reforms would have improved the country's prospects. Given the strength of elite opposition and the deep fragmentation of the public, it seems equally plausible, if not more likely, that liberalization would merely have resulted in a sort of illiberal autocratic or oligarchic rule that proved all too common in other former communist states such as Russia. Chinese scholars themselves highlighted the peril of oligarchic rule and the examples of Russia and other illiberal democracies when they discussed the risks of liberalizing reforms.[111] Scholars cited the examples of Russia and Mexico when they explained how rapid privatization "quickly produced a group of extremely wealthy tycoons and oligarchs." In a revealing comment about the extent of China's own corruption and oligarchy, a 2013 article in the party journal *Seeking Truth* noted that "if the Chinese telecom industry were to be privatized," the result "would be a tycoon like Carlos Slim with wealth rivaling that of nations."[112]

The country's deep integration into the global economy also helps explain the CCP's obsession with the idea that foreign enterprises could mobilize their workers and clients to advance political changes, which imperiled the regime's control. Chinese commentators betrayed apprehension about the fragile state of the country in their warnings about hostile "international forces" who have "done everything in their power to promote a strategy of westernizing and dividing China." Betraying a deep anxiety about the risks of the country's fragmentation, one article stated, "Only a China that is fractured, chaotic, weak, and lax" would serve the needs of the unnamed foreign forces.[113]

One puzzle that remains concerns the central government's failure to build the cohesiveness of the public and thereby elevate the potential for political mobilization in support of the central leadership's agenda. The pragmatic benefits of such an effort, if successful, could have been substantial. A mobilized and engaged public could have helped hold elites accountable, demand fair access to social welfare benefits, support the central leadership's upgrading reforms, and perhaps even set the stage for successful liberalizing reforms.

But it is the extreme fragmentation of the public that helps explain why authorities could not carry out a political mobilization. In 1988, Joel Migdal described China as a strong state that had established integrated social control due to Mao's mobilization of the people.[114] Yet thirty years later, China's situation had changed dramatically. Migdal's own work provides reasons why China today may more accurately be regarded as a country defined by social fragmentation rather than cohesiveness. As Migdal himself noted, social order can disintegrate over time, and this has happened in China as it has in other countries. The major factors that contribute to disintegration were also anticipated by Migdal, such as the penetration of the local economy by the global market, which introduced new incentives, foreign capital, and disruptive changes that empowered local strongmen and reoriented economies away from local needs to distant consumers. Rapid growth enriched powerful elites, who in turn funded their own patronage networks and even recruited national-level leaders. And as the experience of successive leaders in China has shown, these developments can prove incredibly difficult to change once in place. Xi Jinping's efforts yielded more progress than Hu experienced, but the modest results came at the price of higher repression and potentially destabilizing coercion against elites, not to mention the reproach of an international community appalled by the brutality of the Chinese government.[115] The fact that Xi Jinping can inflict such trauma on China's domestic situation for such little gain raises questions about the prospects of intensive growth in a country facing such an unfavorable political situation as China.

NOTES

1. *BBC*, "China Third Plenum: Leaders Unveil Key Reforms," November 12, 2013.
2. *China Daily*, "Wen Confident in Maintaining Economic Growth," March 16, 2007.
3. *Wall Street Journal*, "China Needs Fundamental Reform."
4. Scissors, "A Stagnant China in 2040, Briefly."

5. Dani Rodrik, "Work and Human Development in a Deindustrializing World," *UNDP Think Piece*, February 2015.

6. John West, "China, a Low Productivity Superpower," *The Interpreter*, October 31, 2019.

7. Andrew Baston, "Fixing China's State Sector," *Paulson Policy Memorandum*, January 2014.

8. McKinesey Global Institute, "China's Choice: Capturing the $5Trillion Productivity Opportunity," June 2016.

9. IMF, "Press Release: IMF Staff Completes 2016 Article IV Mission to China," June 14, 2016. As of January 6, 2021, https://www.imf.org/en/News/Articles/2015/09/14/01/49/pr16277.

10. Fewsmith, "The Third Plenary Session of the 16th Party Congress."

11. *BBC*, "China Third Plenum: Leaders Unveil Key Reforms."

12. Jin Hui, "Government Reform Is the Core of the Present Round of Reforms" [Zhengfu Gaige Shi Ben Lun Gaige De Hexin], *Economic Observer News* [Jingji Cankao Bao], September 23, 2014.

13. Zhang Zhuoyuan, "Comprehensively Understand the Market's Decisive Role" [Quanmian Liaojie Shichang De Juedingxing Zuoyong], *Outlook* [Liaowang], No, 51, December 23, 2013, 46–68.

14. Jiang Zengwei, "To Give Full Play to the Role of the Market, the Market Must First Be Properly Constructed" [Yao Chongfen Fahui Shichang Zuoyong, Bixu Shouxian Zhengque Goujian Shichang], *Seeking Truth* [Qiushi], February 1, 2014.

15. Tucker Van Aken and Orion A. Lewis, "The Political Economy of Noncompliance in China: The Case of Industrial Energy Policy," *Journal of Contemporary China* 24, no. 95 (2015): 798–822.

16. Yuhuan Wang, "Beyond Local Protectionism: China's State-Business Relations in the Last Two Decades," *The China Quarterly* 226 (June 2016): 319–41.

17. Jamil Anderlini, "Chinese Industry: Ambitions in Excess," *Financial Times*, June 16, 2013.

18. Yuhuan Wang, "Beyond Local Protectionism."

19. Taylor Fravel, "Xi Jinping and the PLA," *The Diplomat*, March 19, 2013.

20. *Reuters*, "Former China Security Chief Faces Corruption Probe: Report," August 30, 2013.

21. *Xinhua*, "Full Text of 18th Party Congress Report," November 27, 2012.

22. *Outlook* [Liaowang], "The Power of Adhering to Political Discipline" [Jianchi Zhengzhi Jilu De Liliang], No, 21, May 23, 2011, 38–39.

23. World Inequality Database, "World Inequality Report 2018."

24. Yu Xie and Yongai Jin, "Household Wealth in China," *Chinese Sociological Review* 47, no. 3 (2015): 203–29.

25. *World Bank*, "China 2030: Building a Modern, Harmonious, and Creative Society," February 27, 2012.

26. Jin Hui, "Government Reform Is the Core of the Present Round of Reforms."

27. Minxin Pei, "China's Crony Capitalism: The Dynamics of Regime Decay," *The National Interest*, October 2, 2016.

28. Malcolm Moore, "China's Reforms Stalled by 'Powerful Vested Interests'," *The Telegraph*, January 12, 2012.

29. Fewsmith and Nathan, "Authoritarian Resilience Revisited."

30. *VOA*, "After Bo Xilai Conviction, Mixed Legacy for Chongqing's Anti-Mafia Campaign," April 15, 2014.

31. Lynette H. Ong, "Thugs for Hire: Subcontracting of State Coercion and State Capacity in China," *Perspectives in Politics*, April 2018.

32. Max Zenglein, "China's Overrated Services Sector," MERICS, 2016.

33. Ibid.

34. Richard Freeman, "A Labor Market with Chinese Characteristics," in *The Routledge Handbook of the Chinese Economy*, ed. Gregory C. Chow (London: Routledge, 2015).

35. Swider, *Building China*, 2.

36. Ying Chen and Zhun Xu, "Informal Employment and China's Economic Development," *The Chinese Economy* 50, no. 6 (2017): 425–33.

37. Norwegian Energy and Environment Consortium, "China's Productivity Imperative."

38. Qian Jiwei, "Why Informal Workers are Opting Out of China's Welfare System."

39. Freeman, "A Labor Market with Chinese Characteristics."

40. *The Guardian*, "Chinese Repression of Dissent Intensifies Under Ruthless Xi Jinping," December 30, 2014.

41. *Freedom House*, "Freedom on the Net: A Global Assessment of Internet and Digital Media," 2013.

42. Jin Hui, "Government Reform Is the Core of the Present Round of Reforms."

43. *South China Morning Post*, "How Leading Small Groups Help Xi Jinping and Other Party Leaders Exert Power."

44. Javier C. Hernández, "China's 'Chairman of Everything': Behind Xi Jinping's Many Titles," *The New York Times*, October 25, 2017.

45. *Business Insider*, "China's Crackdown on Corruption and Government Spending: A Timeline," January 23, 2014.

46. *Xinhua*, "Xi Calls for 'Strong Measures' to Cure Corruption," January 13, 2015.

47. *Wall Street Journal*, "China Anti-Corruption Cases Have Quadrupled Since 2013, Study Says," December 11, 2015.

48. *NBC News*, "China's President Xi Beefs Up His Anti-Corruption Crackdown," February 27, 2018. As of May 5, 2022, https://www.nbcnews.com/news/china/china-s-president-xi-beefs-his-anti-corruption-crackdown-n851491.

49. Tom Mitchell, "Xi Jinping's Anti-Corruption Probe Takes Aim at Military," *Financial Times*, March 2, 2015.

50. Timothy R. Heath, *The Consolidation of Political Power in China Under Xi Jinping: Implications for the PLA and Domestic Security Forces* (Santa Monica, CA: RAND Corporation, 2019).

51. Joel Wuthnow and Phillip C. Saunders, "Chinese Military Reforms in the Age of Xi Jinping: Drivers, Challenges, and Implications," *China Strategic Perspectives*, Institute for National Strategic Studies, No. 10, March 2017.

52. Liu Zhen, "China's Military Police Given Control of Coast Guard as Beijing Boosts Maritime Security," *South China Morning Post*, March 21, 2018.

53. Office of the Secretary of Defense, *Annual Report to Congress: Military and Security Developments Involving the People's Republic of China 2016*, Washington, DC, April 2016.

54. Jiayang Fan, Taisu Zhang, and Ying Zhu, "Behind the Personality Cult of Xi Jinping," *Foreign Policy*, March, 8, 2016.

55. Jerome Doyon, "The End of the Road for Xi's Mass Line Campaign: An Assessment," *China Brief* 14, no. 20 (October 23, 2014). As of September 22, 2023: https://jamestown.org/program/the-end-of-the-road-for-xis-mass-line-campaign-an-assessment/.

56. Heike Holbig, Jean Christopher Mittelstaedt, Yevgen Sautin, and Angela Stanzel, "China's 'New Era' With Xi Jinping Characteristics," *European Council on Foreign Affairs* website, December 15, 2017.

57. *Xinhua*, "China Moves to Clear Blockades for Unified Market," December 10, 2013.

58. *Reuters*, "Xi Says China Will Continue to Open its Economy, Deepen Financial Reforms," October 17, 2017.

59. World Inequality Database, "World Inequality Report 2018."

60. *South China Morning Post*, "Coup Plotters Foiled: Xi Jinping Fended Off Threat to 'Save Communist Party'," October 20, 2017.

61. Han Baojiang, "Reform and Opening Up Are the Source of Vitality of the Development and Progress in Contemporary China" [Gaige Kaifang Shi Dangdai Zhongguo Fazhan Jinbu De Shengmingli Yuanquan], *Outlook* [Liaowang] 26 (July 1, 2013): 25–26.

62. Ibid.

63. Bi Jingjing, "The Mass Line Is the Fundamental Work Line for Pooling Our Strength to Realize the Chinese Dream" [Qunzhong Luxian Shi Ningju Liliang Shixian Zhongguomeng De Genben Gongzuo Xian], *Seeking Truth* [Qiushi], No. 15, August 1, 2013.

64. *Xinhua*, "Zhou Yongkang Arrested for Serious Disciplinary Violations," July 29, 2014.

65. *BBC*, "Chinese General Guo Boxiong Sentenced to Life in Prison for Corruption," July 25, 2016; *CBS News*, "China Says 300,000 Punished for Corruption," March 6, 2016.

66. *Bloomberg*, "Is China Growing Services Sector at Expense of Manufacturing?," July 21, 2016.

67. Zenglein, "China's Overrated Services Sector."

68. Jain-Chandra, Khor, Mano, Schauer, Wingender, and Zhuang, "Inequality in China."

69. Denise van der Kamp, Peter Lorentzen, and Daniel Mattingly, "Racing to the Bottom or the Top? Decentralization, Revenue Pressures, and Governance Reform in China," *World Development* 95 (2017): 164–76.

70. Baston, "Fixing China's State Sector."

71. Ibid.

72. Zenglein, "China's Overrated Services Sector."

73. Bi Jingjing, , "The Mass Line Is the Fundamental Work Line for Pooling Our Strength to Realize the Chinese Dream."

74. Ibid.

75. Heath, "Xi's Mass Line."

76. *South China Morning Post*, "Xi Jinping a Reformer and a Nationalist," June 6, 2013.

77. *Wall Street Journal*, "Chinese President Xi Jinping's Extreme Makeover," May 12, 2016.

78. Anne Marie Brady, "China's Foreign Propaganda Machine," *Wilson Center*, October 26, 2015.

79. *China Daily*, "China Outlines Its First Social Credit System," June 27, 2014.

80. Martin Chorzempa, Paul Triolo, and Samm Sacks, "China's Social Credit System: A Mark of Progress or a Threat to Privacy?," Peterson Institute for International Economics Policy Brief, June 2018.

81. *South China Morning Post*, "Human Rights under Xi 'worst since Tiananmen Crackdown'."

82. Chris Buckley, "China Gives Communist Party More Control Over Policy and Media," *The New York Times*, March 21, 2018.

83. Jamie P. Horsley, "What's So Controversial About China's New Anti-Corruption Body?" *The Diplomat*, May 31, 2018.

84. David Gitter, Julia Bowie, and Brock Erdahl, "Quarterly Report 2 | January-April 2018," *The Party Watch Initiative*, June 1, 2018.

85. Alice Lyman Miller, "Only Socialism Can Save China; only Xi Jinping Can Save Socialism," *China Leadership Monitor*, No. 56, May 17, 2018.

86. *Seeking Truth* [Qiushi], "Excerpts of Speech by Xi Jinping at the Second Plenary Meeting of the Sixth Plenary Session of the 18th CPC Central Committee" [Xi Jinping Zai Shiba Jie Liu Zhong Quanhui Di Er Ci Quanti Huiyi Shang De Jianghua Zhaiyao], December 31, 2016.

87. *BBC News*, "China's Anti-corruption Campaign Expands with New Agency."

88. *Reuters*, "China to Launch National Probe into Policy Implementation," August 20, 2018.

89. *Global Times*, "Xi Stresses War Preparedness During PLA Navy Marine Corps Visit," October 14, 2020.

90. Chris Buckley, "Drive the Blade In: Xi Shakes Up China's Law and Order Forces," *New York Times*, August 20, 2020.

91. Buckley and Myers, "China's Legislature Blesses Xi's Indefinite Rule."

92. *Reuters*, "China to Enshrine Xi's Thought into State Constitution Amid National 'Fervor'," January 19, 2018.

93. Wen and Shepherd, "China Cranks Propaganda, Xi Jinping's Cult of Personality into Overdrive Ahead of Party Congress."

94. Wang Qishan, "Comprehensively Administer the Party with Strict Discipline and Shoulder the Party's Mission in the New Age" [Yange Jilu Quanmian Zhizheng Dang Jianfu Xin Shiqi Dang De Shiming], *People's Daily* [Renmin Ribao], November 8, 2016, 3.

95. World Inequality Database, "World Inequality Report 2018."

96. Suparna Goswami, "Study Finds India Is Asia's Most Corrupt Country, While Japan Comes In Last," *Forbes*, March 8, 2017.

97. Ralph Jennings, "Bad for Business? China's Corruption Isn't Getting Any Better," *Forbes*, March 15, 2018.

98. Samantha Eyler-Driscoll, "What Glue Holds Communist Capitalism Together in China? Cronyism," *Pro Market*, March 20, 2018.

99. *South China Morning Post*, "China's War on Organized Crime, Corrupt Officials Sees 79,000 Detained," April 14, 2019.

100. *World Bank*, "China Maintains Strong Growth and Reform Momentum, Says World Bank", December 19, 2017.

101. Wayne M. Morrison, "China's Economic Rise: History, Trends, Challenges, and Implications for the United States," Congressional Research Services, February 5, 2018.

102. Chris Buckley and Keith Bradsher, "China Unveils Superagencies to Fight Pollution and Other Threats to Party Rule," *New York Times*, March 13, 2018.

103. *The Economist*, "For Some Plaintiffs, Courts in China Are Getting Better," September 30, 2017.

104. Tom Phillips, "Chairman Xi Crushes Dissent but Poor Believe He's Making China Great," *The Guardian*, October 14, 2017.

105. *Reuters*, "Xi Says China Will Continue to Open its Economy, Deepen Financial Reforms."

106. West, "China, a Low Productivity Superpower."

107. *The Economist*, "The Struggle to Reform China's Economy," February 21, 2019.

108. Raiser and Soh, "To Sustain Growth, China Can Learn from Previous Transitions to High Income."

109. Morrison, "China's Economic Rise."

110. Robert Lawrence, "China, Like U.S., Faces Challenges in Achieving Inclusive Growth Through Manufacturing," Peterson Institute for International Economics, Policy Brief, August 2019.

111. Lu Wei, "Making Online Public Opinion Work the Top Priority of Propaganda and Ideological Work" [Jiang Wangluo Yulun Gongzuo Zuowei Xuanchuan Sixiang Gongzuo De Zhongzhong Zhi Zhong], *People's Daily* [Renmin Ribao], September 17, 2013, 16.

112. *Seeking Truth* [Qiushi], "Consolidating the Common Ideological Foundation of United Struggle by the Party and the People" [Gongu Dang He Renmin Tuanjie Fendou De Gongtong Sixiang Jichu], October 16, 2013.

113. Ibid.

114. Migdal, *Weak States and Strong Societies*.

115. Jude Blanchette, *China's New Red Guards: The Return of Radicalism and the Rebirth of Mao Zedong* (Oxford: Oxford University Press, 2019).

Chapter 5

Taiwan 1973–1979

Success Amid a Looming Threat of an Elite-Led Popular Mobilization

In the 1970s, Taiwan's leaders, led by President Chiang Ching-kuo, decided to carry out a major, multi-sector policy initiative to bolster growth. As part of this initiative, they launched the "Ten Major Construction Projects," which consisted of a series of government-funded projects to build infrastructure and key industries.

The government of Taiwan faced a favorable set of political factors when it tackled this challenge. The central government had ample resources and maintained sturdy control over subnational governments. Chiang also held a firm grip on the Kuomintang (KMT) ruling party as well as the island's security forces. Elites were relatively weak, differentiated, and featured a low level of collusion. They were also well-disposed toward the proposed economic policies. The populace had a high level of cohesiveness, owing to a mostly formal workforce, an enterprise sector dominated by domestic industries, and responsive political institutions that permitted limited but real political participation. With such favorable political conditions, the central leadership successfully implemented policies that yielded major productivity gains and added another chapter to the story of the "Taiwan economic miracle."

While the central leadership experienced a fairly smooth implementation of its economic initiative, political tensions between the central government and native Taiwanese elites led President Chiang to contemplate political reforms at the end of the 1970s. In particular, the émigré nature of the KMT leadership threatened the regime's unity as the native-born population outnumbered an aging minority mainlander faction. A low level of social inequality had bought the island considerable stability in the preceding decades, but it also raised the prospect of deepening solidarity between ethnic Taiwan elites and a largely ethnic Taiwan populace against the mainlander leadership. The public's cohesiveness thus proved a near-term asset but posed a potential long-term threat to mainlander rule.

To forestall a possible overthrow by a combined force of Taiwanese elites and the public, the mainlander leadership tried to coopt the native elites by expanding opportunities to join the upper ranks of the KMT. When these measures proved inadequate, the government acceded to an organized opposition, which in subsequent decades paved the way for liberalizing democratic reforms.

BACKGROUND

The KMT ruled Taiwan in the 1970s as a quasi-Leninist political party founded by Sun Yat-sen dedicated to the overthrow of the Qing dynasty and the formation of a republic. Following its defeat in the Chinese Civil War in 1949, the KMT remained on Taiwan, where it presided over a closed, single-party authoritarian system. Although the KMT shared some organizational features in common with the CCP, it lacked its communist counterpart's ideological fervor and close relationship with the population.

One of the most distinctive features of the KMT was its status as an émigré regime. The KMT led an exodus of people to Taiwan during the Chinese Civil War. The mainlanders initially comprised about 10 percent of the island's population. The emigres ruthlessly suppressed Taiwan-born elites who could potentially organize resistance to the KMT occupation through brutal purges. In the early 1950s, the KMT carried out a "land to tiller" program that reallocated the land owned by landlords. The redistribution of land weakened the remaining landlord elite and helped shore up the regime's strained ties with the native Taiwanese populace.[1]

The 1970s posed severe political and economic challenges to the KMT regime. In 1972, the US agreed to switch recognition of the legitimate government of "China" from the Republic of China (ROC) on Taiwan to the People's Republic of China (PRC) on the mainland. The loss of US recognition dealt a severe blow to the credibility of the KMT. This loss of prestige galvanized political opposition.[2] The KMT realized that to survive, it had to effectively integrate Taiwan-born natives into the regime.

In addition to these political challenges, technocrats became concerned about the island's economic prospects. In the early 1970s, Taiwan featured a shrinking but productive agricultural sector and a growing manufacturing sector divided into three parts: State-owned enterprises (SOE), large enterprises, and small to medium enterprises (SME). The KMT maintained control of the SOEs, which concentrated on "strategic" industries that supplied power and resources to the island's manufacturers. However, an ideological imperative to maintain its own anticommunist stand and pressure from the United States persuaded the KMT regime to divest itself of some state-owned enterprises and to foster a few private enterprises as early as the 1950s.[3] The KMT encouraged Taiwanese to engage in the vibrant private enterprise sector. The KMT's support for economic opportunity helped maintain a common identity in the face of the perceived threat from mainland China.[4] Indeed, SMEs were major employers, accounting for over 50 percent of all workers during the mid to late 1970s. They were not only major exporters but also a principal driver of the whole Taiwan economy, with extensive linkages to both the SOEs and intermediary large enterprises.[5]

The principal economic hazard lay in a looming slowdown owing to two important trends: the diminishing supply of surplus labor and creeping protectionism in export markets. Moreover, the island experienced the shocks of the oil crisis, which revealed the limits of its export strategy. Although the industrial sector expanded and the agricultural sector shrank in the 1970s, productivity declined and growth slowed. Industrial productivity worsened, with total factor productivity (TFP) dipping into negative territory in the early 1970s.[6] Meanwhile, wages rose as the surplus labor from rural areas diminished.

To improve the country's economic prospects, authorities proposed a US$8 billion infrastructure program known as the "Ten Major Construction Projects." The government also expanded the ranks of SOEs to produce a range of capital-intensive goods on a large scale. Some were finished goods, such as shipbuilding, but most were intermediate goods, such as steel, petrochemicals, and oil refinement. These industries served the large and rapidly growing local market as well as the export sector.[7]

Taiwan's technocrats recommended a strategy of backward linkage for several reasons. First, downstream industries (i.e., makers and distributors of finished goods) had expanded to such a degree that they created huge domestic demand for intermediate and upstream products (i.e., suppliers of raw materials). In addition, the experts judged that expanding the steel, shipbuilding, and petrochemical industries would help maintain a robust defense industry.[8]

The Ten Major Construction Projects aimed to address weaknesses in the basic transportation and power systems while also responding to growing demand for semifinished products. The Ten Major Construction Projects included the development of new port facilities, new super highways linking north to south, and a large-scale and modern airport set in Taoyaun County. The growing demand for electric power for industrial, commercial, and consumer use was also addressed. Nuclear-powered generators were planned and then constructed north of Taipei and in the south.[9]

Developments Related to the Central Leadership

In the 1970s, the KMT state retained a high level of autonomy in relation to the native-born elites due to its control of resources that it looted from the mainland and access to foreign aid, principally from the United States. With its resources, the central leadership could coopt local elites and provide patronage to citizens. The position of the central government was strengthened by the relatively small geographic area administered by the KMT—the island of Taiwan could fit within the province of Fujian across the strait.

Taiwan's political system prominently featured a "strongman," or autocratic military dictator. In the early 1970s, an ailing Chiang Kai-shek, the top leader, handed power to his son, Chiang Ching-kuo, who assumed the office of premier in 1972 and KMT chair in 1976. He subsequently became president in 1978. As of 1974, Chiang Ching-kuo maintained absolute control of the military and security forces.[10]

Although KMT rulers had the ultimate say on policies, they tended to defer to economic specialists on matters related to their expertise.[11] Some observers attributed this deference to the KMT's searing experience on the mainland. Rampant inflation and corruption contributed to the KMT's defeat at the hands of the CCP. Moreover, the KMT regime firmly believed in fiscal and monetary conservatism. To reduce the risks of corruption, they separated political from economic elites and tended to adhere to economic orthodoxy.[12]

The KMT central leadership generally maintained a hands-off approach to the economy, except for the state-owned enterprise (SOE) sector. The importance of SOEs neared its peak in the 1970s and 1980s, but even at the height of their power, Taiwan's SOEs never achieved the dominant presence that they did in communist China. For example, SOEs accounted for 5 percent of GDP in 1951 and peaked in 1981 at around 10 percent.[13]

Ideologically, the KMT was never a coherent party. It upheld a vague ideology and was instead dominated by factions. Chiang Kai-shek's and Chiang Ching-kuo's power was based on the manipulation of rival groups. The autocrats routinely balanced them and used one to check the other. Although most of the political factions were weakened after the KMT retreated to Taiwan, the power struggles continued as new factions emerged when old ones fell away.[14]

Under Chiang Ching-kuo, the principal political division among factions lay between progressives and conservatives.[15] However, although tensions between groups intensified sporadically, party discipline generally held firm. There were no reports, for example, of flagrant defiance of party discipline or overt challenges to Chiang's authority.

In sum, the well-resourced KMT central leadership held a *strong* position in the island's political economy, with firm control of subnational governments, the island's security forces, and the party apparatus. However, key developments had begun to weaken its hold on the KMT political party as Taiwanization introduced new elites with different outlooks and values from the mainlander elite.

Developments Related to Elite Opposition

The island's elite tended to have a moderate share of the nation's resources and featured a high level of differentiation. Although the division between mainlanders and native Taiwanese remained a major cultural barrier, the KMT's political design successfully coopted some Taiwan-born elites through a strategy of corporatism and clientelism. In terms of income and wealth, the Taiwanese elite's share remained relatively modest through this period. According to government statistics, the top 10 percent of income earners earn about 25 percent of national income.[16]

Mainlanders dominated the central government. Native Taiwanese dominated the lower level government offices. Joseph Bosco characterized the local political organization as one featuring "factions," which he defined as groupings that featured "uncertain duration, personalistic leadership, a lack of formal organization, and a greater concern with power and spoils than with ideology or policy." He added, however, that Taiwan's factions had a more fixed nature, with permanent names, a strong sense of identity, and stable leadership. These factions operated as political machines within the KMT, with elected officials distributing goods to supporters.[17]

In addition to vertical segmentation, Taiwan's elites featured a high degree of sectoral differentiation. Through the 1970s, the mainlander KMT officials dominated the military and political sectors. By contrast, the local Taiwanese elites tended to concentrate in the business sector, especially the private sector. Thus, while economic resources were diffused, they came to be held largely by the Taiwanese.[18]

In the early 1970s, the KMT began to experience a dearth of talented personnel when older mainlanders retired or died. To make up the shortfall, the KMT began coopting native Taiwan elites through a strategy of "Taiwanization." The strategy aimed to gradually defuse political opposition by expanding opportunities within the ruling party. When Chiang Ching-kuo assumed the premiership in 1972, six Taiwanese were given positions at the cabinet level in the Executive Yuan. For the first time, a Taiwanese, Hsieh Tung-min, was appointed governor of the province of Taiwan.[19]

In short, elites posed *weak opposition* to the central leadership in this period. The elite share of national income remained fairly modest. The elites were highly differentiated both vertically and horizontally. Moreover, the elites generally supported the central government's ideas for economic upgrading and thus posed little opposition.

Developments Related to Public Cohesiveness

In Taiwan, state control over society had never been absolute, even in the 1950s and 1960s. The KMT did not attempt to control every aspect of its subjects' lives, and the inhabitants of the island generally enjoyed a wide range of personal and nonpolitical liberties. The looseness of the party's ideology also permitted considerable room for discussion and debate within the ranks, so long as taboos such as the legitimacy of KMT rule were not crossed.[20]

The society experienced a significant division between the mainlander émigré population and the local Taiwan natives, but in the initial decades, this difference was eased by a shared fear of the threat posed by the communist mainland. A relatively low level of inequality and ample opportunities for the local population to prosper economically and participate in the political process through local elections also helped facilitate social cohesiveness.

Taiwan experienced relatively low levels of inequality, with a Gini coefficient of about 0.28 in 1975.[21] As an example of how a fairly well-endowed central government employed policy instruments to curry favor with the local population and ease opposition, the central government changed its policy in 1973 from one of squeezing farmers to one of generous subsidies. This helped bolster the central leadership's political relationship with rural populations.[22] Economically, people worked in the formal employment sector, and the informal sector remained small. Taiwan's economy at this point featured a limited foreign investor presence. The domestic business sector featured considerable linkages between upstream and downstream industries.[23]

The populace experienced a higher level of political integration than was the case on the mainland. The KMT may have maintained a quasi-Leninist organization and monopolized political power, but it also tolerated competitive elections at the local level in part to placate its US patron. These elections chose officials to govern at the village and local government levels and were widely regarded as real, competitive, and based on local interests. In these elections, factions within the KMT mobilized voters on a political machine-like basis to gain favors from patrons.[24]

Social segregation between mainlanders and local Taiwanese had eased somewhat by the early 1970s as the island's population learned Mandarin, but distinctive patterns persisted. One difference was vocational. Of the positions related to national security, mainlanders occupied 82 percent. They also dominated in public administration, legal, medical, and university positions. However, their presence in the armed forces had declined. A majority of the

Taiwan enlisted force consisted of the island's natives, although mainlanders continued to dominate the higher ranking officer corps.[25]

In sum, Taiwan had a *cohesive* public at this time. The island had a mostly formally employed workforce and a small informal sector. The enterprises featured mostly domestic industries, with little foreign presence. Politically, the regime offered opportunities for the populace to participate through local elections. Yet the division between mainlanders and local Taiwanese began to grow with the weakening of the KMT's international position following US recognition of mainland China.

Taiwan's political situation comported with the "enabling condition," suggesting that the island faced promising prospects for successful implementation of a major, multi-sector policy initiative. With such a favorable climate, the central leadership also had little incentive to dramatically increase the coercion of the elites or repression of the public.

INTERVENING DEVELOPMENTS, 1974–1976

In this period, the government proceeded with its strategy for economic upgrade. There appeared to be little opposition among either the elites or the public. The mainlanders served primarily in the noneconomic sectors and thus had little reason to oppose an economic strategy recommended by technocrats as a means of improving the country's long-term prospects. Local Taiwanese business elites welcomed the infrastructure development projects and initiatives. Very few elites had a vested interest in resisting the upgrading initiative, given the unpromising alternative of persisting with outdated and uncompetitive industrial arrangements.

Developments Related to the Central Leadership

Generalissimo Chiang Kai-shek died in 1975, and his son Chiang Ching-kuo assumed power. Chiang Ching-kuo had successfully amassed power to become the undisputed leader of the country since 1972. As premier, he assembled a group of forward-looking technocrats.[26] Chiang Ching-kuo accumulated additional powers in this period, including the chairmanship of the KMT, which he gained in late 1975, and the Presidency in 1978. The subordinate bureaucracies did not pose any serious defiance to central government directives. The principal opposition to Chiang's authority tended to derive from factions, a long-standing feature of Taiwanese politics. Chiang Ching-kuo relied on his inner circle and had to manage power struggles between competing groups.[27]

The military experienced a significant increase in membership from the local population. In the mid-late 1970s, about 80 percent of the enlisted force consisted of local Taiwanese. The mainlander KMT retained a tight grip on the most senior posts, but at least some local native Taiwanese entered higher ranks. There was no sign of disaffection or disobedience among the military and security forces to the autocrat's authority.

In sum, the central government remained *strong* in this period. Chiang Ching-kuo consolidated control of the government, party, and military. Factional power struggles within KMT remained fairly modest and did not significantly impede the government's operation.

Developments Related to Elite Opposition

In this period, the elites continued to prosper, although their share of income remained relatively unchanged from the previous period. While the mainlanders continued to control key political posts, the Taiwan natives dominated the economy, especially the SME sector. By contrast, the SOEs provided the KMT with a degree of autonomy and control over the domestic economy but did not generate as much revenue as the export-oriented SMEs. While the Taiwanese business elites continued to participate in the political system, they also pressed for greater representation. However, there was no evidence of widespread defiance or resistance to the central leadership's economic leadership or of its efforts to carry out the Ten Major Construction Projects.

The local-level elections grew in importance as a funnel for local elites to enter higher level offices. The central leadership slowly expanded the scope of the political contests and loosened control of the political system. Despite periodic crackdowns, the KMT party-state incrementally expanded the electoral process and relaxed election rules.[28]

As the country prospered, a new intellectual and business elite arose. To coopt these individuals, the KMT introduced new elections and recruited many promising young people into party and government positions. However, the KMT could not offer enough high-level positions due to its desire to maintain control of the most important positions. Dissatisfied with the limited opportunities, ambitious local Taiwanese began to form an opposition, the "Tang-Wai."[29]

As Taiwan became more integrated with the world market, private businesses sought capital and other resources from foreign partners. The dependence of local businesses on the government for credit and other assistance has greatly declined. This in turn reduced the leverage mainlanders had over Taiwanese businessmen through their control of the island's finances. Businessmen became empowered to demand more freedom and pressed for further liberalization of the economy under state control. Rapid economic changes thus occurred at a time when the KMT's institutional capacity for mobilization and control eroded. In an earlier period, the regime had attempted to eliminate or control any social groups. However, the increasing complexity of social and economic life resulted in an ever-expanding number of civic and social associations, which were beyond the capacity of the party to monitor and control.[30]

In sum, elite opposition remained *weak*. Elites remained divided by sector and generally held a modest share of income and wealth. Taiwanization increased local business elites' access to higher level government offices. Although the economic elites generally approved of an economic strategy designed to improve the competitiveness of the island's industries, local elites began to articulate an opposing policy agenda. Resentment also grew over the mainlanders' resistance to opening higher level offices to the local elites. Nevertheless, the central government's need for vibrant growth as a source of legitimacy and elite support for a more competitive economy resulted in a general alignment of interests between central leaders and the elites on the issue of intensive growth policies.

Developments Related to Public Cohesiveness

The fallout from the party's loss of international recognition added fuel to a growing Taiwan identity movement. The ROC government's claim to represent all of China no longer held any credibility. And with the government's de facto control narrowed to Taiwan, the question of who should rule and to what end became more salient. Local Taiwanese people began to demand more concessions from a mainlander-dominated central government intent on promoting a common "Chinese" identity and culture. Reflecting their weakened position, authorities loosened some restrictions and allowed more critical publications to circulate.

At the same time, the employment sector remained relatively unchanged, with the non-rural workforce generally engaged in formal work and the corporate sector featuring a growing but still limited foreign enterprise presence. The electoral opportunities provided opportunities for the public to demonstrate its support for political leaders who showed a greater willingness to question KMT orthodoxies. In a few cities, non-KMT officials were elected to office for the first time.[31]

Moreover, the central leadership's position regarding the populace weakened considerably as the economy's dependence on the SME sector deepened. The KMT regime recognized that exports from the SME sector had become critical to the economy. The mainlander-dominated leadership also viewed the SMEs as a potent force that could help restrain the Taiwan-owned large enterprises that were becoming increasingly influential. Eager to cultivate their support, Chiang Ching-kuo's promoted policies that helped SMEs.[32] Thus, the interests of the central leadership, Taiwan-dominated economic elites, and the workforce aligned in support of a more active promotion of SMEs.

In sum, the population continued to experience a fairly high level of *cohesiveness*, with a fairly low level of social inequality, high levels of formal employment, and an economy featuring domestic companies with clear linkages that incentivized coordination for upgrading policies. The electoral process provided a means for the public to organize and articulate its views on the imperative of accommodating local identity, which central leaders accommodated. Cultural and social distinctions grew somewhat sharper in the aftermath of the KMT's loss of international recognition.

The central leadership retained a firm grip, but they also recognized that time was not on their side. The economic elites, dominated by the Taiwanese, had grown powerful while the strength of the mainlanders waned. Society remained generally cohesive, which suggested a high potential for political mobilization. The KMT central leadership succeeded in temporarily buying off discontent with its policies regarding SMEs and rural populations, but this conciliated the population without undermining its high potential for political mobilization. The problem for the KMT mainlander-dominated central leadership was that its ability to lead a mobilization was rapidly declining while that of the local Taiwan elite was growing stronger.

Although the central leadership's position was weakening, the convergence of interests between the central leadership and elite, as well as actions taken by the central leadership to maintain the cohesiveness of the public, resulted in a favorable political condition for realizing the major, multi-sector policies for economic upgrading.

INTERVENING DEVELOPMENTS, 1977–1979

In this period, the weakening political position of the mainlander-dominated central government faced severe tests. The central leadership made additional concessions to conciliate the local Taiwanese elite, but this did not address their underlying weakness. However, in regard to the economic development strategy, the central leadership continued to experience fairly strong support from the elites and the public. Authorities successfully implemented the major, multi-sector policy initiatives.

Development Related to the Central Leadership

Chiang Ching-kuo continued to maintain a strong grip on the central government and on the military. However, his control over lower level governments weakened as more local native Taiwanese entered office. In some cases, elected officials did not belong to the KMT. In the KMT itself, the ascendance of a wealthy and assertive middle class and other autonomous social groups upended the established electoral system based on strict KMT control and patronage. When elected officials and representatives could succeed in the political arena without depending exclusively on the party's resources and support, they began to assert more autonomy. However, in this period, no elected KMT officials openly defied the central leadership.[33]

To strengthen his connection with the people, Chiang cultivated an image as a down-to-earth popular leader. At the same time, he maintained a firm grip on the security forces. He put close allies in charge of top military positions, and most observers of the time conceded that the central leadership held undisputed control over the nation's security forces.[34]

In sum, the central leadership remained *strong* but trended toward fragility. Chiang maintained a tight grip on the government and security forces, but his control of the KMT and political networks continued to atrophy as more and more local Taiwan natives began to challenge the mainlanders' monopoly on power.

Developments Related to Elite Opposition

Years of rapid growth had resulted in an increasingly pluralistic society and a wealthier, well-informed middle class. Observers noted the remarkable autonomy of the business class. Individual small and medium enterprises were unorganized and appeared generally beyond the capture of the party state. However, the share of income by the top 10 percent of earners increased only slightly, resulting in a still relatively equitable society.[35]

Political opposition crystallized into anti-regime protests that erupted following President Chiang Ching-kuo's decision to suspend elections in 1978, angering an increasingly powerful Tang-Wai opposition. Efforts to expand the publication of media critical of the KMT's abuses resulted in street protests, clashes with police, and a crackdown the following year. The divergence between central authorities and the Taiwanese elite continued to grow, despite general support for the country's economic development strategy.[36]

In short, elite opposition to the central leadership's economic policies remained *weak*. However, opposition to the monopoly on power exercised by the mainlander-dominated central leadership grew. The local Taiwan-dominated elite continued to have a modest share of the country's income and wealth, thus limiting the resources with which they might challenge the central leadership. Elite differentiation declined as more native-born Taiwanese entered higher offices, but the highest offices remained largely in the hands of mainlanders. Moreover, growing sympathy among native-born Taiwanese officials for the Tang-Wai opposition raised the risk that the mainlanders might face a powerful coalition. All elites generally supported the KMT-led economic development strategy, but political differences intensified, especially in the wake of the protests of 1978–1999.

Developments Related to Public Cohesiveness

Economically, the fruit of the economic upgrading strategy began to bear fruit, with GDP growth rebounding in the late 1970s and wages experiencing further gains. The workforce remained largely defined by formal employment in the industrial sector. The island began to reduce its dependence on exports and increase domestic consumption as a driver of growth. In 1975, about 35 percent of the economy's GNP came from exports, which represented a decline from 1973, when the ratio reached 47 percent.[37]

These changes were occurring at the same time that the KMT's institutional capacity for mobilization and control had eroded. The ever-expanding variety of civil society organizations exceeded the capacity of the KMT to monitor, much less to control. Moreover, the KMT's security forces struggled to penetrate internationally oriented organizations, such as the Junior Chambers of Commerce, the Lions Clubs, and the Rotary Clubs.[38]

In sum, the public remained *cohesive*, with low-income inequality and opportunities for political participation through elections. However, the social and cultural differences between mainlanders and native-born Taiwan sharpened. The risk grew that the Tang-Wai might mobilize the public against the embattled mainlander minority.

The central government retained a favorable but fading political situation as it implemented the Ten Major Construction Projects upgrading initiative. Successful implementation would likely accelerate these trends since it would weaken the mainlander-dominated central leadership's position as the Taiwan-born economic elites grew wealthier and stronger. The high mobilization potential of the public and the fact that so many people shared a common social and ethnic identity with the Taiwan-born elites raised the danger that excessive repression and violence by the central leadership to shatter the power of the Tang-Wai could backfire and instead energize country-wide opposition.

CONCLUSION

The case of Taiwan demonstrates how favorable political conditions can facilitate the implementation of major economic upgrading policies. A strong central leadership, weak elite opposition, and cohesive public facilitated the Taiwan leadership's implementation of the Ten Major Construction Projects. By 1980, the structure of Taiwan's economy had changed dramatically. Industry increased its share of GDP from 31.7 percent in 1972 to 42.8

percent in 1977. Industrial products increased as a share from 56 percent to 86.3 percent in the same period.[39] At the same time, the economy eased its dependence on exports, with the export sector dropping to below 35 percent of GNP in 1976 after reaching a high of 47 percent in 1973.[40] Over the six-year period, GDP growth averaged around 9 percent, adding to the island's reputation as the "Taiwan miracle."[41]

The configuration of the three political factors favored the successful implementation of the economic development strategy outlined by Chiang and his advisors in the early 1970s. With the central government in firm control of security forces and experiencing generally consistent compliance from lower level governments and discipline within the KMT ranks, the central leadership was well positioned to implement a major, multi-sector policy initiative. Taiwan's central leadership also benefited from a largely compliant elite, which recognized the imperative of improving the export industry upon which the island's economy had come to depend. Although there is little evidence of organized opposition to the economic policy, the native Taiwanese elite did oppose the mainlander's monopoly on power. The elites experienced divisions both vertically and horizontally that impaired coordinated opposition. However, the cohesiveness of the public was a critical factor in the evolution of the island's politics. The public's low level of inequality, labor's mostly formal work force, and the business sector's linkages between the various sized domestic industries, as well as the existence of an established electoral system, resulted in a stable, cohesive public with a high potential for political mobilization.

Ironically, although these features favored the KMT's grip on power in the early decades, the public's cohesiveness eventually became a major liability for mainlander-dominated central leadership. As tensions with Taiwan-born elites intensified, the public and the elite began to form a potent opposition. The mainlander-dominated central leadership, aware of the vulnerability of its position, tried numerous strategies to coopt and placate the native-born elites, including more strongly backing the SME exporters who had become the backbone of the economy. Under persistent pressure, the central leadership grudgingly accepted the formation of an opposition force, the Tang-Wai. An eroding central capacity to monitor and control civil society also enabled civil society to flourish, laying the foundations for liberal democratic reforms years later.

NOTES

1. Pan-Long Tsai, "Explaining Taiwan's Economic Miracle: Are the Revisionists Right?," *Agenda* 6, no. 1 (1999): 69–82.

2. Jim W. Ko, "Cold War Triumph – Taiwan Democratized in Spite of U.S. Efforts," *Case Western Reserve Journal of International Law* 36, no. 1 (2004): 137–82.

3. Cheng Tun-jen, "Democratizing the Quasi-Leninist Regime in Taiwan," *World Politics* 41, no. 4 (July 1989): 471–99.

4. Hung-mao Tien, "Taiwan in Transition: Prospects for Socio-Political Change," *The China Quarterly* 64 (December 1975): 617.

5. Yongping Wu, "Rethinking the Taiwanese Developmental State," *The China Quarterly* 177 (March 2004): 103.

6. Cheng Tun-jen, "Transforming Taiwan's Economic Structure in the 20th Century," *The China Quarterly* 165 (March 2001): 19–36.

7. Ian Davies, "The Economic Significance of the Industrialization Program," *The Australian Journal of Chinese Affairs* 6 (July 1981): 1–20.

8. Tun-jen, "Transforming Taiwan's Economic Structure in the 20th Century."

9. Murray Rubenstein, "Chapter 2: The Evolution of Taiwan's Economic Miracle 1945-2000: Personal Accounts and Political Narratives," in *Technology Transfer Between the US, China and Taiwan*, ed. Douglas B. Fuller and Murray A. Rubenstein (London: Routledge, 2013).

10. Wu, "Rethinking the Taiwanese Developmental State."

11. Edwin Winkler, "Institutionalization and Participation on Taiwan: From Hard to Soft Authoritarianism," *China Quarterly* 99 (1984): 481–99.

12. Tun-jen, "Transforming Taiwan's Economic Structure in the 20th Century."

13. Huei-Wen Pao, Hsueh-Liang Wu, and Wei-Hwa Pan, "The Road to Liberalization: Policy Design and Implementation of Taiwan's Privatization," *International Economics and Economic Policy* 5 (2008): 323–44.

14. Wu, "Rethinking the Taiwanese Developmental State."

15. Winkler, "Institutionalization and Participation on Taiwan."

16. World Inequality Database, "World Inequality Report 2018."

17. Joseph Bosco, "Taiwan Factions: Guanxi, Patronage, and the State in Local Politics," *Ethnology* 31, no. 2 (April 1992): 157–83.

18. Alan Cole, "The Political Roles of Taiwanese Entrepreneurs," *Asian Survey* 88 (September 1968): 645–54.

19. Winkler, "Institutionalization and Participation on Taiwan."

20. Peter R. Moody, *Opposition and Dissent in Contemporary China* (Stanford, CA: Hoover Institution Press, 1977), 246.

21. Republic of China Council for Economic Planning and Development, *Taiwan Statistical Data Book, 1998* (Taipei: ROC Council for Economic Planning and Development, 1998).

22. Cheng, "Democratizing the Quasi-Leninist Regime in Taiwan."

23. Cole, "The Political Roles of Taiwanese Entrepreneurs."

24. Bruce J. Jacobs, "Paradoxes in the Politics of Taiwan: Lessons for Comparative Politics," *The Journal of the Australian Political Science Association* 13 (November 1978): 239–47.

25. Tien, "Taiwan in Transition."

26. Ibid.

27. Wu, "Rethinking the Taiwanese Developmental State."

28. Hung-mao Tien and Tun-jen Cheng, "Crafting Democratic Institutions in Taiwan," *The China Journal* 37 (January 1997): 1–27.

29. Cheng, "Democratizing the Quasi-Leninist Regime in Taiwan."

30. Ngo Tak-wing, "Civil Society and Political Liberalization in Taiwan," *Bulletin of Concerned Asian Scholars* 25 (1993): 3–16.

31. Winkler, "Institutionalization and Participation on Taiwan."

32. Wu, "Rethinking the Taiwanese Developmental State."

33. Michael Ying-Mao Kau, "The Power Structure in Taiwan's Political Economy," *Asian Survey* 36, no. 3 (March 1996): 287–305.

34. Tien, "Taiwan in Transition."

35. Cheng, "Democratizing the Quasi-Leninist Regime in Taiwan."

36. Diane Ying, "Taiwan Is Planning Open Trials Soon for Dissidents," *New York Times*, January 24, 1980.

37. Thomas J. Bellows, "Taiwan's Foreign Policy in the 1970s: A Case of Adaptation and Viability," *Asian Survey* 16, no. 7 (July 1976): 593–610.

38. Cheng, "Democratizing the Quasi-Leninist Regime in Taiwan."

39. Tsai, "Explaining Taiwan's Economic Miracle."

40. Ramon H. Myers, "The Economic Transformation of the Republic of China on Taiwan," *The China Quarterly* 99 (September 1984): 500–28.

41. IMF website, "Data Mapper." As of January 31, 2020, https://www.imf.org/external/datamapper/NGDP_RPCH@WEO/TWN.

Chapter 6

Soviet Union 1985–1990

Weak Central Leadership, Strong Elite Opposition Dooms Perestroika

Upon ascending to power, Soviet leader Mikhail Gorbachev attempted to bolster intensive growth. The Soviet economy had performed poorly for years when Mikhail Gorbachev outlined his ambitious "perestroika" agenda aimed at accelerating political, social, and economic restructuring. Among his priorities, Gorbachev highlighted the need to overhaul a bloated and inefficient state sector, increase incentives for companies to produce higher quality consumer goods, and improve the productivity of the agricultural sector.

However, Gorbachev encountered severe opposition from vested interests within the government, party, industry, and military. Despite efforts to consolidate his position through purges, bureaucratic maneuvers, and other measures, Gorbachev and his allies in the central government failed to overcome this opposition. The only way Gorbachev could gain the acquiescence of the opposition was to buy their support with massive subsidies and to scale back the proposed changes.

The exorbitant payoffs, persistent feuding among elites, and the leadership's inability to take decisive action fueled runaway inflation, an acute shortage of most goods, and destabilizing levels of debt. Desperate to gain leverage over his opponents, Gorbachev promoted democratic reforms to involve the public. However, he misjudged the level of public support, and his efforts backfired. Liberalization accelerated the nation's dissolution. A desperate coup attempt in 1991 by elites to stave off the inevitable precipitated the collapse of the Soviet Union.

BACKGROUND

When Gorbachev became general secretary in May 1985, the Soviet economy had stagnated. The Soviet people had for years experienced minimal gains in their quality of life. The low quality of Soviet-manufactured goods made them uncompetitive on western markets. Moreover, the West continued to significantly outpace the Soviet Union in technology.[1] The official economy's inability to produce sufficient quantities of food, consumer goods, and services fostered a black market, but even this failed to provide adequate quantities of goods and services.[2]

The Soviet economy suffered most prominently from the two interrelated problems of debt and low productivity. The Soviet Union's enormous debt was owed in part to the country's costly approach to industrialization under Stalin, which saddled the country with a massive long-term debt burden. The problem was compounded by the reliance on central planning, which provided little incentive for individuals or enterprises to act efficiently. In 1965, Alexei Kosygin, chairman of the Council of Ministers, attempted to improve productivity by introducing a more responsive pricing mechanism. The effort failed, however, in large part due to opposition from elites. In particular, enterprise managers, who enjoyed privileges and influence, resisted change.[3] Soviet planners followed Kosygin's failure with fifteen years of almost continuous incremental modifications that left the system intact. Although they persisted in seeking more effective ways to incentivize enterprises without transforming the system, the results proved invariably disappointing. Symptomatic of the government's failed approach was the multiplication of bureaucracies to deal with issues of production. From 1966 to 1985, the number of industrial ministries increased from thirty-one to fifty-seven, and total employment in state administration rose by 82 percent.[4]

Western economists and international advisory groups noted the interrelated problems of low productivity, inefficiency, debt, and slow growth.[5] Echoing a view commonly seen in western writings, one analyst of the time observed that Moscow could "no longer sustain the high growth rates of the past that were based on the established practice of injecting ever-larger quantities of investment capital and labor resources into the economy."[6] A 1984 report by the Brookings Institute highlighted three persistent problems: Enterprise security, employment security, and the reliance on central planning. It noted that the Soviet system minimized competition between enterprises, limited imports, and featured a massive number of redundant enterprises. The state also provided generous subsidies for unproductive enterprises. The state's commitment to full employment meant companies had little incentive to reduce payrolls, and workers had little incentive to work hard. And due to the importance of central plans that prioritized production above all, enterprises regarded central government bureaucrats as the only customers who mattered.[7]

Soviet economists and some officials also recognized that their country needed to improve productivity. They noted that the reliance on debt-fueled growth carried a high "externality" cost in the form of worsening environmental degradation and soaring debt levels. Worker health suffered in other ways too. Many drank heavily when they relocated to distant industries in Siberia.[8] Gorbachev observed in his 1987 book *Perestroika*,

> The country in the latter half of the seventies began losing momentum. Economic failures became more frequent. Difficulties began to accumulate and deteriorate, and unresolved problems to multiply. Elements of what we call stagnation and other phenomena alien to socialism began to appear in the life of society.[9]

A sign of the problems of low productivity could be seen in the agriculture sector. In the early 1970s, the Soviet Union exported 7 million tons of grain per year, but by 1982, the USSR had to import 45 million tons. In 1981 and 1982, the food situation was so dire that some large cities had to reintroduce food rationing. Yet the disappointing production coincided with massive state subsidies. Although higher prices provided an incentive for farms to turn over crops to the state, they provided no incentive to improve an inefficient agricultural system, which in 1982 already used far more fertilizer than its more efficient Western counterparts.[10]

The Soviets debated two ways to improve productivity. One approach, preferred by the elites who worked in industry and the bureaucracy, relied on upgrades to the production processes and investments in technology. Recognizing the outdated and rusting state of many factories, this approach sought to increase capital investment, build and buy new machinery, and adopt more capital-intensive manufacturing processes. But while this approach did have some economic logic, it also carried a political logic that appealed to the same elites. For bureaucrats and managers in each sector, more funds meant more opportunities for patronage and corruption and more resources to spend on pet projects.

A contrasting approach, favored by some Soviet economists, sought to improve efficiency by making better use of existing capabilities. Related ideas sought to modify incentives, change how enterprises were structured, and revise how the government interacted with enterprises. This approach was based on the insight that the planned economy provided few individuals or enterprises with incentives to behave efficiently. Enterprises were judged by dozens of different indicators, a few of which required productivity. Unlike the preceding approach, the latter had the distinct political disadvantage of lacking powerful interest groups to lobby in its favor.[11]

Developments Related to the Central Leadership

Gorbachev's tenure as General Secretary started from a position of weakness relative to the party, government, and military, all of which were dominated by conservatives who resisted change. A hint of the strength of this opposition could be seen in the tentative experiments with market-friendly incentives that occurred in the early 1980s. The resistance from ministries and industries proved so strong that the experimentation had largely died out by the time Gorbachev became general secretary in 1985.[12]

Party unity and discipline had seriously eroded by the time Gorbachev assumed power. By the mid-1980s, the Communist Party had become dominated by interest groups that wielded immense power, particularly when defending their bureaucratic turf. On economic questions, industrial interest groups and economic bureaucrats, operating through the Communist Party apparatus, often played the most important roles. Long-serving officials in Soviet industrial ministries developed power bases and patronage networks that let them implement policies independently of, and sometimes in contradiction to, Moscow's wishes.[13] Corruption flourished as well. CIA sources reported that the use of political influence in the job market had steadily increased and that corruption had become especially prevalent in the housing sector. Moreover, illegal trade flourished in agricultural products, consumer goods, and automobiles.[14]

Gorbachev started his tenure from a position of weakness relative to the military as well. He lacked any military experience and did not have a client network in the military. The military-industrial complex had grown to become among the most powerful interest groups. Tensions had grown between civilian and military leaders as the decline in the rate of growth after 1975 raised questions about the massive allocation of resources to defense expenditures. The Soviet Union's war in Afghanistan, which began in 1979, compounded the problem. To fight the war, the Defense Ministry demanded more resources and resisted demands to curtail military spending. Despite pressing needs in the civilian economy, the military leadership succeeded in gaining an increase in the share of gross national product allocated for military spending from the mid-1970s to the mid-1980s.[15]

Perhaps reflecting an awareness of the forces arrayed against change, Gorbachev initially focused on conventional measures to improve the economy's performance. His first economic reform consisted of the "uskorenie," or "acceleration," of economic development. This approach emphasized capital investment and tighter central control, the usual prescription adopted by Soviet leaders.[16] Like his predecessors, Gorbachev quickly learned that these measures did not materially improve the situation.

In sum, the central leadership started the period relatively *weak*. Gorbachev entered office as the General Secretary with few allies in the highest echelons of government. While purges and an anticorruption drive allowed him to increase the number of allies in the Politburo, he had at best partial authority over the government ministries and their associated industrial complexes, the military, and the Communist Party of the Soviet Union (CPSU).

Developments Related to Elite Opposition

By the time Gorbachev entered office, the elites of the country had become entrenched. The strength of the elites could, in some ways, be difficult to assess. As a communist society, after all, the elites held a smaller share of income than their counterparts in the west. The top 10 percent income share was about 23 percent in 1985, far lower than France (30 percent) and the US (37 percent) at that time. Moreover, the elites had little private wealth since private property was outlawed.[17] However, elites maintained privileges that underscored their status and power. In particular, the elites maintained formidable political influence and numerous "perks," such as a superior standard of accommodation, access to special shops, and holidays in exclusive resorts. Individuals in higher level bureaucratic positions gained even more privileges. Although the official salary remained low in monetary terms, high-level officials could supplement their incomes through corruption and bribery.[18] Elites also enjoyed access to superior health care unavailable to the masses and luxuries such as imported automobiles. Some even had private airplanes.[19]

The level of collusion, both horizontally and in terms of collaboration between industry and government, had solidified. In horizontal terms, collusion between government and industry has been present as a feature of the political economy since the early years of the USSR. Beginning in the 1930s, political leaders tightly controlled economic activity. A multilevel, highly specialized state hierarchy governed the economy. And the State Planning Committee (Gosplan) oversaw economic planning under the general supervision of the Council of Ministers, within guidelines approved by the Politburo. The Soviet Union's government aimed to ensure the CPSU absolutely controlled the "commanding heights" of the economy. Over time, the political apparatus focused on securing more resources for patronage and corruption. About fifty ministries directed the activities of enterprises, many of which developed elaborate patronage networks.[20]

Similarly, elite networks of patronage reaching the highest levels of government developed over decades. Under Stalin, party cadres experienced significant violence, and many were killed. Stalin's bloody methods ensured the circulation of elites, promoted a sense of accountability, and prevented the formation of cliques that could oppose him. But it also proved dangerously volatile, as elites naturally opposed such cruel treatment. To stabilize the political system, Leonid Brezhnev offered a "stability of the cadres" policy that granted job security and assurances against random violence. But Brezhnev did not offer a clear mechanism to achieve cadre accountability. Accordingly, in subsequent years, elite groups solidified and patronage networks flourished. Party discipline grew lax, and the failure to achieve production targets occurred frequently. The new policy also provided political cover for cadres to abuse their powers.[21]

Declassified CIA reports of the time described the entrenched power of elites. One 1985 report concluded that Gorbachev would likely encounter resistance from

> segments of the elite who stand to lose most: the venal members of the entrenched bureaucracy who have survived earlier corruption campaigns; regional party officials who may see the anticorruption campaign as part of a larger policy of tightening central regulation of republic party organizations; and the economic bureaucracy (especially the ministries), which may fear that moves against corruption will go hand in hand with some kind of economic reform.[22]

Three interest groups stood out as among the most powerful: agriculture, energy, and the military. These industries have been labeled by both Soviet and western analysts as the agro-industrial complex, the fuel-energy complex, and the military-industrial complex. Each of these collusive networks of government, industry, and party members featured its own bureaucracy. Personnel often spent their entire career within a single industrial complex, creating intricate patronage networks strengthened by relationships, favors, and loyalty. The prominence of these three groups owed in part to the real needs that they addressed: Energy exports provided a major source of revenue for the country, agriculture employed and sustained large parts of the population, and the military protected the nation, especially given the Cold War with the United States and an active war in Afghanistan. However, the bureaucracies at the heart of each of these industrial complexes abused their positions of importance for gain and tenaciously defended their interests.[23]

As an example, the strength of the military-industrial complex could be seen in the disproportionate access to the nation's resources that it enjoyed. It alone constituted about 20 percent of Soviet economic output and about 40 percent of the state budget. It employed at least 15 million people, almost one-tenth of the Soviet workforce. Most of the Soviet Union's scientific and technological research took place within the defense sector.[24] The details of the size of the military-industrial complex could be hard to discern, even for the nation's leaders. To fight the war in Afghanistan, military leaders demanded more resources. They also resisted orders by the central leadership to make their economic footprint more transparent.[25]

Similarly, Gorbachev ran into serious resistance from the agricultural lobby when he proposed an incentive system to improve the productivity of farms. Local party leaders benefitted from patronage networks that reached from the top of the Politburo down to collective farms. Managers of industries that produced tractors, fertilizer, and irrigation depended on high levels of agricultural investment for political power and economic well-being. Ministry officials knew that decentralization would reduce their influence. All of these groups vigorously opposed change, arguing that Gorbachev's ideas were naive. Despite his own background in agriculture, Gorbachev made little progress in compelling these groups to adopt more efficient farming practices.[26]

In sum, elite *opposition* to any change was *strong*. Gorbachev entered office confronted by a large and powerful network of party, government, military, and industry elites who benefited from inefficient and unsustainable practices. Sensing the opposition, Gorbachev initially advanced conventional investment-based policies that did not challenge the elites but quickly realized the inadequacy of those measures. This set up a confrontation between Gorbachev's allies and the elites.

Developments Related to Public Cohesiveness

Economically, Soviet society remained cohesive but trended toward fragmentation. Officially, all workers were employed and enjoyed welfare benefits. Indeed, the state went to great lengths to avoid cutting employment rolls. But rising inflation, widespread shortages, and price controls eroded the value of those guarantees. These trends also spurred the creation of a large and growing gray market (different from a black market in that traded goods may not be illegal, but they are distributed outside official channels). The gray market, or "second economy," consisted of markets and employees who did not pay tax, draw benefits, or work in the formal economy. Goods and services were sold in non-approved markets and channels. The second economy played a large role in agriculture, with the output of collective farmers' personal plots providing 30–42 percent of total agricultural output. Soviet press reports stated that 80–85 percent of all gasoline ended up on the gray market, 25 percent of the internal fish catch originated from illegal catches on state lands, and that 25 percent of all distilled alcohol was produced and sold outside the state sector.[27]

Politically, the public remained fragmented, with few venues for participation. But widespread circumvention of official controls suggested people were beginning to build new forms of political association outside formal channels. The controls exercised by the state had begun to break down by this time. Extensive controls on the dissemination of information remained in effect, but Soviet citizens routinely evaded them. The populace relied so extensively on audio tapes and video cassette recorders to evade political control that the state resorted to producing and selling them. Individuals also experienced a considerable expansion in personal choices, such as in the selection of a career, employer, and place of residence.[28]

Inequality remained relatively modest compared to western democracies, but political pluralism intensified. According to Mcauley, around 40 percent of the entire population in 1967 would be considered poor by the Soviet standards of 1974. The Gini coefficient in the USSR increased from 0.229 in 1967 to 0.288 in 1974, which is low compared to western countries.[29] But the sense of solidarity with the party had largely dissipated. Observers of the time noted that ideology appeared to have lost much of its relevance for many people and that a proliferation of diverse new ideas seemed to gain wider currency. Protests emerged, for example, over ecological and other issues that the party appeared to disregard. In the republics, ethnic and religious identities that had long been suppressed returned with vigor, leading to a balkanization of communities in many regions.[30]

In sum, the public remained *cohesive* in 1985 in terms of the economy, but trended toward *fragmentation* owing to the failures of the economy and a lack of opportunity for political participation. Political controls remained in place, but the populace already experienced greater pluralization and diversity of views as the country's stagnation eroded the CPSU's credibility. High levels of government spending resulted in nominally generous employment and welfare benefits, but inflation and an inadequate production system robbed those benefits of meaning. The economy's ineffectiveness fueled a large and growing informal economy. The Soviet Union also experienced a high level of fragmentation along ethnic lines, especially in the republics. This ethnic fragmentation was severe enough that the situation may be judged both "fragmented" at the regional level and "cohesive" at the national level.

The Soviet Union faced a politically unfavorable situation for enacting major policy changes. In particular, the weakness of Gorbachev and his allies in the central government and the strength of the elite opposition augured ill for any effort to carry out a major restructuring. The relative cohesiveness of the public, while fragile and clearly headed toward fragmentation, suggested some possibility of political mobilization. However, whether a politically mobilized populace would choose to back a weak and embattled central CPSU leadership, entrenched bureaucratic elites, or some other option remained far from clear. At the very least, one might expect Gorbachev to step up efforts to centralize power, gain control of the ministries and subnational levels of government, strengthen the discipline and unity of the CPSU, and assert his control of the military while taking action to diminish the strength of the elites. To improve prospects for successful mobilization of the public, Gorbachev would need to deliver tangible benefits from his leadership. Successful action along these lines could move the country closer to the enabling condition and thereby raise prospects for successful policy implementation.

INTERVENING DEVELOPMENTS, 1986–1988

In this period, Gorbachev began to pursue more radical efforts to restructure the economy. His strategy was based on two insights. First, he noted that the Soviet Union's high-quality education system created impressive levels of human capital but that the country failed to take advantage of its workers' skills. Second, he and his advisers concluded that the global economy was increasingly driven by high-tech industries requiring skilled labor. Gorbachev was especially impressed by the successes enjoyed by China, Japan, and the Asian Tigers.[31]

Gorbachev had hinted at more radical ideas even before assuming the position of General Secretary of the CPSU. The term "perestroika," which means "transformation," first appeared in Gorbachev's 1984 report to the All-Union economic conference on problems of the agro-industrial complex. The term "perestroika" refers to the "transformation of productive relations, changing the social and economic organization of the late Soviet system," and it became a key slogan that embodied aspirations to significantly improve the nation's economic performance.[32] In a famous speech in December 1984, he called for a "profound transformation" of the economy and the "entire system of social relations." He also spoke of the need to develop "socialist self-government by the people" and to enlist the "interests and energies of the masses." Hinting at anticipated opposition, he criticized "formalism" and bureaucracy as "the fierce enemy of action."[33]

At the Twenty-Seventh Party Congress in February 1986, Gorbachev declared the need for "radical reform of the economic mechanism," including a reexamination of the nature of property ownership under socialism, a topic long viewed as taboo. A law adopted in 1986 enlarged the permissible scope of private economic activity, albeit simultaneously with another one aimed at curtailing corruption and "unearned incomes" from gray market activities. The government passed measures to encourage groups of individuals to produce consumer goods and services. A sweeping reform of the wage and salary system was introduced, with financing linked to a firm's ability to pay higher wages from its own earnings. Gorbachev also introduced reforms that permitted a few ministries and enterprises to engage in international trade independent of the state monopoly. This law also authorized joint ventures with foreign partners on Soviet soil.[34] Other policy initiatives included measures to overhaul enterprise management, which the CPSU Central Committee approved in June 1987. These spelled out a strategy of enterprise reform that gave directors increased autonomy in setting prices, wages, and output targets. The following year, Gorbachev and his government introduced measures that, for the first time, legalized private economic activity, including contracting with employees and the retention of profits by individual owners.[35] Gorbachev had a timeline in mind for achieving the goals of all of these policy initiatives. He hoped to shepherd the economy onto a new growth model featuring intensive growth by 1991, the beginning of the Thirteenth Five-Year Plan.[36]

Critics immediately noted problems with Gorbachev's policy agenda. Ambiguities and a lack of clarity plagued his policy statements. Contradictory goals appeared throughout. Most problematic was the insistence on overhauling the economy without causing a decline in the welfare of the people. An example concerned the contradictory goals of Gorbachev's effort to control the country's drinking problem. To improve productivity, the government launched a campaign against drinking. This helped reduce absenteeism and improved some health measures, but it removed a major source of tax revenue, which impaired Gorbachev's ability to pay for perestroika reforms.[37] Other problems included a dearth of qualified economists, a lack of reliable statistical data, and widespread false reporting about production.[38]

Gorbachev's struggle to overhaul a sclerotic economy was exacerbated by the severity of the country's financial situation. The country's budget deficit had grown alarmingly, in part due to a fall in oil prices in the 1970s and, after 1979, the war in Afghanistan. But officials acknowledged that the burden of state subsidies played a large role as well. The total cost of subsidies threatened to reach 100 billion rubles by 1990. This raised a painful dilemma. The Kremlin could reduce the deficit by raising taxes or cutting spending. Both of these measures would fall hardest on the powerful, vested interest groups that rejected such possibilities out of hand. Politburo records showed that Soviet leaders understood their options in 1986 and 1987, but they could not agree on either tax increases or spending cuts. Instead, they chose the worst option, which was to print money to fill the gap. This proved disastrous, leading to painful shortages and hyperinflation. Fear of public outcry also discouraged the Politburo from liberalizing prices as a way to reduce spending on subsidies and thereby narrow the deficit. The issue came up repeatedly at the highest levels of government, but no decision was made.[39]

Developments Related to the Central Leadership

To overcome these difficulties and enact his policy agenda, Gorbachev needed favorable political conditions. In the first few years, he acted to consolidate his authority in the party, government, and military. However, these efforts scarcely proved inadequate against a formidable opposition.

To strengthen his grip on the party, he carried out a purge. He removed opponents from both the Politburo and the Central Committee. Less than a year after taking power, Gorbachev had replaced almost half of the Party's top leadership (Politburo and Secretariat). Personnel changes within the Central Committee took a longer time because he feared provoking them.[40] To help bolster popular support and his control of the party, he also launched an anticorruption campaign. The CIA assessed at the time that the effort may have "improved the regime's image in the eyes of the population" and possibly "rejuvenated" the CPSU to a degree. More pragmatically, the charge of corruption provided Gorbachev with a convenient excuse to remove political opponents of his agenda.[41]

In 1988, Gorbachev took additional measures to strengthen his influence over policy. He eliminated most economic divisions within the Central Committee except for agriculture and the military industrial complex, drastically reducing the party's influence over economic management. His successful campaign against conservatives within the Party apparatus was punctuated by the mass resignation of seventy-four central committee members in April 1989.[42] Regarding the government, Gorbachev replaced some of the top officials, but he saw little progress in gaining control of the central ministries and subnational bureaucracies. After becoming general secretary, he abolished five ministries and a state committee that worked with agriculture, replacing them with a unified state committee for the agro-industrial complex. However, the newly installed officials resisted Gorbachev's proposed policies.[43]

Gorbachev attempted to strengthen his control over the military, but he moved cautiously. With the war still continuing in Afghanistan, Gorbachev could ill-afford appearing to diminish and weaken the military. Nonetheless, observers noted several symbolic denigrations of the Soviet military, such as the absence of military officers at the March 13, 1985, funeral service for Konstantin Chernenko and the small number of uniformed personnel who accompanied the civilian leadership at the 1986 parade marking the anniversary of the October revolution. However, the military's membership in the Central Committee remained largely unchanged, underscoring its strength.[44]

The purges and anticorruption campaign did not seriously weaken the opposition. Party officials opposed Gorbachev's economic reforms because increased autonomy for enterprise directors meant decreased power for Party bureaucrats responsible for monitoring (and taking bribes from) enterprise activity.[45] Even after the purges, the Politburo proved to be a bastion of political opposition to Gorbachev's efforts. The initiatives associated with perestroika all faced intense opposition from Gorbachev's Politburo colleagues, who accused him of rolling back socialism's gains, threatening to impoverish the population, and—worst of all—reintroducing capitalism. Gorbachev's Politburo opponents managed to subvert many of his reforms, and they severely delayed each of his major initiatives, a problem about which he complained regularly.[46] State officials also resisted perestroika reforms, especially decentralization, due to fears of a loss of power. They slow-rolled the implementation of Gorbachev's policies accordingly.[47]

The difficulty Gorbachev encountered could be seen in the struggles he experienced in carrying out the major structural changes. For example, Gorbachev regarded SOE reform as a top priority in 1986, but the Politburo refused to enact legislation for a year, despite Gorbachev's repeated exhortations. Many Soviet leaders simply did not see the need for change. By the second year, Gorbachev frequently harangued the Politburo on the merits of decentralization and the economic imperative for change. Yet many of Gorbachev's colleagues, especially those with close ties to industries, rejected his proposals. They preferred, instead, to address problems by increasing subsidies and investment in the SOEs. Gorbachev persisted and finally cajoled the Politburo into passing the Law on State Enterprises in June 1987, a full year after he began pushing for such changes. Even so, to get the law passed, Gorbachev had to repeatedly compromise and promise massive cash subsidies to industries.[48] Capital investment averaged less than 170 billion rubles per year from 1981–1985, but under the acceleration program, which was needed to retain industrial support, capital spending reached 206 billion rubles in 1987 and surpassed 218 billion rubles in 1988. The increase in capital spending was equivalent to over 5 percent of GDP—an extravagant amount given the fact that the budget was spiraling out of control.[49]

A similar story characterized Gorbachev's efforts to ease shortages. Gorbachev and his economic advisers knew that the only way to eliminate shortages was to increase prices, allowing enterprises to make more money and thereby increasing their incentive to bring products to market. But there were no significant price increases until 1990. Even as inflation raced out of control, shortages spread, and lines lengthened, the Politburo declined to loosen consumer price regulations.[50]

Gorbachev's power relative to the military was tested. The General Secretary wanted to cut the military budget. Even though the country remained at war in Afghanistan, Gorbachev had sound reasons for seeking defense cuts: Military spending was growing faster than the economy, and resources were urgently needed elsewhere. But he backed away from the idea. CIA reports noted that efforts by the top leadership to direct the defense industry to convert more production to consumer goods failed through 1988 because the military resisted the demands.[51] Gorbachev later wrote that "even a mention" of the idea of a budget cut would "mean immediate dismissal."[52]

Gorbachev concluded that his best hopes lay in reducing the CPSU's control over the government. Accordingly, he began to seek ways of building a government that had more independence from the party through political reforms. As conceived by Gorbachev, the overriding objective of political reforms was to enable economic restructuring.[53]

In sum, the central leadership, led by Gorbachev, remained *weak*. Gorbachev attempted to strengthen control of the government, military, and party through purges, reshuffling, and the abolition of offices and committees, but this proved insufficient. Central authority remained deeply divided and paralyzed by gridlock.

Developments Related to Elite Opposition

The strength of the elite opposition showed little change in this period. The top 10 percent share of income remained at around 23 percent.[54] However, the elites continued to enjoy the same perks and privileges of serving in the government bureaucracy. The fact that they succeeded in securing largesse from the state despite a worsening financial picture illustrates the power that they wielded.

Horizontal collusion between party cadres, government bureaucracies, enterprises, and industries remained robust. The strong opposition of Politburo members to Gorbachev's agenda and advocacy on behalf of their clients in the industrial complexes also demonstrated the strength of vertical collusive networks.

An illustration of the depth of political opposition can be seen in the repeated compromises Gorbachev had to make when he sought to reorganize agriculture on a more efficient basis. In many instances, farm groups succeeded in obstructing the implementation of changes agreed to by top leaders. The farm lobby succeeded in gaining a pledge from Gorbachev to prohibit bankruptcy among farms in exchange for support for restructuring efforts, but this compromise undercut any financial gains that could be made from the changes. Moreover, Politburo members repeatedly dismissed Gorbachev's structural changes as a distraction and argued instead for more investment as the solution to agriculture's problems. Gorbachev agreed to provide higher agricultural subsidies in exchange for additional market-oriented reforms. The subsidies and compromises undermined the effect of the reforms and added to the state's already unsustainable debt problem.[55]

In short, elite opposition to Gorbachev's economic reform agenda remained *strong*. Elites within the party state remained well entrenched and vigorously opposed Gorbachev's efforts. They extracted concessions in the form of payoffs but did not implement the policies. Their access to privileges and perks did not diminish during this time period.

Developments Related to Public Cohesiveness

Gorbachev recognized the importance of popular support for his restructuring efforts. Initially, he relied on propaganda to whip up enthusiasm. Observers described relentless messages that extolled restructuring. Throughout the country, giant billboards featured slogans such as "Comrade—what have you done for perestroika?" Yet the propaganda yielded disappointing results. On the one hand, polls showed strong support for restructuring. However, Soviet media also carried numerous reports of popular resistance to changes.[56] A major impediment to wider popular support was the lack of material evidence that the changes could improve the lives of people. Gorbachev's promotion of perestroika was accompanied by inflation that wiped out savings and exacerbated shortages. An observer of the time noted, "Housing in urban areas remains in desperately short supply. And promised consumer goods—stereos, cars, washing machines—still remain largely unavailable."[57]

Economically, the public remained relatively cohesive, but the living conditions of most people worsened. The opening of the economy to individual labor marked an important innovation, but its impact was blunted by provisions that restricted its applicability to individuals without formal work, such as housewives, pensioners, students, and the disabled, and it prohibited individuals from employing others.[58] Inflation and shortages of most consumer goods imposed severe hardships that Gorbachev had little power to alleviate, owing to the standoff with his political opponents.

Eventually, Gorbachev took the radical step of activating what he called the "human factor." By giving society a new public voice and a greater political role within the state, Gorbachev hoped he could rely on the public and state institutions rather than the party as his own political power base for furthering the process of perestroika. As Gorbachev stated,

> Since at the time the bureaucrats still controlled the main levers of power, there were only two ways of assuring success of reform: creating significant pressure on them from the majority of society, which was in favor of change, and cutting off the most conservative elements of the nomenklatura.[59]

Gorbachev's policy initiative was called glasnost, or *openness*. In June 1986, he relaxed censorship and granted greater freedom of expression in the press, arts, and sciences, and eventually on the streets. In 1987, the government narrowed the definition of treasonous behavior and released hundreds of political prisoners, expanding the scope of permissible political activity.[60] In 1988, the party adopted several measures to increase participation in politics. The Congress of People's Deputies was to be elected in a democratic fashion. Moreover, the CPSU approved measures designed to revive the power of the local Soviets and broaden the range of issues they were empowered to deal with.[61]

Socially, glasnost facilitated new cultural freedoms, encouraged pluralization, and strengthened subnational identities. Given the low appeal of Soviet communism, this relaxation contributed to the strengthening of ethnic and minority communities, especially in the Soviet republics. Inter-ethnic conflicts had arisen in the first years of perestroika and were aggravated by the growth of separatist sentiment.[62] More independent political clubs and groups throughout the country began to gain adherents as well.[63] Social fragmentation increased, especially among ethnic minority populations in the republics.

Whether the public would use its new freedoms to voice support for Gorbachev remained far from clear. The rampant shortages, hyperinflation, and other economic difficulties severely eroded public support for Gorbachev and spurred labor and other protests. Many observers worried that the contradictory goals of maintaining unsustainable practices to ensure full employment and the pursuit of restructuring reforms could lead to a crisis.[64]

In sum, public cohesiveness remained divided. Formal employment and low inequality ensured a measure of economic *cohesiveness*, albeit on a financially unsustainable basis. However, the country experienced deepening political *fragmentation*, and divisions along ethnic lines worsened as well, especially in the republics. The public experienced a basic level of cohesiveness owing to the state's obligations to provide jobs and welfare, although the benefits appeared increasingly hollow. Gorbachev expanded the political cohesiveness of the public through institutional innovations in hopes that a grateful public might back his policy agenda. But the same loosening of repression also facilitated the unraveling of the nation as pluralization accelerated and ethnic and other minorities in the republics pursued greater autonomy.

After a spurt of growth, the Soviet economy grew by about 1.5 percent in both 1987 and 1988. This is similar to the "stagnation" years of 1981–1985, according to CIA estimates. Moreover, Soviet media reports indicate that after three full years, Gorbachev's program to reequip Soviet industry with more modern machinery had failed to live up to expectations.[65] Analysts observed that after three years of reforms, there was little evidence of progress. Indeed, by most measures, the economy appeared to be in worse shape than it was in 1985.[66]

Gorbachev desperately needed to strengthen the power of the central leadership to direct the government bureaucracy and compel elites to carry out policies without debilitating concessions. It was a measure of his desperation that Gorbachev began to pursue liberalizing political reforms to help him in this struggle. However, Gorbachev grossly overestimated the level of public support for the reformist faction of the CPSU. The ensuing years would see the rapidly unraveling of the state as a consequence of the gridlock and passivity of the government in the face of crisis.

INTERVENING DEVELOPMENTS, 1989–1991

This period saw the central leadership lose control of the country's economic and political situation. Paralysis over how to control state spending or raise revenues resulted in accelerating deficits. In 1989, the budget deficit reached an alarming 11 percent of GDP.[67] In 1991, inflation soared to 200 percent, and the deficit reached perhaps 30 percent of GDP.[68] The inflation eroded incomes and exacerbated shortages. The government continued to set prices far below market levels, so businesses lacked incentive to increase production.

In the agricultural sector, supply chains simply stopped functioning. For example, during the second half of the 1980s, the Soviet Union produced, on average, nearly 200 million tons of grain per year. In 1991, authorities expected a harvest of no more than 50–60 million tons. Some of this grain had been hidden by farmers seeking to avoid taxes and eventually made its way to the black markets. But, as in most other parts of the economy, production simply halted because there was no incentive otherwise. Acute shortages began affecting all types of products—not just luxuries but even basic foods.[69] Gorbachev's efforts to reform trade, enterprises, and agriculture had been eclipsed by the financial crisis. By 1991, economic collapse precipitated a desperate and futile coup by the vested interests threatened by Gorbachev's reforms. The dissolution of the Soviet Union followed shortly thereafter.

Developments Related to the Central Leadership

Gridlock in the Politburo and the deterioration in the country's fiscal situation starkly revealed the lack of unity and pervasive conflict that convulsed the CPSU. The situation did not improve in the final years and, in fact, worsened. No decisions were made to reverse the budget deficit. The severe weakness of the ruling party had profound implications for the unity of the state. Once it became clear that the party was far from united, the republics began to reconsider their own futures.

The party-state bureaucracy rejected Gorbachev's leadership and tried to reassert control over a disintegrating economy. Many of Gorbachev's reforms were overturned in practice. Central authorities interfered in contracts, imposed mandatory enterprise production targets to address shortages, and rescinded incremental measures to liberalize prices among some firms.[70] Subnational governments, especially in the republics and ethnic-minority regions, began to withhold tax revenue from Moscow. Managers at state enterprises similarly exploited the feuding among top leaders to seize control of their firms. These developments resulted in less revenue flow to Moscow, which in turn worsened the fiscal situation.[71]

Gorbachev continued to struggle to compel the military to cut its budgets. Citing the need to fight the war in Afghanistan and deter NATO, military officials resisted the demands. Instead, they promised in 1990 to produce more civilian goods to address the shortages. But despite much talk about the conversion of defense factories to civilian production, little happened. Even as late as 1989, the Soviet military managed to fend off serious defense cuts. Defense spending was probably reduced—though only slightly—in 1990 and 1991.[72]

In sum, the central leadership remained *weak*. Gorbachev made little progress in asserting his authority or in controlling the various state-industrial complexes. Failure to carry out reforms led to the dissolution of the Soviet Union.

Developments Related to Elite Opposition

The position of the elites in the country appeared unchanged until the collapse of the system. Indeed, the ability of elites in enterprises, industries, and governments to maintain subsidies at the expense of a disintegrating economy underscored the immense power that they wielded.

Collusion remained strong as well, especially between the party, government, and industries. Evidence could be seen in the way industries extracted hikes in industrial subsidies in exchange for tolerating Gorbachev's reforms. Industries maintained powerful patrons within the Politburo who ensured the subsidies continued to flow, even amid national crises. By 1989, capital expenditure was 20 percent higher than in 1985, even though the additional investment made virtually no improvement to the nation's economic situation.[73]

Elite opposition to Gorbachev's reform agenda culminated in the coup in 1991, when the army imprisoned Gorbachev at his summer home in Crimea. Yet it was not just a military coup. Industrial leaders also strongly backed the putsch. Oleg Baklanov, first deputy chairman of the Defense Council, which represented the military-industrial complex; Aleksandr Tizyakov, president of the Association of the USSR State Enterprises; and Vasily Starodubtsev, chairman of the USSR Union of Peasants, which represented the agro-industrial complex, were all prominent supporters of the coup. These elites feared that the next round of economic pain would fall on them. In particular, they feared the loss of subsidies, reductions in budgets, and tax hikes.[74]

Elite resistance remained *strong* until the end of the Soviet Union. Opposition compelled Gorbachev to provide massive subsidies, which aggravated the economic crisis. Moreover, the political impasse encouraged political actors to assert their own interests, which in the end meant a futile coup.

Developments Related to Public Cohesiveness

Economically, the public remained formally divided between cohesion at the national level and fragmentation by region. Economically, the majority of state employment remained in place. Inflation and rampant shortages undermined the meaning of such employment, however. The informal economy surged. By 1990, it was estimated to account for 15 to 20 percent of GDP.[75]

Politically, the public had more opportunities than ever to participate in politics, thanks to loosening controls on expression and democratic reforms. People began to form new social groups outside the control of the CPSU. In 1988, there were more than 30,000 grassroots voluntary associations dedicated to various types of civic causes.[76] In the final years, however, the social forces became polarized as a result of the economic crisis. In the summer of 1989, mass strikes erupted and spread across most sectors and spheres of production, further destabilizing the country.[77]

Gorbachev misjudged the 1990 elections. He and his associates approved of elections at lower levels of the state, believing that elected officials to Soviets at the republic, oblast, city, and district levels would weaken the grip of conservative party bureaucrats. Instead, the elections enhanced the autonomy of the Soviets, not only for conservative party officials but for liberal ones as well. The increased autonomy gave officials greater freedom to resist any demands from Moscow.[78]

In social terms, the political mobilization of the public led to polarization and fragmentation along the lines of interest groups and ethnic minorities. The profound weakness of the central leadership also prompted republics to seek a way out of the crisis independently. The Baltic republics wanted to form modern market democracies of the western type. Others had different views, but few wanted to continue under the old Soviet system. The conflict intensified sharply after elections were held in 1990. Some republics drew up economic programs that defied communist orthodoxy.[79]

In sum, the public became *fragmented* in the last years of the Soviet Union. Economically, the old Soviet system of full employment and welfare benefits, already largely meaningless amid persistent crises, collapsed completely. Glasnost policies and the establishment of democratic elections aimed to mitigate the crumbling of the economy. However, an environment of conflict and crisis meant that Gorbachev's efforts to mobilize public sentiment resulted in an acceleration of polarization and fragmentation, resulting in the Soviet Union's disintegration.

CONCLUSION

Mikhail Gorbachev's efforts to restructure the Soviet economy failed. Due to the weakness of his political position and the strength of the elite opposition, he did not succeed in implementing the perestroika policy initiative. Total production continued to decline, and industrial production fell by 40 percent by the late 1980s. Per capita GDP continued its decline in the early 1970s.

Productivity fell 0.5 percent from an already low level during 1980–1985.[80] Despite a goal of 100 percent of SOEs being self-financed by 1988, only 60 percent reported reaching that goal. Efforts to incentivize enterprises to generate output in response to demand as opposed to state orders failed as well. The state sought to reduce its role in ordering industrial production to 40 percent, but in 1988, state orders still made up 86 percent. The GDP growth rate averaged under 2 percent over the five-year period.[81]

A principal reason why perestroika failed was due to an unfavorable political situation. A key factor was the weakness of the pro-perestroika central leadership in the Politburo and central government. Gorbachev was a young leader who lacked revolutionary credentials or the personal authority of Vladimir Lenin, Joseph Stalin, or Nikita Kruschev. This made him highly vulnerable to being ousted by powerful adversaries in the central government. Accordingly, Gorbachev frequently hesitated to push through difficult but financially imperative policies such as pricing reform. The public outcry over price increases would have given his political opponents a convenient reason to remove him from office. Gorbachev never gained firm control of the military either. This raised the persistent danger of military overthrow if Gorbachev pushed too hard for the country's elite to sacrifice their interests for the sake of the nation, especially given the ongoing war in Afghanistan. The threat proved all too real, of course, when the military collaborated with other interest groups to overthrow Gorbachev in the 1991 coup.

The strength of the elites proved a second major factor. Much of the government bureaucracy, the Communist Party, and industrial managers opposed Gorbachev's reforms due to fears that they might entail losses in income and privileges. Because of their political power, the industrial complexes routinely defied Gorbachev. The military, farms, and energy sectors were untouched by cuts proportional to their size until the Soviet Union's final demise. These interest groups succeeded in delaying change and extracting expensive payoffs in return for their acquiescence.[82]

Finally, the cohesiveness of the public, ironically, may have played a role in accelerating the Soviet Union's demise. The Soviet government's anxiety about popular unrest motivated it to maintain an unaffordable level of social welfare spending in the form of food subsidies, subsidies for enterprises to maintain full employment, and other major outlays. This exacerbated the financial crisis. But the economic cohesiveness of the public also provided hope for Gorbachev that an expansion of political participation might result in a mobilized public that could back his agenda. This proved a disastrous miscalculation, since economic cohesiveness obscured the reality of deepening social fragmentation along political, social, ethnic, and other lines. Even the degree of economic cohesiveness could be overstated. The failures of the official economy robbed the benefits of meaning for most people and spawned a sprawling informal sector. Moreover, shortages, inflation, and economic crises polarized the populace. Political mobilization by a public disenchanted with the ruling CPSU and busy creating new identities and communities could only have accelerated political fragmentation, a process helped by the lack of strong central leadership and the paralyzing effects of intra-elite conflict.

This last point raises the possibility that ideology may have played a role in Gorbachev's failure to adequately appreciate the strength of interest-group opposition. Some scholars have pointed out that Gorbachev and his allies maintained a "whole series of illusions" concerning the possibilities of improving the effectiveness of a sclerotic and dysfunctional economic system. One of the biggest delusions was the mistaken belief that few people would oppose the reforms.[83] Evidence that the leadership clung to such delusions could be seen in the way authorities promoted policies that were contradictory in their nature and in their overestimation of the prospects for popular support.

NOTES

1. Gertrude Schroeder, "Economic Reform of Socialism: The Soviet Record," *The Annals of the American Academy of Political and Social Science* 507 (January 1990): 35–43.

2. Central Intelligence Agency, *The Soviet Anticorruption Campaign: Causes, Consequences, and Prospects: An Intelligence Assessment*, August 1985.

3. Mervyn Matthews, *Privilege in the Soviet Union: A Study of Elite Life-Styles Under Communism* (Milton Park: Routledge, 2011), Chapter 2.

4. Schroeder, "Economic Reform of Socialism."

5. International Monetary Fund, "A Study of the Soviet Economy," December 15, 1991.

6. Seweryn Bialer, "The Harsh Decade: Soviet Policies in the 1980s," *Foreign Affairs*, Summer 1981.

7. Ed. A. Hewett, "Economic Reform in the Soviet Union," *The Brookings Review* 2, no. 3 (Spring 1984): 8–11.

8. Central Intelligence Agency, *Soviet Intensive Economic Development in Perspective: A Research Paper*, 1998.

9. Mikhail Gorbachev, *Perestroika: New Thinking for Our Country and the World* (New York: Harper Collins and Row, 1987), 18–19.

10. Marshall Goldman, *Gorbachev's Challenge: Economic Reform in the Age of High Technology* (New York: W. W. Norton, 1987), 65.

11. Vladimir Mau, "Perestroika: Theoretical and Political Problems of Economic Reforms in the USSR," *Europe-Asia Studies* 47, no. 3 (1995): 387–411.

12. Chris Miller, *The Struggle to Save the Soviet Economy* (Chapel Hill, NC: University of North Carolina Press, 2016), 85.
13. Ibid., 56.
14. Central Intelligence Agency, *The Soviet Anticorruption Campaign.*
15. *Adelphi Papers*, "Brezhnev's Alliance with the Military and its Erosion," 31, no. 258: 5–10.
16. Michael McFaul, *Russia's Unfinished Revolution: Political Change from Gorbachev to Putin* (Ithaca, NY: Cornell University Press, 2001), 40.
17. Filip Novokmet, Thomas Piketty, and Gabriel Zucman, "From Soviets to Oligarchs: Inequality and Property in Russia, 1905-2016," *VOX EU* website, November 9, 2017.
18. Matthews, *Privilege in the Soviet Union.*
19. Eleanor Randolph, "Soviet System of Privileges Examined," *Washington Post*, August 10, 1991.
20. Hewett, "Economic Reform in the Soviet Union."
21. Yoram Gorlizki, "Too Much Trust: Regional Party Leaders and Local Political Networks Under Brezhnev," *Slavic Review* 69, no. 3 (Fall 2010): 676–700.
22. Central Intelligence Agency, *The Soviet Anticorruption Campaign.*
23. Michael Ellman and Vladimir Konorovich, *The Destruction of the Soviet Economic System* (Milton Park: Routledge, 1998), 157.
24. Mikhail Agursky, *The Soviet Military-Industrial Complex* (Jerusalem, Israel: Magnes Press, 1980).
25. Miller, *The Struggle to Save the Soviet Economy*, 60.
26. Chris Miller, "Gorbachev's Agriculture Agenda: De-collectivization and the Politics of Perestroika," *Critical Explorations in Russian and Eurasian History* 17, no.1 (2016): 95–118.
27. Steven L. Sampson, "The Second Economy of the Soviet Union and Eastern Europe," *The Annals of the American Academy of Political Science* 493 (September 1987): 120–36.
28. Robert Sharklet, "Soviet Dissent Since Brezhnev," *Current History* 85, no. 513 (October 1, 1986): 321.
29. José Luis Ricón, "The Soviet Union: Poverty and Inequality," *Nintil*, March 14, 2017.
30. Frederick Starr, "Soviet Union: A Civil Society," *Foreign Policy* 70 (Spring 1988): 26–41.
31. Miller, *The Struggle to Save the Soviet Economy*, 60.
32. Mau, "Perestroika."
33. Gorbachev, *Perestroika*, 25–26.
34. Schroeder, "Economic Reform of Socialism."
35. McFaul, *Russia's Unfinished Revolution*, 42.
36. Michael McGwire, *Perestroika and Soviet National Security* (Washington, DC: Brookings Institution Press, 1997), 175.
37. Anders Aslund, "Perestroika: The Great Awakening 1985-1987," in *Russia's Capitalist Revolution* (Washington, DC: Peterson Institute for International Economics, 2007).

38. Yuri N. Maltsey, "Soviet Economic Reforms: An Inside Perspective," *Foundation for Economic Education*, March 1, 1990.

39. Miller, *The Struggle to Save the Soviet Economy*, 69.

40. Mary Kessler, "The Paradox of Perestroika," *World Policy Journal* 5, no. 4 (Fall, 1988): 651–76.

41. Central Intelligence Agency, *The Soviet Anticorruption Campaign.*

42. McFaul, *Russia's Unfinished Revolution*, 45.

43. *Los Angeles Times*, "Stiff Opposition to Perestroika Reported," November 16, 1989.

44. Dale R. Herspring, "Gorbachev and the Soviet Military," *Proceedings of the Academy of Political Science* 36, no. 4 (1987): 42–53.

45. McFaul, *Russia's Unfinished Revolution*, 42.

46. Miller, *The Struggle to Save the Soviet Economy*, 87.

47. McFaul, *Russia's Unfinished Revolution*, 42.

48. William Moskoff, *Impoverishment and Protest in the Perestroika Years* (The National Council for Soviet and East European Research, September 18, 1992), 4.

49. Miller, "Gorbachev's Agriculture Agenda," 100.

50. Miller, *The Struggle to Save the Soviet Economy*, 67.

51. Central Intelligence Agency, *The Soviet Economy in 1988: Gorbachev Changes Course*, April 1989.

52. Gorbachev, *Memoirs* (New York: Doubleday, 1996), 121.

53. McFaul, *Russia's Unfinished Revolution*, 47.

54. Novokmet, Piketty, and Zucman, "From Soviets to Oligarchs."

55. Michael Ellman, "Soviet Agricultural Policy," *Economic and Political Weekly* 23, no. 24 (June 11, 1988): 1208–10.

56. Robert D. Grey, Lauri A. Jennisch, and Alanna S. Tyler, "Soviet Public Opinion and the Gorbachev Reforms," *Slavic Review* 49, no. 2 (Summer 1990): 261–71.

57. Kessler, "The Paradox of Perestroika."

58. Karin Plokker, "The Development of Individual and Cooperative Labor Activity in the Soviet Union," *Soviet Studies* 42, no. 3 (July 1990): 403–28.

59. McFaul, *Russia's Unfinished Revolution*, 46.

60. R. G. Gidadhubli, "Perestroika and Glasnost," *Economic and Political Weekly* 22, no. 18 (May 2, 1987): 784–87.

61. Brendan Kiernan and Joseph Aistrup, "The 1989 Elections to the Congress of People's Deputies in Moscow," *Soviet Studies* 43, no. 6 (1991): 1049–64.

62. Kaarel Piirimae, "Gorbachev's New Thinking and How its Interaction with Perestroika in the Republics Catalysed the Soviet Collapse," *Scandinavian Journal of History*, August 18, 2020.

63. Thomas Remington, "A Socialist Pluralism of Opinions: Glasnost and Policy-Making Under Gorbachev," *The Russian Review* 48, no. 3 (July 1989): 271–304.

64. Kessler, "The Paradox of Perestroika."

65. Central Intelligence Agency, *The Soviet Economy in 1988.*

66. Schroeder, "Economic Reform of Socialism."

67. *New York Times*, "Soviets Foresee Budget Deficit of $162 Billion," January 22, 1989.

68. Igor Filatochev and Roy Bradshaw, "The Soviet Hyperinflation: Its Origins and Impact Throughout the Former Republics," *Soviet Studies* 44, no. 5 (1992): 739–59.

69. Richard Parker, "Inside the Collapsing Soviet Economy," *The Atlantic*, June 1990.

70. Schroeder, "Economic Reform of Socialism," 40.

71. Miller, "Gorbachev's Agriculture Agenda," 155.

72. Clifford G. Gaddy, *The Price of the Past: Russia's Struggle with the Legacy of a Militarized Economy* (Washington, DC: Brookings Institute, 1997), 56.

73. Miller, "Gorbachev's Agriculture Agenda," 97.

74. Ibid., 168.

75. David Remnick, "Vast 'Shadow Economy' Permeates Soviet Life," *Washington Post*, September 21, 1990.

76. Joel C. Moses, "Democratic Reform in the Gorbachev Era: Dimensions of Reform in the Soviet Union, 1986-1989," *The Russian Review* 48, no. 3 (July 1989): 235–69.

77. *Christian Science Monitor*, "Miners Strike to Bring Down Gorbachev," April 9, 1991.

78. Gidadhubli, "Perestroika and Glasnost."

79. James Boughton, "After the Fall: Building Nations Out of the Soviet Union," in *Tearing Down Walls* (Washington, DC: IMF, 2012).

80. Robert C. Allen, "The Rise and Decline of the Soviet Economy," *Canadian Journal of Economics* 34, no. 4 (November 2001): 869–81.

81. Central Intelligence Agency, *The Soviet Economy in 1988*, 2.

82. Miller, "Gorbachev's Agriculture Agenda, 150.

83. Mau, "Perestroika," 389.

Chapter 7

Comparative Analysis

The preceding chapters reviewed five cases in which single-party authoritarian regimes attempted to implement major policy initiatives to improve intensive growth. The cases resulted in two successes and three failures. How do these cases compare? What lessons can we draw from their experiences? This chapter will compare the cases with similar outcomes and then contrast the two groups.

FAILED OUTCOMES COMPARISON

The cases that resulted in failed policy implementation shared features in common (table 7.1). In the case of China in 2004 and China in 2013, the starting political factors were identical: A weak central leadership, a strong elite opposition, and a fragmented public. The configuration faced by Chinese leaders was especially inauspicious because the central leadership faces formidable opposition yet is handicapped by both its own weakness and the low mobilization potential of the people.

Table 7.1 Starting Political Factor Values for Failed Policy Implementation Cases

Case	*Central Leadership Strength*	*Strength of Elite Opposition*	*Public Cohesiveness*
China 2004	Weak	Strong	Fragmented
China 2013	Weak	Strong	Fragmented
Soviet Union 1985	Weak	Strong	Cohesive (economic)/ fragmented (ethnic/republics)

Source: Data summarizes findings from chapters 3, 4, and 6.

In the case of the Soviet Union, the first two factors were similar, but the public was split between national economic *cohesiveness* and *fragmentation* along largely ethnic lines in the republics. The mobilization potential may have been theoretically higher, but the weakness of the central leadership, the strength of elites, the fragility of the public's economic cohesiveness, and ethnic fragmentation in the republics posed a formidable obstacle to popular mobilization. Moreover, the years of poor economic performance eroded the appeal of the Soviet regime. The net effect was that central leaders in the Soviet and Chinese cases faced powerful elites from a position of weakness yet had little ability to mobilize the public as an ally. In all cases, mobilization of a fragmented populace raised the risk of national breakdown. In the Soviet case, the mobilization of the public facilitated efforts by party bosses and local strongmen to build power bases at odds with Moscow's intent. Indeed, Gorbachev's promotion of glasnost accelerated the Soviet Union's breakup when leaders in the union republics exploited the deep fragmentation along ethnic lines to assert independence.

In all three cases, the central leadership took similar steps to consolidate central power, weaken elite opposition, and strengthen the cohesiveness of the public as well as the central leadership's connection to the public. Incoming central leaders swapped out personnel and carried out purges. Xi Jinping went the furthest in consolidating power. He carried out a large-scale anti-corruption purge that allowed him to both consolidate his grip on the party, government, and military and eliminate rival elites. Xi also oversaw a major centralization of power and a concerted propaganda effort that bolstered his personal authority. Of the three cases, Xi was the only one to experience a significant improvement in the value of the central leadership's strength. This positioned Xi to more aggressively confront elites and strengthen his base of popular support.

Xi's centralizing efforts only succeeded because of the work of his predecessor. Hu's tenure ended with a growing consensus among central leaders that the country required greater centralization, a consensus that did not appear to exist when Hu took office. Moreover, Xi benefited from the many steps undertaken by Hu Jintao to standardize and regularize procedures and political processes. These measures failed to bring recalcitrant elites to heel, but they helped improve the overall competence of government officials and permitted Xi to manipulate the rules, standards, and procedures to discipline recalcitrant elites to some extent.

Hu Jintao experienced less success in centralizing power, owing in part to his inheritance of a politically disadvantageous situation. He also faced personal limitations. The bland technocrat lacked Deng's revolutionary background or personal charisma. Nor did Hu have a strong constituency of supporters in the military. Formally, he became the most powerful person.

However, appearances were deceiving. Although the CCP no longer featured the sorts of well-defined ideological factions that persisted in the Deng era, that did not mean that those institutions had become unfailingly compliant and obedient. Hu's authority became difficult to gauge because, while overt defiance became rare, so did consistent compliance. Instead, throughout his tenure, Hu wrestled with the intractable problem of officials who only partly complied or quietly ignored Beijing's mandates. Symptomatic of his troubles was the routine disregard of central directives by subnational governments. Hu sought to overcome this problem in part by standardizing procedures, instituting meritocratic norms, and improving the quality of training for officials. This failed to bring elites to heel, however, because it did not resolve the central leadership's fundamental dependence on the same individuals. The elites easily outmaneuvered Hu by feigning compliance while selectively implementing measures that did not threaten their interests while passively undermining those that did.

The privatization of wealth and retreat from Marxist orthodoxy allowed elites in China under both Hu and Xi to openly accumulate vast fortunes and secure a larger share of the nation's income and wealth than may have been the case in the Soviet Union. Yet the similarities in how the elites operated overshadow the differences. In all three cases, the elites enjoyed a disproportionate share of power, which they used to protect their own interests. The elites established robust collusive networks both horizontally across government, party, and commercial sectors and vertically from local to national-level offices. Having coopted and gained control of many levers of government, these elite networks grew entrenched and resisted demands for change. The party's monopoly on power ironically became the bulwark of elite privilege. In all three cases, central leaders found they had only limited means to discipline and control elites upon whom they depended to govern the state and manage the economy. The centralized Soviet economy meant that the elites in the central ministries posed the most formidable opposition, while in the decentralized Chinese economy, the most powerful elites were generally those in the subnational governments.

In the Chinese cases, elites encouraged an illusion of government performance that obscured the reality of bureaucratic dysfunction. The elites ensured the basic operation of day-to-day economic activity and government operations to facilitate the extraction of rent. Moreover, the cadres had an incentive to implement some policies and appear compliant because doing so helped deflect scrutiny from the central leadership and thus undercut political arguments for their discipline and removal. Paradoxically, Hu's reforms may have actually strengthened the position of entrenched elites by improving the appearance of increasingly institutionalized, competent governance and thereby obscure the reality of official malfeasance and systematic self-dealing.

The elites under Hu Jintao and Xi Jinping showed an impressive measure of strength, but their rise really took off under the last years of Deng Xiaoping. As noted in the case study, Deng's successful implementation of his major policy initiative contributed directly to both the significant enrichment of elites and the expansion of collusive networks among elites. By the time Deng died, the elites had already grown quite powerful, but this strength was disguised by the congruence between the central leadership's growth agenda and the governance strategy of the subnational elites, both of which prioritized rapid growth. Once Hu Jintao began to seek a new, more efficient, "intensive" mode of growth, however, the power of the elites revealed itself. Hu recognized the problem and tried to overcome elite opposition through non-confrontational methods such as extensive training, education, and regularization of procedures and norms to govern decision-making and political processes. However, without the political will to break the power of elites, these measures proved only superficially effective in disciplining elites. While they did help address real problems among the cadre corps by introducing long-overdue meritocratic standards and elevating the level of professionalism, they did not curb official malfeasance or compel compliance.

Xi Jinping took a more brutal and coercive approach to breaking the power of elites through his anticorruption purge. But although he made progress in dismantling at least some rival networks, the regime's dependence on subnational elites to govern the country and manage the economy proved impossible to overcome. The central leadership could not afford to disrupt the normal operation of government and economy by coercing too many officials, and in any case, the central authorities faced severe limitations in their ability to oversee and discipline the vast armies of subnational government officials. The immense wealth held by elites also provided opportunities to lobby for relief or pay off disciplinary efforts. As a sign of the strength of the party-state elites, the inefficient state sector ballooned under Xi Jinping, despite the central leadership's avowed goals of building a more productive and competitive economy.

Gorbachev abolished some bureaucracies and tried to bolster his position with extensive propaganda. But his position was the weakest, since he could not even secure the façade of unity in the Politburo that his Chinese counterparts had. Moreover, he never imposed his will on the various bureaucracies. Accordingly, officials across multiple levels of party, military, industry, and government repeatedly undermined the perestroika reforms. The only way he could secure their assent was to provide unaffordable payoffs, and even then, the powerful interest groups rarely complied with the new policies. Gorbachev's inability to substantially improve his position vis-à-vis the elites doomed his policy initiatives.

The grounds for pessimism about the Soviet Union case were amplified by the strength of the elite opposition. Unusual in this case was the relatively modest share of income enjoyed by the top 10 percent of earners, at least officially. Ideological resistance to a frank discussion of Soviet inequality makes it difficult to measure how much of the country's wealth the elites controlled, but their ability to consistently extract massive transfers from the state to sustain their lifestyles suggests that the available statistics do not adequately convey the extent of their privileges. In the case of the Soviet Union, it may be the case that control of the government's authority may have been as vital a measure of power as that of wealth and income since many of the privileges of the elite extended beyond official salaries and because private property remained illegal.

In addition to their dominance in the party-state bureaucracy, elite opposition to Gorbachev stemmed from an exceptionally strong collusion between party, government, military, and industrial elites. These collusive networks had depended on state handouts and thus had little incentive to go along with Gorbachev's restructuring. Gorbachev never found a way to significantly weaken the grip of these elites.

The Soviet elites fortified the defense of their interests with ideological arguments against the sort of market-friendly changes sought by Gorbachev. Secure in their positions, elites felt little reason to uphold the façade of compliance, and their opposition remained overt and public. But the willingness of elites to repeatedly and consistently defy Gorbachev contributed greatly to the fatal weakening of the state. The ability of elites to successfully extract crippling amounts of transfers exacerbated the country's economic crisis and contributed directly to its eventual collapse.

Of the autocrats, Gorbachev made the least progress in his efforts to discipline and control recalcitrant elites. He relied on exhortation, argument, and persuasion to wear down resistance in the Politburo, but this merely underscored the feebleness of his position. Because Gorbachev never gained control of the military and security forces, he could not risk taking more coercive and aggressive approaches to dealing with the elite opposition. Underscoring this point, he had to rely on massive cash transfers to purchase support when exhortation failed. Often, the elites would respond by pocketing the transfers and ignoring Gorbachev's directives.

Securely entrenched in the party-state bureaucracy, elites in all three cases had considerable freedom to pick and choose which policies they wished to implement and which they did not. The principal problem faced by central leaders in all three cases was not one of consistent defiance. Rather, the principal problem was that elites arrogated for themselves the power to decide which policies merited implementation and which did not. In the case of China, elites accompanied their non-compliance with a farcical political performance that promoted the image of subservience and enthusiastic support for the central leadership's agenda. They could get away with this deception because the central leaders, Hu and Xi, valued the illusion of bureaucratic obedience as a basis for their own personal authority.

Central leaders also faced the challenge of monitoring the behavior of vast numbers of bureaucrats and officials. Partial compliance complicated efforts to ferret out which individuals merited punishment and which did not. Moreover, the elites in government frequently cultivated influential patrons who provided protection. In contemplating disciplinary actions, central leaders had to consider the political risks of antagonizing powerful patrons. So long as the elites could credibly argue that they were doing their jobs, central leaders could be persuaded that the removal of individuals backed by powerful patrons was not worth the political cost and risk. But this, of course, merely aggravated the problem of partial and incomplete policy implementation.

One notable difference between the Soviet and Chinese cases of 2004 and 2013 lay in the state of cohesiveness of the public. In the Soviet case, the government's commitment to maintaining a full employment economy, basic welfare benefits, and its severe constraints on foreign enterprises and private businesses resulted in a much more economically cohesive workforce and enterprise sector compared to the Chinese cases. However, this cohesiveness came at a great cost. The state could not afford the massive subsidies for the public or an industrial sector burdened with redundant and inefficient enterprises. The burden of maintaining the statist economy contributed directly to runaway debt, devastating shortages, and hyperinflation that destroyed the economy. The CPSU squandered much of the public's goodwill through its failure to materially improve the standard of living. Clear evidence of political paralysis and infighting eroded what little confidence the people may have had. Moreover, the country remained deeply fragmented along ethnic lines, especially in the republics. The acceleration of competing identities and loyalties in ethnic minority republics had already introduced new forces that would adeptly exploit the fragile state of society for anti-regime purposes. When Gorbachev began pushing democratic reforms as a desperate measure to control hardliner opponents, the CPSU had arguably already long since lost the ability to inspire popular enthusiasm. Political mobilization merely accelerated the dissolution of the state and the formation of new political entities.

The Chinese government relieved itself of an ideological commitment to costly welfare obligations in the 1990s when Deng oversaw a massive downsizing of the SOE workforce. This measure significantly improved the fiscal situation and allowed China to avoid the Soviet Union's fate, but it seriously damaged the cohesiveness of urban populations. Fragmentation intensified as China deepened its integration into the global economy, since many of the jobs created by a globalizing production network centered on the processing trade. The rapid expansion of the informal sector allowed China to compete on the basis of cheap labor and low-cost production. Moreover, the poor integration of domestic industries was exacerbated by the increased presence of foreign companies that had little interest in funding a social safety net or paying for Chinese industrial upgrades. With an economy based on low-wage, foreign-employed, province-dominated activity, the workforce became deeply fragmented. Surging inequality exacerbated fragmentation. Rural and urban divisions, inland and coastal regions, and social classes all experienced widening gaps, despite central government efforts to reduce them. Severe underfunding of local services only aggravated the problem.

Both Hu Jintao and Xi Jinping grappled with how to improve the cohesiveness of the public, in part due to their interest in reducing popular unrest. But they also recognized the importance of gaining popular support for holding elites accountable. Hu Jintao introduced ideological messages of a "harmonious society" that aimed in part to persuade officials to govern more responsibly and for the people to cooperate peaceably. He also oversaw the extension of social welfare benefits to help offset the loss of benefits from shed SOE jobs. However, the atrophy of the party's ideology undercut the appeal of its "harmonious messages," and the meagre funding for social welfare benefits limited their effectiveness. Xi Jinping tried to more directly align popular support with the central leadership's agenda by reorienting propaganda efforts away from upholding the general authority of the party (since that benefited the elites' authority as much as the central leadership) to a message more tightly focused on the authority of Xi Jinping. This proved a useful tactic for separating popular support from that of local elites. However, Xi Jinping discovered the same fundamental constraint that confounded Hu Jintao: The central leadership's dependence on subnational elites to manage the economy and ensure social stability constrained its ability to discipline them. Moreover, no matter how popular Xi may have been personally, many people remained dependent on local elites to survive. If forced to choose, it is not clear that the central authorities could count on the populace to back Xi against the local patrons who directly controlled access to goods and services.

Public anger over worsening inequality, a lack of government services, and the abuses of local authorities disinclined central leaders to expand opportunities for political involvement. Instead, the government stepped up repression. But elevated repression and severe public fragmentation bought stability at the price of weakening the central leadership's position vis-à-vis an increasingly well-resourced and entrenched elite, as Hu learned to his dismay. Efforts to build up a sense of political cohesiveness through nationalism and appeals to ethical values achieved little in light of severe economic, political, and social fragmentation.

The situation continued to deteriorate under Xi Jinping when the country began to prematurely deindustrialize starting in 2013. With half the population still in rural areas, Beijing faced the prospect of a labor force dominated by low-productivity workers in agriculture and service sectors and a shrinking industry still dominated by the processing trade. Industry, even as it began to shrink, remained segmented and featured poor linkages. To increase economic cohesiveness, Xi would have to vastly increase funding for social welfare programs nationwide. However, doing so required the transfer of resources from the nation's elites—a politically perilous option. To help slow the further fragmentation of the public and maintain growth, the government instead relied on SOEs, but this merely worsened the country's low productivity and debt. Politically, Xi tried to rebuild the central leadership's political ties with the public through a number of measures, including the promotion of personalistic politics, digital technologies, and nationalism. These political measures slightly shored up the central leadership's ties with the public but, as with his predecessor, could not alone overcome the effects of deep economic and social fragmentation.

The starting values of the political factors influenced the choice of political strategies undertaken by the three leaders as they sought to implement their respective major policy initiatives. But the individual personality of each leader and the state of official ideology played important roles as well.

Gorbachev's personality led him to rely extensively on exhortation and admonishment to try and prod his Politburo colleagues into supporting his agenda. However, his approach was also driven by an acute awareness of the weakness of his political position and the strength of the opposition arrayed against him, a fact he lamented frequently in his memoirs and writings. The ideology of the CPSU played an important role in Gorbachev's struggle with opposing elites as well. Interest groups exploited stale communist formulas to oppose Gorbachev's liberalizing reforms and demand greater state spending. Political illusions affected Gorbachev and his allies as well, since they mistakenly assumed a higher level of public support for their political agenda than in fact existed. Moscow's commitment to ensuring the economic cohesiveness of the people by sustaining an unaffordable social welfare program likely fueled the illusion that the regime's legitimacy could be purchased and its obvious failings forgiven.

Hu Jintao's technocratic background and conflict-averse personality encouraged him to rely on a political strategy that avoided confrontation. Given the power of opposing collusive networks and the weakness of public support, confrontation between the central leadership and elites carried serious risks of political conflict, which Hu had good reason to fear. He may have also been partly deceived into overestimating the potential of his strategy of elite transformation because it did address a real need to improve the professionalism of officials and formalize political processes. The appeal of a strategy to transform elites from opponents to facilitators of an upgrading policy agenda through training, education, and exhortation offered the additional benefit of reinforcing the consensus decision-making features of the political system that had worked reasonably in eras in which the central leadership and elites shared common interests in an extensive growth strategy.

However, the premise of Hu's strategy of elite transformation proved deeply flawed. In an era of antagonism between central leaders and elites over economic policy, consensus was simply not possible. A political strategy premised on consensus-building, no matter how refined by training, education, and institution-building, was a recipe for gridlock and inaction. The elites easily exploited the strategy by promoting a façade of compliance while undermining policies that they opposed in practice. Hu's misguided attachment to the obsolete consensus-building approach of his predecessors merely provided elites with the veto power they needed to frustrate Beijing's designs.

Xi appeared to have the confidence and background to more aggressively challenge rival elites. Hailing from an aristocratic background and trained in politics, he seemed to relish opportunities to accrue power, exalt hiimself, and humble opponents. His more combative personality served well in his strategy of selective confrontation with elites. However, it came at the price of alienating the international community and aggravating tensions with rival elites, who in turn learned to hide their disaffection.

The outcomes in China and the Soviet Union shared some similarities as well as obvious differences. In all three cases, central leaders oversaw only incremental and marginal progress in the implementation of their respective major policy initiatives. In particular, the governments saw little progress in rectifying the gross inefficiencies and waste that supported the position of elites, although at the same time the economy continued to grow in most cases. In the Soviet case, of course, a steadily worsening economic situation, especially after 1985, eventually led to a crisis and the dissolution of the government.

SUCCESSFUL OUTCOMES COMPARISON

The two cases of successful policy implementation shared several features in common. Most notably, the central leaders in both cases succeeded in shaping a favorable political environment, that is, they achieved the "enabling condition" by the midpoint of the implementation period (table 7.2).

In the case of China in 1991, Deng Xiaoping and his allies initially appeared weak. Deng lacked control of the security forces and remained at a disadvantage in the government and in the party leadership. That year, Deng

Table 7.2 Starting Political Factor Values for Successful Policy Implementation Cases

Case	*Central Leadership Strength*	*Strength of Elite Opposition*	*Public Cohesiveness*
China 1991	Weak	Weak	Cohesive
Taiwan 1974	Strong	Weak	Cohesive

Source: Data summarizes findings from chapters 2 and 5.

suffered repeated defeats in his efforts to carry out his socialist market policy agenda, most notably at plenary and central economic planning meetings. However, subsequent developments revealed Deng's position to be stronger than it appeared. He enjoyed a broad base of support in the government, party, and military. Crucially, he also retained considerable goodwill among the public, which he shrewdly exploited in the Southern Trip in 1992. It took only the momentum of good publicity and the repeated displays of strong public support to overcome the feeble resistance of the hardliner faction. By 1993, Deng had quickly consolidated power in the government, military, and party. Implementation of his plans followed soon after.

Taiwan's strongman in the mid to late 1970s, Chiang Ching-kuo, started the implementation period from a position of strength. He held indisputable power in the government, military, and party. Moreover, the central leadership under Chiang retained enormous riches, due to the wealth that KMT emigres looted from China and to generous US backing. The top leadership further bolstered their position by eliminating potential rivals among the Taiwanese elite. The exclusion of native-born Taiwanese from the highest levels of government also allowed the central leadership to operate with some degree of cohesion and unity of purpose, independent of the elites responsible for economic activity. Of course, in later years, the KMT could not sustain the arrangement, but in 1973, the central leadership relied on these features to retain a strong grip on power.

The political opposition facing Deng proved weak. The opposition to Deng consisted primarily of a handful of ideologically motivated hardliners and conservatives. They had personal convictions and reputations at stake, and they controlled a few key offices, primarily in the central government. However, they lacked the support of the military. Nor did the hardliner opposition experience much support among the critical audience of elites who controlled the subnational governments. Despite efforts to elicit support, the hardliners also lacked the backing of the public. The Chinese people had grown tired of the debilitating political conflicts that Deng's opponents seemed intent on reviving and the destitution that the hardliners' ideals offered little hope of changing. Collusion among elites was limited in part due to restrictions on the presence of entrepreneurs in the communist party and the limitations on property rights, which inhibited cadres from accumulating wealth. Through the mid to late 1990s, these restrictions would be lifted, enabling subnational elites who backed Deng to grow fabulously wealthy and deepen their collusive networks. However, throughout this period, their interests converged with those of Deng and his ally Jiang Zemin, who promoted rapid growth. The problem of dealing with a powerful and entrenched elite would be left to subsequent administrations, who would have to deal with the more politically contentious politics of intensive growth policies.

Taiwan's leaders also faced a relatively weak opposition. The KMT decimated the local elites in the 1940s, and their land to the tiller reforms further weakened the power of the landed elite in the 1950s. Moreover, as an émigré regime, the mainlanders maintained a firm grip on the nation's most important political and security-related bureaucracies. Indeed, the island's elites were largely differentiated into mainlander-dominated government and military sectors and native Taiwan-dominated commercial sectors. Elites in general held a modest share of national wealth and income and featured a low level of collusion. Not only were they relatively weak, the native-born Taiwanese elites also did not have an incentive to oppose the economic upgrading policy initiative advanced by Chiang. He did not even need to mobilize public support due to the lack of political opposition to his economic initiative.

In the case of China in the early 1990s, the public's cohesiveness was in transition. In the Maoist period, the CCP's focus on mass politics and an economy dominated by the state resulted in a generally high level of cohesiveness. Fragmentation increased, however, when the CCP politically demobilized the populace and began to dismantle the state sector. By 1991, the people had been largely depoliticized. However, the CCP had not completely abandoned the mobilization of public sentiment. Indeed, both Deng Xiaoping and his hardliner opponents in the central government solicited public support through mass media and other high-profile events. Deng's popularity and the public's fatigue from Maoist politics provided the reformers with a decisive edge, but the failure of the hardliners to garner public sympathy did not negate the lingering importance of popular involvement in politics. Deng's passing and the party's disinterest in reviving mass politics definitely ended the period of political cohesiveness at the end of the 1990s. Economically, SOEs still employed over half of the workers in 1991, but massive downsizing—a consequence of Deng's socialist market policies—resulted in the shedding of tens of millions of jobs. By the early 2000s, urban labor began to be characterized by informality. The business sector also grew increasingly fragmented, with foreign companies in the late 1990s playing an increasingly larger role. The domestic economy featured poorly integrated industries dominated by sub-contractors and cellularized provincial economies. Growing social inequality intensified as well, especially after the SOE downsizing. Not coincidentally, competing groups like *Falun Gong* and separatist ethnic movements began to gain traction in the later 1990s amid the country's severe economic, political, and social fragmentation.

In the case of Taiwan, a low level of inequality, a largely formal workforce, and a business sector dominated by domestic companies with fairly robust linkages between SMEs, large enterprises, and SOEs ensured economic cohesiveness. The political system provided limited but real participation in the selection of local leaders, and this yielded considerable political cohesiveness as well. The main cleavage was ethnic, with a minority mainlander expat community governing the more numerous Taiwan-born populace. Through the early 1970s, repression and a shared opposition to the threat of communist China helped keep these differences in check. However, decades of rapid growth and the aging of the expat community led to an erosion in the ability of the security forces to control society. Moreover, the US decision to change recognition to Beijing in the early 1970s brought latent tension to the forefront. The differentiation of elites facilitated the strengthening of bonds between the native Taiwanese economic elites and the public, resulting in a high potential for mobilized political opposition to mainlander dominance. By the mid-1970s, the ruling KMT regime found it had little choice but to accommodate a populace that chafed under expat rule. The mainlander strategy of cooptation through "Taiwanization" proved to be insufficient, and an opposition formally emerged at the end of the period. However, in terms of economic policy, the cohesiveness of the public and lack of elite opposition facilitated central leadership-led efforts to successfully carry out the economic upgrading policy initiatives.

The political strategies adopted by both leaders centered on building supporting coalitions and managing the relatively modest opposition to proposed policies. Deng's personal prestige enabled him to mobilize the support of the public, as well as that of many subnational elites, in favor of the new policies. Taiwan's strongman permitted economic technocrats to carry out their work of upgrading the country's infrastructure while the central government used its wealth to buy support from key constituencies. The problem of increasing pressure for greater access to top leadership posts by native-born Taiwan elites grew during this period, but central leaders relied on selective recruitment and payoffs to key constituencies to relieve some of the pressure. This strategy would eventually prove inadequate, but future leaders would bear the brunt of coping with the political demands for democratic change.

SUCCESSFUL AND FAILED OUTCOMES COMPARISON

Comparing and contrasting the cases of success with those of failure can illuminate some of the political dynamics that accompanied efforts to implement intensive growth policies. Important differences include contrasting political factors, differences in the nature of the economic challenge, and variation in the choices of political strategies.

The difference in the three political factors stands out as one striking difference (table 7.3). The cases of successful policy implementation featured strong central leadership by the midpoint of the implementation period. Deng started from a weak central leadership position, but this obscured his real strengths, which he quickly capitalized on. Both cases of successful policy implementation featured fairly weak elite opposition. In the case of China in 1991, the hardliners who opposed Deng failed to inspire subnational elites. On the contrary, subnational elites generally backed Deng's economic policy agenda since they regarded the proposed change as far more lucrative. In the case of Taiwan, low inequality and the differentiation of elites resulted in a generally weak Taiwanese elite, and these individuals generally did not oppose the government's upgrading policy initiative. These two cases also tended to feature cohesive publics, at least initially. In the case of China in 1991, for example, a legacy large state sector and minimal private and foreign investor presence in the enterprise sector resulted in a non-farm economy defined by formal employment, good benefits, and domestic industry. Although officially the government encouraged depoliticization of the people, both Deng and his hardliner opponents regularly solicited popular support against each other, underscoring a degree of political cohesiveness.

By contrast, all of the cases of policy implementation failure featured weak central leadership, at least initially. In the case of China in 2013, Xi Jinping succeeded in building a strong central leadership. However, Hu and Gorbachev failed in their respective cases to overcome the weakness of their positions. Perhaps the most distinctive feature of the failed cases consisted of strong elite opposition. In all cases, powerful and wealthy elites dominated the party-state apparatus and exploited the ruling party's monopoly on power

Table 7.3 Summary of Starting Political Factor Values for All Cases

Case	*Central Leadership Strength*	*Strength of Elite Opposition*	*Public Cohesiveness*
Successful cases (2 cases)	Strong/weak	Weak	Cohesive
Failure cases (3 cases)	Weak	Strong	Fragmented

Source: Data summarizes findings from chapters 2–6.

to great advantage. Building collusive networks spanning government, parties, the military, and industry and reaching patrons at the highest levels of government, entrenched elites were well positioned to defend their interests and fend off efforts to change the status quo. The three cases of failure also featured either fragmented publics or, in the Soviet case, an economically cohesive but ethnically fragmented populace that, in all cases, had grown alienated from the ruling party. Thus, in all three cases, the central leadership lacked a feasible way to mobilize popular support against recalcitrant elites.

Differences in Political and Economic Challenges

Differences in the political and economic challenges between the successful and failed cases can help explain the variation in outcomes and the political strategies adopted by the different leaders. In the successful cases of China in 1991–1998 and Taiwan, the challenges were arguably easier than those faced by Moscow in 1985 and Chinese leaders in 2004 and 2013. The challenges owed to contrasting levels of development and to the relative varying degrees to which intensive growth measures were part of the policy initiatives.

In the case of China in 1991, the country faced decelerating growth and inflation. But it also faced favorable prospects for expansion. In terms of its level of development, the country had considerable potential for "extensive" growth. Nearly 75 percent of the population remained in rural areas, indicating potentially high gains from reallocating labor from low-productivity agriculture to manufacturing. Financial repression and strong interest from foreign investors suggested a high possibility of growth from capital inputs as well.

In the case of Taiwan, the island faced a higher level of development. The gains from sectoral reallocation from rural to industrial jobs had been largely exhausted, and a sudden shift to a less favorable international environment provided a strong incentive for the island to carry out an upgrade of its export industries and infrastructure to maintain a strong competitive advantage. The threat to the island's survival posed by communist China, exacerbated by the US decision to change formal recognition to Beijing, provided a strong incentive for the island's economic actors to support the upgrading policy. The central government's access to vast resources, thanks to its rich US backers and the loot it had carried from mainland China, facilitated their efforts to carry out major capital investments. In both cases, productivity gains resulted from the policy initiatives, but the strong element of "extensive" growth measures likely played an important role in the feasibility of success since extensive growth measures are generally easier to carry out.

The cases of the Soviet Union and China in 2004 and 2013 featured significantly more demanding challenges. In each case, the country had industrialized and faced a diminishing ability to rely on extensive growth methods. In both Chinese cases, the saturation of global markets and erosion of the country's labor cost advantage meant that future growth would have to come from a more efficient use of existing capabilities. As in the Soviet case, this would require shutting down excess capacity from redundant factories and inefficient SOEs, which could result in job losses in the tens of millions and income and power for elites. Finding ways to improve productivity through such means was inherently contentious.

The contrasting challenges were matched with policy responses of varying levels of political risk. The initiatives advanced by Deng Xiaoping and Chiang Ching-kuo offered to unlock growth in a way that did not necessarily require antagonizing powerful interest groups. In the case of China, Deng's reforms shut down many inefficient SOEs but also opened opportunities for workers to find new jobs in newly created, more efficient private industries. The change also lifted restrictions on property ownership and commercial activity, creating new opportunities for elites to exploit their privileged status for profit. The central leadership tolerated all sorts of wasteful and inefficient behavior on the part of local elites so long as they maintained high growth rates. In the case of Taiwan, massive investments generally met approval from business executives eager to elevate the country's economic competitiveness. The spending created many jobs and did not incur major political opposition.

By contrast, the cases of failure all featured policy initiatives that primarily sought to unlock "intensive" growth through the reduction of wasteful, inefficient, and low-productivity practices. This mode of growth required a substantial reallocation of resources away from the state sector toward more efficient channels. By their nature, these initiatives would unavoidably entail massive losses for powerful, entrenched elites, and accordingly, they faced intense resistance. The fact that the leaders in all three cases experienced at most incremental change underscores the broader finding in developmental studies that unlocking economic growth through intensive methods may prove politically difficult.

COMPARISON OF POLITICAL STRATEGIES

The nature of the problems faced by the central leadership and the contrasting values of the political factors help explain the political strategies undertaken by the different authoritarian governments. In all cases, authoritarian leaders proceeded with caution, especially against powerful elites. The central leaders generally sought to avoid conflict with elites if possible but had less hesitation to step up repression of the public (table 7.4).

Table 7.4 Variation in Political Coerciveness Toward Elites, Public Repression in Cases

Type of Coercion/Repression	*China 1991 (Success)*	*China 2004 (Failure)*	*China 2013 (Failure)*	*Taiwan 1973 (Success)*	*USSR 1985 (Failure)*
Central leadership-elite			Elevated		Elevated
Central leadership-public	Elevated	Elevated	Elevated		

Source: Data collected from chapters 2–6.

Where political situations proved favorable and elite opposition generally weak, autocrats relied on generally less coercive means to coax elites into supporting their agenda. In the case of Taiwan, the weakness of the elite opposition and cohesiveness of society enabled the central leadership to oversee the implementation of its economic agenda with little need to elevate coercion or repression. Authorities relied on political controls until the reality of demographics and a weakening legitimacy owing to international developments in the early 1970s made accommodation for Taiwanese opponents unavoidable.

Deng Xiaoping and his allies relied on political maneuver and the mobilization of public sentiment to oust their opponents from top-level positions and compel them to concede. The weakness of the hardliner faction and their lack of support among subnational elites and the public allowed the ailing Deng to prevail without the need to resort to violence. However, the effects of Deng's upgrading reforms resulted in greater public unrest, to which the government responded with greater repression.

Hu Jintao's political strategy was informed by the reality of an unfavorable political situation that he inherited as well as his own personal inclinations. He also recognized a dire need for the regime to upgrade its governance capacity to address the needs of a maturing economy. His strategy of transforming elites into professional, competent, and compliant partners held great appeal to an autocrat who had good reason to fear conflict with powerful elites and who personally favored technocratic solutions. Authorities under Hu stepped up repression of the public as their dependence on subnational elites increased and unrest spread.

Xi Jinping's strategy was informed by the failures of Hu's approach. Xi inherited and upheld the paradigm of the CCP as a governing party, and he maintained the central leadership's close alliance with the elites. Progress in institutionalizing and stabilizing CCP rules provided an important foundation upon which Xi could build more aggressive strategies. Xi astutely perceived the need to strengthen the central leadership's power relative to the elites. He also recognized that strengthening central power alone was unlikely to reverse the situation. Aggressive action to weaken elites and reinvigorate party ties with the public could give the central leadership the upper hand. The anticorruption campaign helped with the first goal. For the latter goal, the central leadership promoted a political mobilization centered on Xi's personal authority. The reinvigoration of the CCP's ideological authority, the promotion of a Xi cult of personality, and the advocacy of nationalist foreign policy—which the central leadership was responsible for, not local elites—served many purposes, but they all also contributed to the broader goal of bolstering the power of the central leadership vis a vis the nation's elites.

These innovative aspects of Xi's approach yielded substantive results. Xi's efforts reduced the danger of elites conspiring to overthrow the central leadership. However, the effort faced hard limits. The central leadership's dependence on elites constrained how much they could afford to risk antagonizing the officials who directly managed economic growth and political stability. Efforts to encourage political cohesiveness may have boosted Xi's popularity, but the reality of economic fragmentation and deep inequality left the public dependent on local elites. Moreover, Xi's political strategy carried its own risks. The centralizing measures alarmed domestic rival elites, some members of the public, and many international observers. Threatened elites began to flee or cultivate international support. The political instability generated by Xi's political strategy thus threatened to undo his standing, and he eventually had to relax the pace of the centralizing and coercive measures. As a result, the central leadership lacked sufficient leverage, and the elites, while too weak to overcome the central leadership, also proved strong enough to maintain their position. The public, meanwhile, remained too weak to play a decisive role. The result under Xi has mostly been a stalemate, with only slightly better results than Hu experienced.

This chapter has provided an overview of some of the points of similarity and difference between the five cases. To summarize, the cases of failure generally featured much more intractable and difficult-to-achieve policy goals related to the pursuit of intensive methods of elevating economic growth. The difficulty of the challenge was intricately related to the value of the political factors related to the political task of setting the necessary conditions for realizing economic revitalization. In all the cases of policy implementation failure, central leaders confronted a daunting political situation. By contrast, the cases featuring successful outcomes featured both an easier economic policy challenge and far more favorable political circumstances.

Conclusion

This book has argued that favorable political conditions are essential to the successful implementation of major, multi-sector policy initiatives that seek to raise intensive growth. The theory stated that a government needed to achieve a favorable political situation resembling an "enabling condition" characterized by strong central leadership, weak elite opposition, and a cohesive public by the midway point of a designated period for implementation. If the central leadership failed to shape something like the enabling condition within the posited time span, then the policy initiative would not succeed. However, building the enabling condition is a necessary, not sufficient, condition. Achieving the configuration alone might not result in the hoped for economic gains since other factors, such as the competence of the bureaucracy, also affect economic outcomes. Analysis of these other factors lies outside the scope of the book, but their importance should be kept in mind when evaluating the evidence about the enabling condition.

The results in the case studies were consistent with the theory (table C.1). In the cases of China (1991–1979) and Taiwan (1973–1979), the central leaders shaped a political environment that resembled the enabling condition by the third year of the six-year period observed for policy implementation. Productivity improved substantially, and the leaders met their priority goals. The successes ushered in periods of sustained economic growth lasting a decade or more.

The negative cases also supported the theory. In the cases of China (2004–2009 and 2013–2019) and the Soviet Union (1985–1991), a failure to build an enabling condition resulted in disappointing or failed policy implementation. In these cases, the leadership experienced a regression in some ways as the state sector expanded and problems of bad debt and excess capacity worsened.

Table C.1 Variation in Policy Implementation among Select Single Party Authoritarian Regimes

	China 1991	*China 2004*	*China 2013*	*Taiwan 1973*	*USSR 1985*
Main economic problem	Slowing growth, inefficient and bloated state sector	Unsustainable growth model, externalities; debt	Unsustainable growth model, high externalities; debt	Unsustainable growth model	Slow growth, inefficient state sector, weak markets; debt
Economic policy goal	Establish a socialist market (increase private sector)	Shift to sustainable growth (rebalance toward consumption, reduce debt)	Shift to sustainable growth model (rebalance toward consumption, reduce debt)	Upgrade infrastructure, industry	Expand market mechanisms, increase labor productivity
Time frame (GDP growth rate average)	1991–1997 (12%)	2004–2010 (10%)	2013–2019 (7%)	1973–1979 (9%)	1985–91 (<2%)
Change in key measurement of goal achievement	Increase of market mechanisms (93% of retail in 1996 from 53% in 1990); Productivity growth (5%)	Change in consumption as % of GDP (41–42%); reduce debt/GDP (debt grows from 150% to 200% GDP); productivity growth (–2%);	Change in consumption as % of GDP (42–45%); reduce debt/GDP (debt grows from 200% to 260% GDP); productivity growth (1%)	Industry increased its share of GDP from 31.7% in 1972 to 42.8% in 1977; industry share of exports (56% to 86%); productivity growth (2.5%)	Market liberalization, productivity growth (<1%); improve production (declined); SOEs completely self-reliant (60% met goal)
Assessment	Success	Failure	Failure	Success	Failure

Source: Data for the China 1991 column adapted from World Bank database, Qian and Wu, 2000; data for the China 2004 column adapted from World Bank database, "Full Text of 18th Party Congress Report," 2012, Cary and Li, 2011, Mohanty, 2012; data for the China 2013 column adapted from the World Bank database, Lawrence, 2019, Raiser and Soh, 2019, World Bank, 2017; data for the Taiwan 1973 column adapted from Myers, 1984, Cheng, 1989, Tsai, 1999; and data for the USSR 1985 column adapted from Allen, 2001, Miller, 2016, Aslund, 2007.

Yet caveats are in order. The sample size was small—a mere five cases. Moreover, the intricate relationship between the economic challenge and the value of the political factors merits emphasis. The leaders of the Soviet Union and China in 2004 and 2013 faced formidable challenges both politically and economically. The fact that no single-party authoritarian closed government has succeeded in upgrading its economy through primarily intensive methods raises questions about whether such governments can achieve the highest levels of productivity and per capita income.

Other scholars have noted that China's development challenges share far more in common with those of other large developing countries in Asia than the small, early-industrializing "Asian Tigers" such as Taiwan.[1] Some experts have noted that the qualities of informalization of the work force, fragmented industrial chains, and powerful elites characteristic of late industrializing countries, including China, suggest that the success of the Asian Tigers may be the last to have enjoyed such a mode of equitable industrialization. This could mean an increase in inequality and long-term, slow growth for the world economy.[2]

THE POLITICAL CHALLENGE OF INTENSIVE GROWTH

Distinctive features of single-party, authoritarian states may make them especially vulnerable to political pressures that arise from the implementation of intensive growth strategies, but lessons from their experience could be applied more broadly. This study has proposed a theory of policy implementation that could help illuminate trends observed in many other countries. Other scholars have noted, for example, the tendency of prospering economies to yield worsening economic inequality, increasingly wealthy and powerful elites, and fragmented publics.[3] Long a feature of many developing countries, these trends have manifested in many of the wealthiest and most liberal democracies in recent years. Perhaps not coincidentally, both developed and developing countries have often struggled in recent years to improve productivity. While the reasons continue to be debated, the results of this study suggest politics could be an important factor. The findings emphasize the extremely challenging task of establishing favorable political conditions for intensive growth policies and the fragility of such a situation even if successfully realized. And this theory represents only one possible "necessary" condition. Scholars have already identified other essential ingredients for successful economic development, such as a competent bureaucracy and productive relationships between the state and society.[4] Perhaps the reason countries have struggled to become rich in recent years is that the combination of favorable necessary conditions may have become harder to achieve.

All countries face the risk that wealthy and powerful interest groups may grow strong enough to distort policy for purposes of self-enrichment with little benefit to the public. The same trends that accelerate economic fragmentation in China and other authoritarian regimes featured in this study can appear in liberal and wealthy as well as developing countries, too. The effects of automation have already devastated the industrial sectors of many advanced countries, which have in turn struggled to replace relatively well-paying manufacturing jobs. In the developing world, the situation is even more dispiriting, with informality predominating in the workforce. These economic trends can further aggravate political and socio-ethnic fragmentation. Although democracies offer a mechanism for political participation, elections do not by themselves negate the problem of political fragmentation. The key question is whether people believe participation opportunities are meaningful. Where large segments of the public have concluded that voting will make little difference in improving their lives, the result is likely to be political fragmentation. And with the public fragmented, central governments in liberal democracies may find their ability to prevail over an increasingly powerful elite opposition constrained. This in turn could result in political gridlock, the spread of extremist politics, and diminishing prospects for implementing intensive growth measures.

AUTOCRATIC POLICY IMPLEMENTATION: THE ROLE OF COERCION AND REPRESSION

While the study focused primarily on the question of whether and how authoritarian states could successfully implement major policy initiatives, a secondary question centered on the incentives for political actors to intensify the coercion of elites and repression of the public. The results of the case study analysis offer sobering food for thought. In four of the five cases, the central leadership's effort to implement the major policy initiative coincided with increased state coercion or repression involving the central leadership, elites, and/or the public. The most common form involved an increase in repression against the people. This happened in all three cases in China. The case studies suggest that increased repression owed to reasons related to the pursuit of major policy initiatives. China experienced substantial productivity gains under Deng Xiaoping and the restoration of fiscal stability by imposing the cost of an economic overhaul on the populace. The government slashed jobs, social welfare benefits, and services, which reduced government spending and debt. It resulted, however, in a significant increase in insecurity and hardship for many Chinese people. Moreover, the central government's close alliance with subnational elites proved a critical enabler of rapid growth policies, but the central leadership's backing also meant that local elites were freed to abuse their authority and neglect public needs. As the central government implemented its upgrading policies, public resentment over problems of malfeasance sparked unrest. Because fully funding the services and correcting the abuses would have sharply reduced China's competitiveness and attractiveness as a destination for foreign investment, the government responded to the demands with heightened repression. One potential conclusion is that societies facing high levels of public fragmentation may find it difficult to resist an increase in repression as part of their efforts to implement major upgrading policies, especially if the central leadership has become heavily dependent on elites to sustain economic activity.

The cases of the Soviet Union and Taiwan did not feature heightened repression of the public, but for different reasons. In the case of the Soviet Union, Gorbachev cultivated the support of the public and encouraged more criticism of the status quo in hopes of pressuring political opponents in the Politburo and government to accept the need for change. In the case of Taiwan, authorities experienced a diminishing ability to monitor and control a rapidly pluralizing society. Faced with increasing solidarity among the Taiwanese population and criticism of the mainlander monopoly on power, the central government tried to placate the public with loosened controls and increased efforts to coopt native elites through recruitment into the KMT. The outcome suggests only societies featuring a high level of cohesiveness and weak elites are best positioned to build stable and liberal democracies. By contrast, the Soviet case suggests liberalizing changes in a deeply fragmented society featuring powerful elites carries a high risk of social and political upheaval and a potential transformation into illiberal regimes.

Coercion involving the central leadership and elites occurred in only two cases, underscoring the trepidation of central leaders toward openly confronting powerful elite adversaries. Xi Jinping significantly increased the coercion of elites through an extensive anti-corruption campaign that swept up many high-level officials and elites throughout the party-state. Yet despite the coercion, the elites saw little actual reduction in their wealth and incomes. One possible lesson is that the threat of political conflict imposes real limits on the ability of central leaders to break power and significantly downgrade the status and privileges of elites.

The other case involved violence by elites against the central leadership, as seen in the Soviet Union case. Gorbachev understood that he lacked the political power to coerce elites into compliance with the perestroika reforms. He tried nonviolent approaches to winning their support, but his apprehension proved well-founded when the elites rebelled in 1991 and seized power to forestall the prospect of a massive downgrade in their status and privileges. This outcome underscores the danger of antagonizing powerful elites.

China under Deng and Taiwan did not experience elevated levels of coercion between elites and the central leadership, but for different reasons. Deng's political strength and the fragility of his hardliner's political position meant the revolutionary leader could rely on political maneuver and the help of his supporters to overcome his opponents without recourse to bloodshed. The strength of the KMT regime and the congruence between the central leadership's policy agenda and the interests of economic elite meant that Taipei had little incentive for coercion. The lesson here is that weak elites and a cohesive public offer more favorable prospects for central leaders to achieve their goals without risking intra-elite violence.

All of the cases studied provided evidence that autocrats that contemplated major policy initiatives went to great lengths to avoid provoking conflict with powerful elites if possible. Only when other, less confrontational methods proved ineffective did they begin to consider more confrontational and coercive approaches. While this study focused on autocratic states, this finding raises unsettling questions about the noncoercive possibilities for intensive growth policies in all societies, especially those featuring unfavorable political conditions characterized by weak central leadership, powerful elite opposition, and a fragmented public. If autocrats, who have at their disposal the power to arbitrarily inflict violence on any individual without regard to due process, cannot control elites, what hope do other government types have? Although a full analysis lies beyond the scope of this study, its findings suggest a more thorough analysis of potential political strategies may be in order for countries that seek intensive growth.

IMPLICATIONS FOR CHINA'S PROSPECTS

What do the study's findings suggest for China's prospects as an original impetus for the research? One finding is that China faces daunting prospects for carrying out intensive growth policies. In general, this study concludes pessimistically that Beijing will not be able to realize the intensive growth strategies prescribed by many economists and that the country will continue to significantly lag behind the "frontier" productive economies. Problems of ballooning debt, underfunded social services, excessive capacity, and low productivity could persist for the foreseeable future. Premature deindustrialization and the persistence of a large rural work force have resulted in severe economic fragmentation that is unlikely to be reversed. Moreover, the central government's dependence on the provinces for economic growth has resulted in an increase in power and leverage by subnational elite that appears unlikely to change outside of some dramatic and potentially destabilizing shock.

Even so, this analysis suggests the political situation as achieved under Xi Jinping may be more stable than is frequently assumed and that the dangers of dissolution and collapse are probably overstated. Xi's centralizing and repressive measures, although controversial and provocative, have at least reduced the risk that elites might overthrow the central leadership. The danger of severe political conflict was higher under Hu Jintao, whose tolerance of elite power permitted the formation of formidable networks—exemplified by the rise of Bo Xilai and Zhou Yongkang—with the potential to someday challenge the central leadership's grip on power.

Over the long term, the case study comparison suggests that if China fails to resolve its productivity issues, its future could resemble something like that of the Soviet Union in Gorbachev's day. In particular, Beijing might someday face the risk of powerful, entrenched elites who routinely distort policy for purposes of self-enrichment and rent and who promote policies that incrementally undermine the nation's economic performance. If a future top leader decided to roll back the centralizing measures undertaken by Xi, the leader might find his position weakened to the point that he might struggle, as Gorbachev did, to impose his or her will on the elites who control the party-state bureaucracy. Chinese leaders are acutely aware of the failings of the CPSU and how the Soviet Union collapsed. China's situation differs from that of the Soviet Union in many ways, of course, a top one being that China's economy is far more decentralized and dynamic than the Soviet economy ever was. The main threat posed by elites to the central government will differ accordingly from that faced by Gorbachev. Powerful, entrenched subnational elites could, for example, pursue greater autonomy within China. National disintegration could pose as a greater threat than a coup. To avoid such a fate, future Chinese leaders will likely have a strong incentive to continue policies of centralization and coercion by elites. They may also try to bolster ties between the autocrat and the public as a form of counterpressure against centrifugal tendencies.

Given the trajectory of China's political and economic evolution, in retrospect, it should not be surprising that Xi Jinping pursued the form of politics he did. In fact, this study has concluded that the political path undertaken by Xi Jinping, far from irrational and erratic, in many ways represented a rational response to a difficult situation, given limited options. The example of Gorbachev and, more proximately, that of Hu Jintao showed the high risk of failure that a path of consensus-building, non-confrontation, and elaboration of procedures, institutions, and processes unavoidably entailed. Popular prescriptions of a shift toward democratic reform and liberalizing change upon closer analysis probably would not have helped Beijing achieve intensive growth either. Such recommendations are usually informed by misguided comparisons with Asian Tigers, which, as this study has suggested, featured far more favorable political conditions. The similarities in China's contemporary situation with that of the Soviet Union under Gorbachev suggest a more compelling model. The Soviet Union did, after all, adopt economic and political restructuring after Gorbachev, which resulted in the dismantling of the state sector and political democratization. But it resulted in a more fragmented populace and rule by oligarchs who exploited the liberalizing changes for self-gain, resulting in an illiberal and authoritarian rule.

For analysts of Chinese elite politics, this study carries some implications as well. Analysis of the evolution of China's political economy over the past few decades suggests that the changing nature of elites merits closer attention. There is confusion in the China watching community over whether the country has experienced greater institutionalization of politics or if its political system remains fundamentally defined by factional alignments, and behind the scenes power struggles may be incorrectly framing the problem. Chinese politics has experienced both greater efforts to regularize and institutionalize processes and procedures and ongoing struggles between groups of elites. What is changing is how these elite groups are being organized and exercising power. Struggles between ideologically aligned networks led by powerful personalities such as Mao or Deng have long since passed. The future of Chinese elite politics may be glimpsed in the late Soviet Union. In the Soviet Union, politics became dominated by competing interest groups defined by interlocking elites in industry, government, and the party. These were sometimes called "industrial complexes," and they proved to be formidable combinations of political power and state capital. In China, Zhou Yongkang's career, before his downfall, provides a glimpse of how such complexes could propel patrons to the highest levels of government and become powerful players in elite politics. Zhou's base of power consisted of the energy industry, which he assiduously cultivated and protected. The massive infusion of cash into China's political system raises the possibility that similar interest groups featuring mutually collusive networks could become a powerful force in politics. However, unlike the Soviet Union, China's industry-state networks of elites are likely to overlap with regional concentrations of power, reflecting its more decentralized economy.

The analysis suggests China will continue to face challenges in upgrading its economy. It is not only growing old before growing rich but also de-industrializing well before it has grown rich. This suggests that productivity gains will become more difficult as the economy transitions into a more service-based economy. Even if China can successfully innovate and become a technological leader, it does not appear likely to reverse the trends toward a shrinking industrial base. More likely, China could evolve in a direction reminiscent of the US economy in the 1990s, when US tech companies dominated internet-related technologies. A tiny proportion of the population grew wealthy and prosperous, but inequality deepened, and the rest of the population experienced comparatively little gain.

If this is China's fate, the central government could continue to face the challenge of managing a numerically small but powerful and well-resourced elite with little help from a fragmented, insecure, and disaffected populace. The incentive to maintain illiberal politics, ally with elites, and repress the public will remain strong even after Xi inevitably leaves power. This could mean the US faces long-term competition with an authoritarian China that will continue to be highly repressive. The long-term persistence of an unfavorable political configuration for implementation of upgrading policies means that the possibility that China might repeat the success of Asian Tiger economies and unleash high productivity growth looks improbable. More likely, China will struggle with suboptimal results in its pursuit of intensive growth and continue to rely on extensive injections of capital. This mode of growth will continue to be wasteful and inefficient, but the results will be tolerable, especially for the central leadership and elite, who will be able to maintain their privilege and status through extractive policies. Moreover, China's case may paradoxically become attractive as a model for many economies that suffer from similar structural constraints as China, such as a large informal sector, premature industrialization, a fractured business sector with poor domestic linkages, and powerful and entrenched elites. A combination of Hu's approach, which prioritized building up the professional competence of officials, and Xi's approach, which centralized power in order to balance elite power and bolster the central leadership's connection with the people, offers the potential to balance domestic political stability, modest growth, and the control of elites. It may not achieve an optimal outcome of high productivity growth, but leaders in such countries may conclude that such an outcome is beyond their reach in any case due to their unfavorable political conditions. Given the alternatives of either elite dominance of the central leadership or economic collapse, China's modest achievements may prove more attractive in coming years as an illiberal model of growth.

A China that achieved suboptimal results in its implementation of major policy initiatives may still have sufficient resources to generously fund its military and foreign policies, due to the central government's ability to capture a larger share of GDP under Xi than was the case with previous leaders Jiang and Hu. The subnational governments may suffer shortfalls in funding for social welfare programs and government services, but Beijing can step up repression to control discontent over these local issues while maintaining generous funding for central priorities such as the military and foreign policy initiatives such as BRI-related activities. Beijing might seek to maintain its uneasy alliance with elites by tolerating considerable graft and corruption, so long as the elites make some incremental progress toward Beijing's goals.

If China's political situation proves insurmountable and it never realizes the levels of intensive growth leaders have sought to provide far higher per capita incomes to the populace, this does not mean China may not pose a challenge to the United States. Power is relative, after all. A slow-growing China may still see its power gain relative to that of the United States, especially if Washington struggles to implement its own intensive growth policies. Rival major powers such as Japan, India, and the European Union are also experiencing, in their own distinctive ways, trends that augur ill for high-productivity growth. In such a case, China may prove less of a giant than if it had successfully overcome its difficulties and implemented contentious, intensive growth policies. But this may matter less than it seems if China's rivals experience even slower growth. If current trends continue, the future of US-China competition could even see a reversion to a pattern common to premodern interstate rivalries, in which central rulers and their elite allies must balance competition with the rival state with careful management of a fragile polity characterized by high inequality and a fragmented and discontented populace.

NOTES

1. Huang, "China's Neglected Informal Economy," 405–38.
2. Rodrik, "Work and Human Development in a Deindustrializing World."
3. Walter Scheidel, *The Great Leveler: Violence and the History of Inequality from the Stone Age to the Twenty-First Century* (Princeton, NJ: Princeton University Press, 2017).
4. Peter Evans, *Embedded Autonomy: States and Industrial Transformation* (Princeton, NJ: Princeton University Press, 1995).

References

Acemoglu, Daron, Suresh Naidu, Pascual Restrepo, and James A. Robinson. "Democracy Does Cause Growth," *Journal of Political Economy*, Vol. 127, No. 1, 2019, pp. 47–100.

Acemoglu, Daron and James A. Robinson. *Why Nations Fail: The Origins of Power, Prosperity, and Poverty*, New York, NY: Crown Business, 2012.

Adelphi Papers. "Brezhnev's Alliance with the Military and its Erosion," Vol. 31, No. 258, 1991, pp. 5–10.

Agenor, Pierre-Richard and Otaviano Canuto. "Middle Income Growth Traps," World Bank Policy Research Paper 6210, World Bank, 2012.

Aghion, Philippe, Alberto Alesina, and Francesco Trebbi. "Democracy, Technology, and Growth," NBER, Working Paper 13180, June 2007.

Agursky, Mikhail. *The Soviet Military-Industrial Complex*, Jerusalem: Magnes Press, 1980.

Aken, Tucker Van and Orion A. Lewis. "The Political Economy of Noncompliance in China: The Case of Industrial Energy Policy," *Journal of Contemporary China*, Vol. 24, No. 95, 2015, pp. 798–822.

Allen, Robert C. "The Rise and Decline of the Soviet Economy," *Canadian Journal of Economics*, Vol. 34, No. 4, November, 2001, pp. 869–881.

Amiti, Aaron and Caroline Freund. "China's Export Boom," *Finance and Development*, Vol. 44, No. 3, 2007, pp. 38–41.

Anderlini, Jamil. "Chinese Industry: Ambitions in Excess," *Financial Times*, June 16, 2013.

Aslund, Anders. "Perestroika: The Great Awakening 1985–1987," in *Russia's Capitalist Revolution*, Washington, DC: Peterson Institute for International Economics, 2007, pp. 11–42.

Barboza, David. "Food Safety Crackdown in China," *New York Times*, June 28, 2007.

Baston, Andrew. "Fixing China's State Sector," *Paulson Policy Memorandum*, January 2014.

Baum, Richard. *Burying Mao: Chinese Politics in the Age of Deng Xiaoping*, Princeton, NJ: Princeton University Press, 1996.

Baumgartner, Frank R., Christian Breunig, Christopher Green-Pedersen, Bryan D. Jones, Peter B. Mortensen, Michiel Nutemans, and Stefaan Walgrave. "Punctuated Equilibrium in Comparative Perpective," *American Journal of Political Science*, Vol. 53, No. 3, 2009, pp. 603–620.

BBC News. "China's Anti-Corruption Campaign Expands with New Agency," March 20, 2018.

———. "China Third Plenum: Leaders Unveil Key Reforms," November 12, 2013.

———. "Chinese General Guo Boxiong Sentenced to Life in Prison for Corruption," July 25, 2016.

Bellows, Thomas J. "Taiwan's Foreign Policy in the 1970s: A Case of Adaptation and Viability," *Asian Survey*, Vol. 16, No. 7, July 1976, pp. 593–610.

Bertsch, Gary K., Robert B. Clark, and David M. Wood. *Comparative Political Systems: Power and Policy in Three Worlds*, New York: John Wiley, 1986, p. 472.

Bi, Jingjing. "The Mass Line Is the Fundamental Work Line for Pooling Our Strength To Realize the Chinese Dream" [Qunzhong Luxian Shi Ningju Liliang Shixian Zhongguomeng De Genben Gongzuo Xian], *Seeking Truth* [Qiushi], Vol. 53, No. 15, August 1, 2013, pp. 22–26.

Bialer, Seweryn. "The Harsh Decade: Soviet Policies in the 1980s," *Foreign Affairs*, Summer 1981.

Blanchette, Jude. *China's New Red Guards: The Return of Radicalism and the Rebirth of Mao Zedong*, Oxford: Oxford University Press, 2019.

Bloom, Peter. *Authoritarian Capitalism in the Age of Globalization*, Cheltenham: Edward Elgar Publications, May, 2016.

Bloomberg. "Is China Growing Services Sector at Expense of Manufacturing?" July 21, 2016.

Boddin, Dominik. "The Role of Newly Industrialized Economies in the Global Value Chain," IMF Working Paper, No. 207, October 2016.

Boltho, Andrea and Maria Weber. "Did China Follow the East Asian Development Model?" *The European Journal of Comparative Economics*, Vol. 6, No. 2, 2018, pp. 267–286.

Borst, Nicholas. "The Link Between China's Property Market and Local Government Finances," China Economic Watch, Peterson Institute for International Economics website, October 18, 2011. As of August 30, 2020: https://www.piie.com/blogs/china-economic-watch/link-between-chinas-property-market-and-local-government-finances.

Bosco, Joseph. "Taiwan Factions: Guanxi, Patronage, and the State in Local Politics," *Ethnology*, Vol. 31, No. 2, April, 1992, pp. 157–183.

Boughton, James. *Tearing Down Walls: The International Monetary Fund, 1990–1999*, Washington, DC: IMF, 2012.

Brady, Anne Marie. "China's Foreign Propaganda Machine," *Wilson Center*, October 26, 2015.

Buckley, Chris. "China Gives Communist Party More Control Over Policy and Media," *The New York Times*, March 21, 2018.

———. "Drive the Blade In: Xi Shakes Up China's Law and Order Forces," *New York Times*, August 20, 2020.

Buckley, Chris and Keith Bradsher. "China Unveils Superagencies to Fight Pollution and Other Threats to Party Rule," *New York Times*, March 13, 2018.

Buckley, Chris and Steven Lee Myers. "China's Legislature Blesses Xi's Indefinite Rule. It Was 2,958 to 2," *The New York Times*, March 11, 2018.

Bunker, Stephen. "Policy Implementation in an Authoritarian State: The Case of Brazil," *Latin American Research Review*, Vol. 18, No. 1, 1983, pp. 33–58.

Business Insider. "China's Crackdown on Corruption and Government Spending: A Timeline," January 23, 2014. As of November 5, 2020: https://www.chinabusinessreview.com/chinas-crackdown-on-corruption-and-government-spending-a-timeline/.

Cai, Hongbin and Daniel Treisman. "Did Government Decentralization Cause China's Economic Miracle?" *World Politics*, Vol. 58, No. 4, July, 2006, pp. 505–535.

Cary, Eve and Cheng Li. "The Last Year of Hu's Leadership: Hu's to Blame?" Brookings Institution, December 20, 2011. As of January 3, 2021: https://www.brookings.edu/articles/the-last-year-of-hus-leadership-hus-to-blame/.

CBS News. "China Says 300,000 Punished for Corruption," March 6, 2016.

Central Intelligence Agency (CIA). *The Soviet Anticorruption Campaign: Causes, Consequences, and Prospects: An Intelligence Assessment*, August 1985.

———. *The Soviet Economy in 1988: Gorbachev Changes Course*, April 1989.

———. *Soviet Intensive Economic Development in Perspective: A Research Paper*, February, 1986.

CGTN. "Historic Changes in China's Economic Structure in Past 40 Years," December 18, 2018. As of January 31, 2020: https://news.cgtn.com/news/3d3d674d77677a4d31457a6333566d54/share_p.html.

Chan, Adrian. "In Search of a Civil Society in China," *Journal of Contemporary Asia*, Vol. 27, No. 2, 2007, pp. 242–251.

Chang, Gordon G. "Xi Jinping's Great Leap Backward," *The American Conservative*, July 9, 2018. As of January 15, 2021: https://www.theamericanconservative.com/articles/xi-jinpings-great-leap-backward/.

Che, Haigang. "Reform Towards the 'Direct Administration of Counties by Provinces' Advances in Depth" [Tuijin Sheng Fen Xian Zhixia Gaige], *Study Times* [Xuexi Shibao], August 3, 2009.

Chen, Cheng. *The Return of Ideology*, Ann Arbor, MI: University of Michigan Press, 2016.

Chen, Jiajian and Qiongwen Zhang. "Fluctuating Policy Implementation and Problems in Grassroots Governance," *The Journal of Chinese Sociology*, Vol. 3, No. 7, 2016, pp. 1–19.

Chen, Renze. "Why Has Credibility Decline?" [Wei Shenme Xinyu Xiajiang?], *People's Daily* [Renmin Ribao], September 8, 2011, p. 17.

Chen, Ying and Zhun Xu. "Informal Employment and China's Economic Development," *The Chinese Economy*, Vol. 50, No. 6, 2017, pp. 425–433.

Chen, Zewei. "Development That Fails To Stress Overall Situation Is Not Scientific Development" [Buneng Qiangdiao Quanjun De Fazhan Bushi Kexue Fazhan], *Outlook* [Liaowang], October 22, 2007, pp. 26–28.

Cheng, Dean. "Xi Jinping Amasses Mao-Like Power in China," *Heritage Foundation*, February 28, 2018.

Cheng, Tun-jen. "Democratizing the Quasi-Leninist Regime in Taiwan," *World Politics*, Vol. 41, No. 4, July 1989, pp. 471–499.

———. "Transforming Taiwan's Economic Structure in the 20th Century," *The China Quarterly*, Vol. 165, March, 2001, pp. 19–36.

China Daily. "China Outlines Its First Social Credit System," June 27, 2014.

China Development Zones Website [Zhongguo kaifaqu wang], September 19, 2010. As of January 5, 2021: http://www.cadz.org.cn/.

China File. "Does Xi Jinping Represent a Return to the Mao Era?" June 16, 2015. As of January 8, 2021: http://www.chinafile.com/reporting-opinion/features/does-xi-jinping-represent-return-mao-era.

China Labor Bulletin. "Reform of State-Owned Enterprises in China," December 19, 2007. As of January 31, 2020: https://clb.org.hk/en/content/reform-state-owned-enterprises-china#part1_3.

Chorzempa, Martin, Paul Triolo, and Samm Sacks. "China's Social Credit System: A Mark of Progress or a Threat to Privacy?" Peterson Institute for International Economics Policy Brief, June 2018.

Christian Science Monitor. "Miners Strike to Bring Down Gorbachev," April 9, 1991.

Cleaves, Peter. "Implementation Amidst Scarcity and Apathy: Political Power and Policy Design," in *Politics and Policy Implementation in the Third World*, Merilee Grindle (ed.), Princeton, NJ: Princeton University Press, 1980, pp. 281–303.

Clover, Charles. "Xi Takes Aim at Military in Anti-Graft Drive," *Financial Times*, February 11, 2018.

Cole, Alan. "The Political Roles of Taiwanese Entrepreneurs," *Asian Survey*, Vol. 88, September 1968, pp. 645–654.

Davies, Ken. "China Investment Policy: An Update," OECD Investment Policy Review of China, 2010. As of November 20, 2020: https://www.oecd.org/china/WP-2013_1.pdf.

Davis, Michael C. "The Case for Chinese Federalism," *Journal of Democracy*, Vol. 10, No. 2, 1999, pp. 124–137.

Delisle, Jacques. "Legalization Without Democratization in China Under Hu Jintao," in *China's Changing Political Landscape*, Cheng Le (ed.), Washington, DC: Brookings Institute Press, 2008, pp. 185–211.

Dickson, Bruce. *Red Capitalists in China: The Party, Private Entrepreneurs, and Prospects for Political Change*, Cambridge: Cambridge University Press, 2003.

Doner, Richard and Ben Ross Schneider. "The Middle Income Trap: More Politics than Economics," *World Politics*, Vol. 68, No. 4, 2016, pp. 608–644.

Dong, Ruifeng. "New Ordeals for the Ruling Party's Mass Work" [ZhiZheng Dang Qunzhong Gongzuo De Xin Kaoyan], *Outlook* [Liaowang], No. 44, November 1, 2010, pp. 32–35.

Doyon, Jerome. "The End of the Road for Xi's Mass Line Campaign: An Assessment," *China Brief*, Vol. 14, No. 20, October 23, 2014. As of September 23, 2023: https://jamestown.org/program/the-end-of-the-road-for-xis-mass-line-campaign-an-assessment/.

D'Souza, Errol. "Collusion in Government and Corruption," *The Journal of Interdisciplinary Economics*, Vol. 21, 2009, pp. 17–33.

Eichengreen, Barry, Donghyun Park, and Kwanho Shin. "When Fast Growing Economies Slow Down: International Evidence and Implications for China," National Bureau of Economic Research, Working Paper 16919, March, 2011.

Ellman, Michael. "Soviet Agricultural Policy," *Economic and Political Weekly*, Vol. 23, No. 24, June 11, 1988, pp. 1208–1210.

Ellman, Michael and Vladimir Konorovich. *The Destruction of the Soviet Economic System*, Milton Park: Routledge, 1998.

Evans, Peter. *Embedded Autonomy: States and Industrial Transformation*, Princeton, NJ: Princeton University Press, 1995.

Eyler-Driscoll, Samantha. "What Glue Holds Communist Capitalism Together in China? Cronyism," Pro Market, March 20, 2018. As of January 8, 2021: https://promarket.org/2018/03/20/glue-holds-communist-capitalism-together-china-cronyism/.

Fan, Yugang. "Cultural Direction of Political Structural Reform" [Zhengzhi Tizhi Gaige De Wenhua Fangxiang], *Outlook* [Liaowang], No. 17, April 25, 2011, p. 71.

Fare, Rolf, Shawna Grosskopf, and Wen-Fu Lee. "Productivity an Technical Change: The Case of Taiwan," *Applied Economics*, Vol. 33, No. 15, 2001, pp. 1911–1925.

Fayoumi, Khalid El, Anta Ndoye, Sanaa Nadeem, and Gregory Auclair. "Structural Reforms and Labor Reallocation: A Cross Country Analysis," *IMF Working Paper*, No. 18/64, 2018.

Ferchen, Matt. "Informality in China and Latin America: Comparisons and Interactions," Carnegie-Tsinghua Center for Global Policy, October 1, 2012. As of September 16, 2020: https://carnegietsinghua.org/2012/10/01/informality-in-china-and-latin-america-comparisons-and-interactions-pub-49981.

Fewsmith, Joseph. *China Since Tiananmen: From Deng Xiaoping to Hu Jintao*, Cambridge: Cambridge University Press, 2008.

———. "Promoting the Scientific Development Concept," *China Leadership Monitor,* No. 11, July 30, 2004. As of November 2, 2020: https://www.hoover.org/research/promoting-scientific-development-concept.

———. "The Politics of Economic Liberalization: Are There Limits?" in *China's Rise and the Balance of Influence in Asia*, William Keller and Thomas Rawski (eds.), Pittsburgh, PA: University of Pittsburgh Press, 2007, pp. 74–94.

———. "The Sixteenth National Party Congress: The Succession That Didn't Happen," *China Quarterly*, Vol. 173, March, 2003, pp. 1–16.

———. "The Third Plenary Session of the 16th Party Congress," *China Leadership Monitor*, No. 9, January 30, 2004. As of November 24, 2020: https://media.hoover.org/sites/default/files/documents/clm9_jf.pdf.

Fewsmith, Joseph and Andrew Nathan. "Authoritarian Resilience Revisited: Joseph Fewsmith with Response from Andrew J. Nathan," *Journal of Contemporary China*, Vol. 28, No. 116, 2019, pp. 167–179.

Filatochev, Igor and Roy Bradshaw. "The Soviet Hyperinflation: Its Origins and Impact Throughout the Former Republics," *Soviet Studies*, Vol. 44, No. 5, 1992, pp. 739–759.

Financial Times. "Bo Xilai: Power, Death, and Politics," July 20, 2012.

———. "China Income Inequality Among World's Worst," January 14, 2016.

———. "China Locked into Investment-Led Growth by GDP Targets," July 22, 2019.

Fox, Eleanor M. "An Anti-Monopoly Law for China: Scaling the Walls of Government Restraint," *Anti-Law Trust Journal*, Vol. 75, No. 1, 2008, pp. 173–194.

Foxley, Alejandro and Fernando Sossdorf. *Making the Transition: From Middle-Income to Advanced Economies*, Carnegie Endowment for International Peace, 2011.

Fravel, Taylor. "Xi Jinping and the PLA," *The Diplomat*, March 19, 2013. As of December 15, 2020: https://thediplomat.com/2013/03/xi-jinping-and-the-pla/.

Freedom House. "Freedom on the Net: A Global Assessment of Internet and Digital Media," 2013. As of December 6, 2020: https://freedomhouse.org/sites/default/files/resources/FOTN%202013_Full%20Report_0.pdf.

Freeman, Richard. "A Labor Market with Chinese Characteristics," in *The Routledge Handbook of the Chinese Economy*, Gregory C. Chow (ed.), London: Routledge, 2015, pp. 1–25.

Gaddy, Clifford G. *The Price of the Past: Russia's Struggle with the Legacy of a Militarized Economy*, Washington, DC: Brookings Institute, 1997.

Gailmard, Sean. "Accountability and Principal Agent Theory," in *Oxford Handbook of Public Accountability*, Oxford: Oxford University Press, 2014, pp. 90–105.

Garnaut, John. "Rotting from Within," *Foreign Policy*, April 16, 2012.

Gel'man, Vladimir and Andrey Starodubtsev. "Opportunities and Constraints of Authoritarian Modernisation: Russian Policy Reforms in the 2000s," *Europe-Asia Studies*, Vol. 68, No. 1, 2016, pp. 97–117.

Gidadhubli, R. G. "Perestroika and Glasnost," *Economic and Political Weekly*, Vol. 22, No. 18, May 2, 1987, pp. 784–787.

Gilley, Bruce. "The 'End of Politics' in Beijing," *The China Journal*, Vol. 51, January 2004, pp. 115–135.

Gitter, David, Julia Bowie, and Brock Erdahl. "Quarterly Report 2 | January–April 2018," *The Party Watch Initiative*, June 1, 2018. As of December 22, 2020: https://www.ccpwatch.org/single-post/2018/06/01/Quarterly-Report-2-January-April-2018.

Global Times. "Xi Stresses War Preparedness During PLA Navy Marine Corps Visit," October 14, 2020. As of December 5, 2020: https://www.globaltimes.cn/content/1203394.shtml.

Goldman, Marshall. *Gorbachev's Challenge: Economic Reform in the Age of High Technology*, New York, NY: W. W. Norton, 1987.

Golley, Jane and Nicolaas Groenewold. "Domestic Market Integration and Inter-Regional Growth Spillovers," in *China: Linking Markets for Growth*, Ross Garnau and Ligong Song (eds.), Canberra: Australian National University Press, 2007, pp 176–196.

Gong, Ting and Alfred Wu. "Central Mandates in Flux: Local Noncompliance in China," *Publius*, Vol. 42, No. 2, 2012, pp. 313–333.

Gorbachev, Mikhail. *Memoirs*, New York, NY: Doubleday, 1996.

———. *Perestroika: New Thinking for Our Country and the World*, New York, NY: Harper Collins and Row, 1987.

Gorlizki, Yoram. "Too Much Trust: Regional Party Leaders and Local Political Networks Under Brezhnev," *Slavic Review*, Vol. 69, No. 3, Fall 2010, pp. 676–700.

Goswami, Suparna. "Study Finds India Is Asia's Most Corrupt Country, While Japan Comes In Last," *Forbes*, March 8, 2017.

Grey, Robert D., Lauri A. Jennisch, and Alanna S. Tyler. "Soviet Public Opinion and the Gorbachev Reforms," *Slavic Review*, Vol. 49, No. 2, Summer 1990, pp. 261–271.

Gries, Thomas and Maargarethe Redlin. "China's Provincial Disparities and the Determinants of Provincial Inequality," *Journal of Chinese Economic and Business Studies*, Vol. 7, No. 2, 2009, pp. 259–281.

Han, Baojiang. "Reform and Opening Up Are the Source of Vitality of the Development and Progress in Contemporary China" [Gaige Kaifang Shi Dangdai Zhongguo Fazhan Jinbu De Shengmingli Yuanquan], *Outlook* [Liaowang], No. 26, July 1, 2013, pp. 25–26.

Hausmann, Ricardo. "Why Are Rich Countries Democratic?" *Project Syndicate*, March 26, 2014.

He, Zhengke. "Institutional Barriers of the Development of Civil Society in Current China," in *The Role of Civil Society Organizations in China and Germany*, Klaus Segbers, Yu Keping, and Ole Jatschek (eds.), Berlin: Center for Global Politics, 2009, pp. 58–66.

Heath, Timothy R. *China's New Governing Party Paradigm: Political Renewal and the Pursuit of National Rejuvenation*, London: Ashgate Publishing, 2014.

———. *The Consolidation of Political Power in China Under Xi Jinping: Implications for the PLA and Domestic Security Forces*, Santa Monica, CA: RAND Corporation, 2019.

———. "Xi's Mass Line: Realigning Party Politics to New Realities," *China Brief*, Vol. 13, No. 16, August 9, 2013.

Hernández, Javier C. "China's 'Chairman of Everything': Behind Xi Jinping's Many Titles," *The New York Times*, October 25, 2017.

Hernandez, Melina. "Democracy and Labor Market Outsides: The Political Consequences of Economic Informality," Dissertation Duke University, 2015.

Hewett, Ed. A. "Economic Reform in the Soviet Union," *The Brookings Review*, Vol. 2, No. 3, Spring 1984, pp. 8–11.

Herspring, Dale R. "Gorbachev and the Soviet Military," *Proceedings of the Academy of Political Science*, Vol. 36, No. 4, 1987, pp. 42–53.

Holbig, Heike. "Ideological Reform and Political Legitimacy in China: Challenges in the Post-Jiang Era," German Institute for Global and Area Studies, Working Paper. No. 18, 2006.

Holbig, Heike, Jean Christopher Mittelstaedt, Yevgen Sautin, and Angela Stanzel. "China's 'New Era' with Xi Jinping Characteristics," European Council on Foreign Affairs Website, December 15, 2017. As of January 23, 2021: https://ecfr.eu/publication/chinas_new_era_with_xi_jinping_characteristics7243/.

Horsley, Jamie P. "What's So Controversial About China's New Anti-Corruption Body?" *The Diplomat*, May 31, 2018. As of December 6, 2020: https://thediplomat.com/2018/05/whats-so-controversial-about-chinas-new-anti-corruption-body/.

Hou, Shaowen. "It Is the Will of the People To Push Forward the Political Structural Reform" [Tuijin Zhengzhi Tizhi Gaige Shi Renmin De Yuanyi], *Study Times* [Xuexi Shibao], September 13, 2010.

Huang, Gengzhi, Desheng Xue, and Bo Wang. "Integrating Theories on Informal Economies: An Examination of Causes of Urban Informal Economies," *Sustainability*, Vol. 12, 2020, pp. 1–16.

Huang, Philip. "China's Neglected Informal Economy," *Modern China*, Vol. 35, No. 4, July, 2009, p. 426.

Huang, Yiping. "Can China Escape the Middle Income Trap?" *China Economic Journal*, Vol. 9, No. 1, 2016, pp. 17–33.

International Monetary Fund. "A Study of the Soviet Economy," December 15, 1991.

———. *China's Economic Outlook*, August 9, 2019.

———. "Data Mapper," As of January 31, 2020: https://www.imf.org/external/datamapper/NGDP_RPCH@WEO/TWN.

———. "Press Release: IMF Staff Completes 2016 Article IV Mission to China," June 14, 2016. As of January 6, 2021: https://www.imf.org/en/News/Articles/2015/09/14/01/49/pr16277.

Jacobs, Bruce J. "Paradoxes in the Politics of Taiwan: Lessons for Comparative Politics," *The Journal of the Australian Political Science Association*, Vol. 13, November 1978, pp. 239–247.

Jain-Chandra, Sonali, Niny Khor, Rui Mano, Johanna Schauer, Philippe Wingender, and Juzhong Zhuang. "Inequality in China: Trends, Drivers, and Policy Remedies," *IMF Working Paper*, WP/18/127, 2018.

Jennings, Ralph. "Bad for Business? China's Corruption Isn't Getting Any Better," *Forbes*, March 15, 2018.

Jia, Xijin and Zhao Yusi. "The Chinese Economic Stimulus Package and Its Impact on Environmental Protection Organizations," *Policy Forum Online,* 09-016A, February 26, 2009. As of January 6, 2021: http://www.nautilus.org/fora/security/09016XijinYusi.html.

Jian, Tianlun, Jeffrey D. Sachs, and Andrew M. Warner. "Trends in Regional Inequality," NBER Working Paper No. 5412, January 1996.

Jiang, Zengwei. "To Give Full Play to the Role of the Market, the Market Must First Be Properly Constructed" [Yao Chongfen Fahui Shichang Zuoyong, Bixu Shouxian Zhengque Goujian Shichang], *Seeking Truth* [Qiushi], February 1, 2014.

Jin, Hui. "Government Reform Is the Core of the Present Round of Reforms" [Zhengfu Gaige Shi Ben Lun Gaige De Hexin], *Economic Observer News* [Jingji Cankao Bao], September 23, 2014.

Jowitt, Ken. *New World Disorder: The Leninist Extinction*, Berkeley, CA: University of California Press, 1991.

Kahn, Joseph. "Hu Takes Military Reins, Completing Shift in China," *New York Times*, September 20, 2004.

Kamp, Denise van der, Peter Lorentzen, and Daniel Mattingly. "Racing to the Bottom or the Top? Decentralization, Revenue Pressures, and Governance Reform in China," *World Development*, Vol. 95, 2017, pp. 164–176.

Kanbur, Ravi, Yue Wang, and Xiaobo Zhang. "The Great Chinese Inequality Turnaround," ECINEQ WP 2017-433, *Society for the Study of Economic Inequality*, April 2017. As of November 5, 2020: http://www.ecineq.org/milano/WP/ECINEQ2017-433.pdf.

Kau, Michael Ying-Mao. "The Power Structure in Taiwan's Political Economy," *Asian Survey*, Vol. 36, No. 3, March 1996, pp. 287–305.

Kessler, Mary. "The Paradox of Perestroika," *World Policy Journal*, Vol. 5, No. 4, Fall, 1988, pp. 651–676.

Kiernan, Brendan and Joseph Aistrup. "The 1989 Elections to the Congress of People's Deputies in Moscow," *Soviet Studies*, Vol. 43, No. 6, 1991, pp. 1049–1064.

Ko, Jim W. "Cold War Triumph-Taiwan Democratized in Spite of U.S. Efforts," *Case Western Reserve Journal of International Law*, Vol. 36, No. 1, 2004, pp. 137–182.

Kroeber, Arthur. "Xi Jinping's Ambitious Agenda for Economic Reform in China," Brookings, November 17, 2013. As of January 6, 2021: https://www.brookings.edu/opinions/xi-jinpings-ambitious-agenda-for-economic-reform-in-china/.

Lampton, David. "Challenger or Challenged?" *Washington Quarterly*, Vol. 39, No. 3, Fall 2016, pp. 107–119.

———. *Following the Leader: Ruling China, from Deng Xiaoping to Xi Jinping*, Berkeley, CA: University of CA Press, 2014.

Lardy, Nicholas. "Financial Repression in China," *Peterson Institute Policy Brief PB08-8*, September 2008. Link: https://www.piie.com/sites/default/files/publications/pb/pb08-8.pdf.

———. "The Role of Foreign Trade and Investment in China's Economic Transformation," *The China Quarterly*, Vol. 144, 1995, pp. 1065–1082.

Lawrence, Robert. "China, Like U.S., Faces Challenges in Achieving Inclusive Growth Through Manufacturing," Peterson Institute for International Economics, Policy Brief, August 2019.

Lee, Pak K. "Local Economic Protectionism in China's Economic Reform," *Development Policy Review*, Vol. 16, 1998, pp. 281–303.

Li, Cheng. "The Powerful Factions Among China's Rulers," Brookings Institute, November 5, 2012. As of November 5, 2020: https://www.brookings.edu/articles/the-powerful-factions-among-chinas-rulers/.

Li, Cheng and Scott W. Harold. "China's New Military Elite," *China Security*, Vol. 3, No. 4, Autumn, 2007, pp. 62–89.

Li, Jingtian. "Development and Justice are Distinctively Written on the Banne of Socialism with Chinese Characteristics" [Fazhan yu Zhengyi Bei Xianming De Xie Zai Zhongguo Tese Shehui Zhuyi Qizhi Shang], *Seeking Truth* [Qiushi], Vol. 51, No. 13, July 1, 2011.

Liao, Felix Haifeng and Yehua Dennis Wei. "Regional Inequality in China: Trends, Scales and Mechanisms," Working Paper No. 202, Territorial Cohesion for Development Program of Rimisp, 2016. As of November 5, 2020: https://www.rimisp.org/wp-content/files_mf/1473279216202_FH_Liao_YD_Wei.pdf.

Linz, Juan. *Totalitarian and Authoritarian Regimes*, London: Lynne Rienner Publishers, 2000.

Liu, Hongbo. "The Practice of Regarding Oneself as an Exception Threatens Unimpeded Transmission of Government Decrees" [Jiang Ziji Shiwei Liewai De Zuofa Hui Zuai Zhengfu Faling De Wuzhangai Zhuanbo], *Outlook* [Liaowang], No. 39, September 25, 2006, p. 3.

Lo, Carlos Wing-Hung and Shui-Yan Tang. "Institutional Reform, Economic Changes, and Local Environmental Management in China: The Case of Guangdong Province," *Environmental Politics*, Vol. 15, No. 2, 2006, pp. 190–210.

Los Angeles Times. "Stiff Opposition to Perestroika Reported," November 16, 1989.

Lu, Wei. "Making Online Public Opinion Work the Top Priority of Propaganda and Ideological Work" [Jiang Wangluo Yulun Gongzuo Zuowei Xuanchuan Sixiang Gongzuo De Zhongzhong Zhi Zhong], *People's Daily* [Renmin Ribao], September 17, 2013, p. 16.

Maltsey, Yuri N. "Soviet Economic Reforms: An Inside Perspective," Foundation for Economic Education, March 1, 1990.

Marelli, Enrico and Marcello Singorelli. "Employment, Productivity, and Models of Growth in the EU," *International Journal of Manpower*, Vol. 31, No. 7, 2010, 732–754.

Mau, Vladimir. "Perestroika: Theoretical and Political Problems of Economic Reforms in the USSR," *Europe-Asia Studies*, Vol. 47, No. 3, 1995, pp. 387–411.

Matthews, Mervyn. *Privilege in the Soviet Union: A Study of Elite Life-Styles Under Communism*, Milton Park: Routledge, 2011, Chapter 2.

McFaul, Michael. *Russia's Unfinished Revolution: Political Change from Gorbachev to Putin*, Ithaca, NY: Cornell University Press, 2001.

McGregor, Richard. "Why Fast Changing China Is Turning Back to Confucius," *Financial Times*, April 11, 2007.

McGwire, Michael. *Perestroika and Soviet National Security*, Washington, DC: Brookings Institution Press, 1997.

McKinesey Global Institute. "China's Choice: Capturing the $5Trillion Productivity Opportunity," June 2016.

Mesquite, Bruce Bueno de, Alastair Smith, Randolph M. Siverson, and James D. Morrow. *The Logic of Political Survival*, Boston, MA: MIT Press, 2005.

Migdal, Joel. *Weak States and Strong Societies*, Princeton, NJ: Princeton University Press, 1988.

Miller, Alice Lyman. "Only Socialism Can Save China; only Xi Jinping Can Save Socialism," *China Leadership Monitor*, No. 56, May 17, 2018. As of December 4, 2020: https://www.hoover.org/sites/default/files/research/docs/clm56am.pdf.

Miller, Chris. "Gorbachev's Agriculture Agenda: De-Collectivization and the Politics of Perestroika," *Critical Explorations in Russian and Eurasian History*, Vol. 17, No. 1, 2016, pp. 95–118.

———. *The Struggle to Save the Soviet Economy*, Chapel Hill, NC: University of North Carolina Press, 2016.

Ministry of Commerce, People's Republic of China. "Brief on China's Imports and Exports 2004," March 11, 2005. As of November 5, 2020: http://english.mofcom.gov.cn/article/statistic/ie/200503/20050300025384.shtml.

Minzer, Carl. *End of An Era*, New York, NY: Oxford University Press, 2018.

Misra, Kalpana. 1998. *From Post Maoism to Post Marxism: The Erosion of Official Ideology in Deng's China*. New York, NY: Routledge.

Mitchell, Tom. "Xi Jinping's Anti-Corruption Probe Takes Aim at Military," *Financial Times*, March 2, 2015.

Mohanty, Manoranjan. "Harmonious Society: Hu Jintao's Vision and the Chinese Party Congress," *Economic and Political Weekly*, Vol. 47, No. 50, December 15, 2012, pp. 12–16.

Mok, Ka Ho and Xiao Fang Wu. "Dual Decentralization in China's Transitional Economy: Welfare Regionalism and Policy Implications for Central-Local Relationship," *Policy and Society*, Vol. 32, No. 1, 2017, pp. 61–75.

Moody, Peter R. *Opposition and Dissent in Contemporary China*, Stanford, CA: Hoover Institution Press, 1977, p. 246.

Moore, Barrington. *Social Origins of Dictatorship and Democracy*, New York, NY: Beacon Press, 1993.

Moore, Malcolm. "China's Reforms Stalled by 'Powerful Vested Interests'," *The Telegraph,* January 12, 2012. As of January 5, 2021: https://www.telegraph.co.uk/news/worldnews/asia/china/9009915/Chinas-reforms-stalled-by-powerful-vested-interests.html.

Morrison, Wayne M. *China's Economic Conditions*. Congressional Research Service, January 12, 2006. As of November 5, 2020: https://fas.org/sgp/crs/row/IB98014.pdf.

Moses, Joel C. "Democratic Reform in the Gorbachev Era: Dimensions of Reform in the Soviet Union, 1986–1989," *The Russian Review*, Vol. 48, No. 3, July 1989, pp. 235–269.

Moskoff, William. *Impoverishment and Protest in the Perestroika Years*, The National Council for Soviet and East European Research, September 18, 1992, p. 4.

Mulvenon, James. "To Get Rich is Unprofessional," *China Leadership Monitor*, No. 6, June, 2003.

Myers, Ramon H. "The Economic Transformation of the Republic of China on Taiwan," *The China Quarterly*, Vol. 99, September 1984, pp. 500–528.

Nathan, Andrew. "China's Changing of the Guard: Authoritarian Resilience," *Journal of Democracy*, Vol. 14, No. 1, 2003, pp. 6–17.

New York Times. "Chinese Official Cuts Short Japan Trip to Protest Shrine Visit," May 24, 2005.

———. "Soviets Foresee Budget Deficit of $162 Billion," January 22, 1989.

Norwegian Energy and Environment Consortium. "China's Productivity Imperative," 2012. As of August 5, 2020: http://www.neec.no/uploads/China-Productivity-Imperative_en[1].pdf.

Novokmet, Filip, Thomas Piketty, and Gabriel Zucman. "From Soviets to Oligarchs: Inequality and Property in Russia, 1905–2016," *VOX EU* website, November 9,

2017. As of January 30, 2021: https://voxeu.org/article/inequality-and-property-russia-1905-2016.

O'Brien, Kevin J. and Lianjiang Li. "Selective Policy Implementation in Rural China," *Comparative Politics*, Vol. 31, No. 2, 1999, pp. 167–186.

OECD, "The New Development Traps," in Latin American Economic Outlook, OECD Publishing, Paris, France, 2019.

Office of the Secretary of Defense. *Annual Report to Congress: Military and Security Developments Involving the People's Republic of China 2016*, Department of Defense: Washington, DC, April 2016.

Ong, Lynette H. "Thugs for Hire: Subcontracting of State Coercion and State Capacity in China," *Perspectives in Politics*, April 2018.

Outlook [Liaowang]. "Overcome the Problems of Restraining Leadership Methods and Capacity" [Kefu Xianzhi Lingdao Fangfa He Nengli De Wenti], No. 36, September 8, 2008, pp. 40–41.

———. "Pooling New Strength for Reform" [Huiju Gaige Xin Liliang], No. 3, January 19, 2009, pp. 32–33.

Page, Jeremy and Lingling Wei. "Bo's Ties to Army Alarmed Beijing," *Wall Street Journal*, May 17, 2012.

Parker, Richard. "Inside the Collapsing Soviet Economy," *The Atlantic*, June 1990. As of January 30, 2021: https://www.theatlantic.com/magazine/archive/1990/06/inside-the-collapsing-soviet-economy/303870/.

Paus, Eva. "Escaping the Middle Income Trap: Innovate or Perish," Asian Development Bank Institute, No. 685, March 2017.

Pei, Minxin. *China's Crony Capitalism*, Cambridge, MA: Harvard University Press, 2016.

———. "China's Crony Capitalism: The Dynamics of Regime Decay," *The National Interest*, October 2, 2016. As of January 22, 2021: https://nationalinterest.org/feature/chinas-crony-capitalism-the-dynamics-regime-decay-17905.

———. "Fighting Corruption: A Difficult Challenge for Chinese Leaders," in *China's Changing Political Landscape: Prospects for Democracy*, Washington, DC: Brookings Institute Press, 2008, pp. 229–250.

———. "The Dark Side of China's Rise," *Foreign Policy*, October 20, 2009.

Pettis, Michael. "How Much Investment Is Optimal?" Carnegie Endowment for International Peace, June 10, 2013. As of January 7, 2021: http://carnegieendowment.org/chinafinancialmarkets/52078.

Phillips, Tom. "Chairman Xi Crushes Dissent but Poor Believe He's Making China Great," *The Guardian*, October 14, 2017. As of December 6, 2020: https://www.theguardian.com/world/2017/oct/14/xi-jinping-crushes-dissent-but-making-china-great-again.

Piirimae, Kaarel. "Gorbachev's New Thinking and How its Interaction with Perestroika in the Republics Catalysed the Soviet Collapse," *Scandinavian Journal of History*, August 18, 2020.

Plokker, Karin. "The Development of Individual and Cooperative Labor Activity in the Soviet Union," *Soviet Studies*, Vol. 42, No. 3, July 1990, pp. 403–428.

Poncet, Sandra. "Measuring Chinese Domestic and International Integration," *China Economic Review*, Vol. 14, 2003, pp. 1–21.

Przeworski, Adam and Fernando Limongi. "Political Regimes and Economic Growth," *Journal of Economic Perspectives*, Vol. 7, No. 3, 1993, pp. 51–69.

Qi, Weiping. "Boosting the Party's Ability to Govern at the Grassroots Level as Viewed from the Characteristics of China's Political Party System" [Cong Zhongguo Zhengdang Zhidu De Tedian Kan Tigao Dangde Jiceng Zhizheng Nengli], *Study Times* [Xuexi Shibao], June 15, 2010.

Qian, Jiwei. "Why Informal Workers are Opting Out of China's Welfare System," *Sixth Tone*, October 9, 2019. As of September 16, 2020: https://www.sixthtone.com/news/1004594/why-informal-workers-are-opting-out-of-chinas-welfare-system.

Qian, Yingyi and Jinglian Wu. "China's Transition to a Market Economy: How Far Across the River?" *Working Paper No. 69*, Stanford Center for International Development, August, 2000.

Quah, Jon and David Seth Jones. "Organizing the Public Bureaucracy to Ensure Effective Implementation and Compliance with ASEAN Commitments," Center for International Law, National University of Singapore, July 4, 2018. As of December 14, 2019: https://cil.nus.edu.sg/wp-content/uploads/2018/07/4.-CIL-ASEAN-Law-and-Policy-Curriculum-and-Training-Programme.-Organising-the-Public-Bureaucracy-to-Ensure-Effective-Implementation-and-Compliance-with-ASEAN-Commitments.pdf.

Raiser, Martin and Hoon Sahib Soh. "To Sustain Growth, China Can Learn from Previous Transitions to High Income," Brookings Institute, October 18, 2019. As of January 20, 2021: https://www.brookings.edu/blog/future-development/2019/10/18/to-sustain-growth-china-can-learn-from-previous-transitions-to-high-income/.

Rajah, Roland and Alyssa Long, *Revising Down the Rise of China*, The Lowy Institute, March 14, 2022.

Ramo, Joshua Cooper. "The Beijing Consensus," Foreign Policy Center, United Kingdom, 2004; Gary Krueger. "China's Authoritarian Market Economy," *Macalester International*, Vol. 18, Article 18, 2007.

Randolph, Eleanor. "Soviet System of Privileges Examined," *Washington Post*, August 10, 1991.

Remington, Thomas. "A Socialist Pluralism of Opinions: Glasnost and Policy-Making Under Gorbachev," *The Russian Review*, Vol. 48, No. 3, July 1989, pp. 271–304.

Remnick, David. "Vast 'Shadow Economy' Permeates Soviet Life," *Washington Post*, September 21, 1990.

Republic of China Council for Economic Planning and Development. *Taiwan Statistical Data Book, 1998*, Taipei: ROC Council for Economic Planning and Development, 1998.

Reuters. "China to Enshrine Xi's Thought into State Constitution Amid National 'Fervor'," January 19, 2018.

———. "China to Launch National Probe Into Policy Implementation," August 20, 2018.

———. "China's Domestic Security Spending Jumps Pass Army Budget," March 4, 2011.

———. "Former China Security Chief Faces Corruption Probe: Report," August 30, 2013

———. "Productivity Stagnant Despite Global Stimulus: WEF," October 8, 2019.

———. "Xi Says China Will Continue to Open its Economy, Deepen Financial Reforms," October 17, 2017.

Ricón, José Luis. "The Soviet Union: Poverty and Inequality," *Nintil*, March 14, 2017. As of January 19, 2021: https://nintil.com/the-soviet-union-poverty-and-inequality/.

Roberts, Dexter. "The Trouble with China's Reform Plan," *Bloomberg News*, November 18, 2013. As of January 15, 2021: http://www.bloomberg.com/news/articles/2013-11-18/the-trouble-with-chinas-reform-plan.

Robinson, Scott E., Foun'say Caver, Kenneth J. Meier, and Laurence J. O'Toole Jr. "Explaining Policy Punctuations: Bureaucratization and Budget Change," *American Journal of Political Science*, Vol. 51, No. 1, January 2007, pp. 140–150.

Rodrik, Dani. "Premature De-industrialization," *Journal of Economic Growth*, Vol. 21, 2016, pp. 1–33.

———. "The Myth of Authoritarian Growth," *Project Syndicate*, August 9, 2010.

Rothstein, Bo, Marcus Samanni, and Jan Teorell. "Explaining the Welfare State: Power Resources vs. The Quality of Government," *European Political Science Review*, Vol. 4, No. 1, February 2012, pp. 1–28.

Rubenstein, Murray. "Chapter 2: The Evolution of Taiwan's Economic Miracle 1945–2000: Personal Accounts and Political Narratives," in *Technology Transfer Between the US, China and Taiwan*, Douglas B. Fuller and Murray A. Rubenstein (eds.), London: Routledge, 2013, pp. 25–47.

Rudd, Kevin. "The Rise of Authoritarian Capitalism," *New York Times*, September 16, 2018.

Rumbaugh, Thomas and Nicolas Blancher. "China: International Trade and WTO Accession," IMF, *Working Paper 04/36*, 2004. As of November 6, 2020: https://www.imf.org/external/pubs/ft/wp/2004/wp0436.pdf.

Sabaltier, Paul and Christopher Weible. "The Advocacy Coalition Framework: Innovations and Clarifications," in *Theories of the Policy Process*, Paul Saultier (ed.), New York, NY: Westview Press, 2007, pp. 129–168.

Saich, Tony. "China in 2005: Hu's in Charge," *Asian Survey*, Vol. 46, No. 1, January 2006, pp. 37–48.

———. "The Fourteenth Party Congress: A Programme for Authoritarian Rule," *The China Quarterly*, Vol. 132, December 1992, pp. 1132–1160.

Sampson, Steven L. "The Second Economy of the Soviet Union and Eastern Europe," *The Annals of the American Academy of Political Science*, September, 1987, Vol. 493, pp. 120–136.

Saultier, Paul. *Theories of the Policy Process*, New York, NY: Westview Press, 2007.

Scissors, Derek. "A Stagnant China in 2040, Briefly," American Enterprise Institute, March 16, 2020. As of October 20, 2020: https://www.aei.org/research-products/report/a-stagnant-china-in-2040-briefly/.

Schroeder, Gertrude. "Economic Reform of Socialism: The Soviet Record," *The Annals of the American Academy of Political and Social Science*, Vol. 507, January 1990, pp. 35–43.

Seeking Truth [Qiushi]. "Consolidating the Common Ideological Foundation of United Struggle by the Party and the People" [Gongu Dang He Renmin Tuanjie Fendou De Gongtong Sixiang Jichu], October 16, 2013.

———. "Excerpts of Speech by Xi Jinping at the Second Plenary Meeting of the Sixth Plenary Session of the 18th CPC Central Committee" [Xi Jinping Zai Shiba Jie Liu Zhong Quanhui Di Er Ci Quanti Huiyi Shang De Jianghua Zhaiyao], December 31, 2016.

Schambaugh, David. *China's Communist Party: Atrophy and Adaptation*, Washington, DC: Woodrow Wilson Press, 2008.

———. "China's Fragile Future," *World Policy Journal*, Vol. 11, No. 3, Fall 1994, pp. 41–45.

———. "Contemplating China's Future," *Washington Quarterly* 39, No. 3, Fall 2016, pp. 121–130.

———. "Deng Xiaoping: The Politician," *The China Quarterly*, Vol. 135, September 1993, pp. 457–490.

———. "The Coming Chinese Crackup," *The Wall Street Journal*, March 6, 2015.

Sharlet, Robert. "Soviet Dissent since Brezhnev," *Current History*, Vol. 85, No. 513, October 1, 1986, pp. 321–324.

Shen, Chunni, Jing Jin, and Heng fun Zou. "Fiscal Decentralization in China: History, Impact, Challenges and Next Steps," *Annals of Economics and Finance*, Vol. 13, No. 1, 2012, pp. 1–51.

Shi, Kaifeng and Luo Shijian. "Oppose Local Protectionism" [*Fandub Defang Boushey*], Outlook [*Liaowang*], No. 12, March 22, 1999, p. 1.

Secular, Terry. "The Challenge of High Inequality in China," World Bank, *Inequality in Focus*, Vol. 2, No. 2, August 2013. As of November 5, 2020: https://www.worldbank.org/content/dam/Worldbank/document/Poverty%20documents/Inequality-In-Focus-0813.pdf.

Skocpol, Theda. *States and Social Revolution: A Comparative Analysis of France, Russia, and China*, Cambridge, MA: Cambridge University Press, 2015.

Smith, Graeme. "Political Machinations in a Rural Country," *China Journal*, Vol. 62, July, pp. 29–59.

Song, Ligang. "State Owned Enterprise Reform in China: Past, Present and Prospects," in *China's Forty Years of Reform and Development 1978–2018*, Ross Garnaut, Ligang Song, and Cai Fang (eds.), Canberra: Australia National University, 2018, pp. 345–374.

South China Morning Post. "China's War on Organized Crime, Corrupt Officials Sees 79,000 Detained," April 14, 2019.

———. "Coup Plotters Foiled: Xi Jinping Fended Off Threat to 'Save Communist Party,'" October 20, 2017.

———. "How Leading Small Groups Help Xi Jinping and Other Party Leaders Exert Power," January 20, 2014.

———. "Human Rights Under Xi 'Worst since Tiananmen Crackdown': Amnesty," November 17, 2017.

———. "Xi Jinping a Reformer and a Nationalist," June 6, 2013.

Starr, Frederick. "Soviet Union: A Civil Society," *Foreign Policy*, Vol. 70, Spring 1988, pp. 26–41.

Sun, Lena. "Deng Completes Major Army Purge," *Washington Post*, February 12, 1993.

Suslova, Elena. "Human Capital, Industrial Growth and Resource Curse," *Human Capital*, October 1, 2012.

Swider, Sarah. *Building China: Informal Work and the New Precariat*, Cornell, NY: Cornell University Press, 2015.

Tak-wing, Ngo. "Civil Society and Political Liberalization in Taiwan," *Bulletin of Concerned Asian Scholars*, Vol. 25, 1993, pp. 3–16.

The Economist. "Beneath the Glacier," April 12, 2014.

———. "Beware the Cult of Xi," April 2, 2016.

———. "For Some Plaintiffs, Courts in China Are Getting Better," September 30, 2017.

———. "The Struggle to Reform China's Economy," February 21, 2019.

The Guardian. "Chinese Repression of Dissent Intensifies Under Ruthless Xi Jinping," December 30, 2014.

Tidrick, Gene. "Productivity Growth and Chinese Industries," World Bank, SWP 761, July 2010.

Tien, Hung-mao. "Taiwan in Transition: Prospects for Socio-Political Change," *The China Quarterly*, Vol. 64, December 1975, p. 617.

Tien, Hung-mao and Tun-jen Cheng. "Crafting Democratic Institutions in Taiwan," *The China Journal*, Vol. 37, January 1997, pp. 1–27.

Tiewes, Frederick. "Peng Dehuai and Mao Zedong," *The Australian Journal of Chinese Affairs*, Vol. 16, July 1986, pp. 81–98.

Tilly, Charles. *Coercion, Capital, and European States, A.D. 990–1990*, New York, NY: Wiley-Blackwell, 1992.

Tsai, Pan-Long. "Explaining Taiwan's Economic Miracle: Are the Revisionists Right?" *Agenda*, Vol. 6, No. 1, 1999, pp. 69–82.

VOA. "After Bo Xilai Conviction, Mixed Legacy for Chongqing's Anti-Mafia Campaign," April 15, 2014.

Vogel, Ezra. *Deng Xiaoping and the Transformation of China*, Cambridge, MA: Belknap Press, 2011.

Wall Street Journal. "China Anti-Corruption Cases Have Quadrupled since 2013, Study Says," December 11, 2015.

———. "China Needs Fundamental Reform," June 30, 2015.

———. "Chinese President Xi Jinping's Extreme Makeover," May 12, 2016.

———. "Rising Wages Pose Dilemma for China," May 17, 2013.

———. "When Democracy Is No Longer the Only Path to Prosperity," March 1, 2019.

Wang, Jianjun and Yang Lin. "Fight a Decisive Battle in Reform to Deal with a Complicated Situation in a Crucial Period" [Yingdui Gaigezhong de Juedingxing Zhandou, Yingdui Dui Guanjian Shiqi De Fuzaa Jumian], *Outlook* [Liaowang], No. 9, March 1, 2004, pp. 18–22.

———. "'Hills of Interests' Are Biggest Resistance to Market Reform" [Liyi Zhi Shan Shi Shichang Gaige De Zuida Zuli], *Outlook* [Liaowang], No. 50, December 11, 2006, pp. 21–23.

Wang, Qishan. "Comprehensively Administer the Party with Strict Discipline and Shoulder the Party's Mission in the New Age" [Yange Jilu Quanmian Zhizheng Dang Jianfu Xin Shiqi Dang De Shiming], *People's Daily* [Renmin Ribao], November 8, 2016, p. 3.

Wang, Yuhuan. "Beyond Local Protectionism: China's State-Business Relations in the Last Two Decades," *The China Quarterly*, Vol. 226, June 2016, pp. 319–341.

Washington Post. "China's Workforce is Expected to Start Shrinking in Next Few Years," May 31, 2011.

Watts, Jonathan. "Mistress Turns in Corrupt Chinese Vice Admiral," *The Guardian*, June 15, 2006.

Wedeman, Andrew. "Corruption in China: Crisis or Constant," in *China's Rise: Challenges and Opportunities*, Fred Bergeston (ed.), Peterson Institute, 2009, pp. 91–104.

Wen, Philip and Christian Shepherd. "China Cranks Propaganda, Xi Jinping's Cult of Personality into Overdrive Ahead of Party Congress," *Business Insider*, October 12, 2017.

West, John. "China, a Low Productivity Superpower," *The Interpreter*, October 31, 2019.

Whalley, John and Xian Xin. "China's FDI and Non-FDI Economies and the Sustainability of Future High Chinese Growth," National Bureau of Economic Research, Working Paper 12249, May 2006. As of November 24, 2020: https://www.nber.org/system/files/working_papers/w12249/w12249.pdf.

Winkler, Edwin. "Institutionalization and Participation on Taiwan: From Hard to Soft Authoritarianism," *China Quarterly*, Vol. 99, 1984, pp. 481–499.

Wong, Anna. "Measuring Trade Barriers: An Application to China's Domestic Trade," Job Market Paper, University of Chicago, 2012.

Woo-Cumings, Meredith (ed.). *The Developmental State*, Los Angeles, CA: Cornell University Press, 1999.

World Bank Website. "China 2030: Building a Modern, Harmonious, and Creative Society," February 27, 2012. As of January 6, 2021: http://www.worldbank.org/en/news/feature/2012/02/27/china-2030-executive-summary.

———. "China Overview," As of January 9, 2021: https://www.worldbank.org/en/country/china/overview.

———. *China: Integration of National Product and Factor Markets, Economic Benefits and Policy Recommendations*, 2005–6. As of January 9, 2021: https://openknowledge.worldbank.org/handle/10986/8690.

———. *China Maintains Strong Growth and Reform Momentum, Says World Bank*, December 19, 2017. As of December 6, 2020: http://www.worldbank.org/en/news/press-release/2017/12/19/china-maintains-strong-growth-and-reform-momentum-says-world-bank.

———. "Developing Country List," 2020. As of January 9, 2021: https://data.worldbank.org/income-level/low-and-middle-income?view=chart.

———. "GDP Per Capita (Current US$): China," As of January 2, 2021: https://data.worldbank.org/indicator/NY.GDP.PCAP.CD?locations=CN.

———. "The Challenge of High Inequality in China," August, 2013. As of January 9, 2021: http://www.worldbank.org/content/dam/Worldbank/document/Poverty%20documents/Inequality-In-Focus-0813.pdf.

World Bank and Development Research Council of China. "Innovative China: New Drivers of Growth," 2019.

World Health Organization Social Development Department of the Development Research Center. "China Health Poverty and Economic Development," December 2005. As of November 9, 2020: https://www.who.int/macrohealth/action/CMH_China.pdf.

World Inequality Database. "World Inequality Report 2018," 2018. As of November 4, 2020: https://wir2018.wid.world/executive-summary.html.

Wu, Guoguang. "China in 2009: Muddling Through Crises," *Asian Survey*, Vol. 50, No. 1, January 2010, pp. 25–39.

———. "China in 2020: Dilemmas of 'Scientific Development'," *Asian Survey*, Vol. 51, No. 1, January 2011, pp. 18–32.

Wu, Yongping. "Rethinking the Taiwanese Developmental State," *The China Quarterly*, Vol. 177, March, 2004, p. 103.

Wuthnow, Joel and Phillip C. Saunders. "Chinese Military Reforms in the Age of Xi Jinping: Drivers, Challenges, and Implications," *China Strategic Perspectives*, Institute for National Strategic Studies, No. 10, March 2017.

Xinhua. "China Moves to Clear Blockades for Unified Market," December 10, 2013.

———. "CPC Announces Decision on Comprehensive Reform," November 13, 2013.

———. "CPC Promoting Reform, Democracy in Local Leadership Elections," May 14, 2006.

———. "Full Text of Hu Jintao's Report at 18th Party Congress," November 17, 2012.

———. "Implementation Outline on Building Ethics Among Citizens" [Gongmin Daode Jianshe Sheshi Gangyao], October 24, 2001.

———. "Wen Jiabao Emphasizes Deepening the Reform of the Administrative and Management Structure and Speeding up Changes in the Government's Functions in His Speech at a Study Class for Cadres at the Provincial Level of the National School of Administration" [Wen Jiabao Zai Guojia Xingzheng Xueyuan Shengji Ganbu Yanjiuban Jianghua Qiangdiao Shenhua Xingzheng Guanli Tizhi Gaige Jiakuai Shixian Zhengfu Zhineng Zhuanbian], September 15, 2003.

———. "Xi Calls for 'Strong Measures' to Cure Corruption," January 13, 2015.

———. "Zhou Yongkang Arrested for Serious Disciplinary Violations," July 29, 2014.

Xu, Chenggang. "The Fundamental Institutions of China's Reforms and Development," *Journal of Economic Literature*, Vol. 49, No. 4, December 2011, pp. 1076–1151.

Xu, Duoduo and Xiaogang Wu. "From Political Power to Personal Wealth: Privatization, Elite Opportunity, and Social Stratification in Post-Reform China," Hong Kong University Working Paper, 2017.

Xu, Vicky Xiuzhong and Bang Xiao. "Falungong: Two Decades After a Deadly Ban, Adherents Still Face Pressure in Australia," ABC News, April 20, 2018. As of November 11, 2020: https://www.abc.net.au/news/2018-04-21/what-is-the-falun-gong-movement-and-does-china-harvest-organs/9679690.

Yang, Jingyu. "Accurately Understanding Several Issues Regarding the Anti-Monopoly Law" [Zhunque Lijie Fan Longduan Fa Ruogan Wenti] *Seeking Truth* [Qiushi], March 11, 2008.

Yang, Song. "Rising Chinese Regional Income Inequality: The Role of Fiscal Decentralization," *China Economic Review*, Vol. 27, 2013, pp. 294–309.

Ying, Diane. "Taiwan Is Planning Open Trials Soon for Dissidents," *New York Times*, January 24, 1980.

You, Ji. "Jiang Zemin's Command of the Military," *The China Journal*, Vol. 45, January, 2001, pp. 131–138.

Yu, Keping. *Democracy Is a Good Thing: Essay on Politics, Society, and Culture in Contemporary China*, Washington, DC: Brookings Institute, 2008.

Yu, Xie and Yongai Jin. "Household Wealth in China," *Chinese Sociological Review*, Vol. 47, No. 3, 2015, pp. 203–29.

Zeng, Qingjie. "Control, Discretion and Bargaining: The Politics of Provincial Leader Rotation in China," *China Political Science Review*, Vol. 1, 2016, pp. 623–644.

Zenglein, Max. "China's Overrated Services Sector," Merics, 2016.

Zhang, Ye. "China's Emerging Civil Society," Brookings Institute Working Paper, June 2003. As of November 4, 2020: https://www.brookings.edu/wp-content/uploads/2016/06/ye2003.pdf.

Zhang, Zhuoyuan. "Comprehensively Understand the Market's Decisive Role" [Quanmian Liaojie Shichang De Juedingxing Zuoyong], *Outlook* [Liaowang], No. 51, December 23, 2013, pp. 46–68.

Zhao, Hongzhu. "Propelling the Work of Inner-Party Supervision Into a New Stage" [Tuijin Dang Nei Jiandu Gongzuo Jinru Xin Jieduan], *People's Daily* [*Renmin Ribao*], February 4, 2018, p. 8.

Zhao, Dingxin. *The Power of Tiananmen: State-Society Relations and the 1989 Beijing Student Movement*, Chicago, IL: University of Chicago Press, 2001, p. 127.

Zhao, Suisheng. "Nationalism's Doubled Edged Sword," *Wilson Quarterly*, Vol. 29, No. 4, Autumn 2005, pp. 76–82.

Zhen, Liu. "China's Military Police Given Control of Coast Guard as Beijing Boosts Maritime Security," *South China Morning Post*, March 21, 2018.

Zheng, Lu and Xiang Deng. "China's Western Development Strategy: Policies, Effects, and Prospects," Munich Personal RePec Archive, December 1, 2011. As of November 4, 2020: https://mpra.ub.uni-muenchen.de/35201/1/.

Zheng, Yongnian. "China in 2012: Troubled Elite, Frustrated Society," *Asian Survey*, Vol. 53, No. 1, January 2013, pp. 162–175.

———. "Power to Dominate, Not to Change: How China's Central-Local Relations Constrain Its Reform," EAI Working Paper 153, July 2009.

Zhou, Xueguang. "The Institutional Logic of Collusion Among Local Governments in China," *Modern China*, Vol. 36, No. 1, pp. 47–78.

Zhu, Min, Longmei Zhang, and Daoju Peng. "China' Productivity Convergence and Growth Potential," IMF Working Paper 19/263, 2019.

Index

Page references for figures are italicized.

Alibaba, 114
"Asian Tigers," 2
authoritarian regimes, 1–12
autocrat, 20, 23, 27

Bo Xilai, 88, 113, 193
Brezhnev, Leonid, 149

central leadership, 9–10, 20, *21*, 29; control of military and security forces, 10, 21; control of political party, 10, 23–24; control of subnational governments, 10, 22–23; weak and strong, 23–24, 26
Chen Yun, 44
Chiang Ching-kuo, 12, 129, 132, 135, 137, 138, 178, 183; power struggles, 135; propaganda, 138
Chiang Kai-shek, 132, 135
China, 1–6, 8–12, 18, 26, 30, 36–37, 41–125, 169, *170*, 176–78, *178*, 180–83, *184*, 187–88, *189*, 192; Anhui province, 75; case studies, compared, 176–81, 187–88, *189*; Central Advisory Commission, 44, 50; central bank, 55; Central Military Commission, 73, 105; central-subnational government relations, 67, 72, 79, 84; Christianity, 75; consumer goods quality issues, 85; crime, 58, 107, 119; Cultural Revolution, 6; debt, 91, 120; decentralization, 43, 50; deindustrialization, 102, 107–9, 113, 119, 121, 176; demographic issues, 89, 120; dissidents, 90, 122; economic growth, 1, 11–12, 69, 120; economic inefficiencies, 60, 69, 70, 104; economic prospects, 1, 11–12, 192–93; Eighth Five Year Plan, 42, 44, 45; elites, 45–47, 60–61, 80–82, 104–6, 119, 171, 173, 177–79 (central elite opposition, 52–54, 56; collusion, 67, 74, 81–82, 103, 106; cooptation of institutions, 69; defiance of central directives, 74–75, 80–82, 85–86, 104, 106, 112, 119, 171, 173; professionalization, 68, 77–78, 91–93, 176–77; share of national wealth, 52, 73–74, 81, 87, 106, 112, 119, 171); Falungong, 58, 75, 180; fiscal reforms, 52; foreign direct investment (FDI), 69–70; Guangdong Province, 43;

Guangzhou, 108; information technology firms, 114; internal security spending, 89, 91; intra-provincial trade, 44, 52, 104, 111; labor share of GDP, 83; land use issues, 89; mass protests, 89, 91; National Peoples Congress, 118; National Security Commission, 110, 111; National Supervisory Commission, 117; nongovernmental organizations (NGOs), 58, 61, 76, 90; People's Armed Police, 111; People's Liberation Army (PLA), 50, 52, 67, 80, 105, 110, 117 (corruption, 86–87); political indoctrination and repression, 58; productivity, 4, 69–70, 91, 102, 113, 120; public cohesiveness, 47–49, 53–54, 57–59, 68, 75, 82, 89, 113, 171, 174, 177–80 (ethnic divisions, 47, 90, 180; foreign invested enterprises, 68, 76, 113; *Hukou* reform, 108–9; inequality, 75, 76, 82, 113, 115; informal labor, 68, 82, 113, 174; social welfare programs, 68, 75; unemployment, 108); regional inequality, 43, 57–58, 71–72, 79, 85, 89; Shanghai city, 44, 75, 107; social credit system, 115; "socialist market economy," 50, 59–60; state owned enterprises (SOE), 42, 43, 47–48, 56, 69, 70, 75, 85, 91, 102, 114, 119, 120, 174, 180, 183 (low productivity, 114, 120; reform and streamlining efforts, 57, 59, 88; service sector companies, 114; social policy, 114; worker unemployment, 61); Tibet, 47, 90; township and village enterprises (tve), 47, 54; trade, 70; Xinjiang, 47, 90
Chinese Civil War, 130
Chinese Communist Party (CCP), 11, 23, 42, 110–18, 171; anti-corruption and, 45, 51, 77, 110, 117, 118, 185; commercial involvement of member, 46, 52; corruption and discipline issues, 44, 54, 60–61, 72–73, 77, 84, 89, 104–7, 110, 118–19; divisions within, 45, 54; Eighteenth Party Congress, 93, 105, 118; Fourteenth CCP Congress, 45, 50; governing party identity, 68, 77, 184; ideology, 58, 67, 72 (systematic overhaul, 80–81); Leading Small Group for Comprehensive Deepening of Reform, 110; mass mobilization, 76, 90, 114, 123; organization department, 86; procedures to improve accountability, 84, 86; revolutionary party identity, 77; Seventeenth Party Congress, 80, 86; Seventh Plenum of the 13th CCP Congress, 43; Sixteenth Party Congress, 74; Sixth Plenum of 18th Party Congress, 118; socialist harmonious society, 84, 175; Third Plenum of 18th CCP Congress, 4, 101, 103, 118; United Front Work Department, 117
Communist Party of the Soviet Union (CPSU), 148, 152, 153, 162–63, 174, 190; Central Committee, 153–55; Politburo, 154–56, 160, 191; Resistance to Gorbachev, 155–56; Twenty-Seventh Party Congress, 153
coups, 24

deindustrialization, 102
democracy, liberal, 1, 11–12, 190; economic performance of, 1, 11; implications of "enabling condition" theory for, 190
Deng Xiaoping, 2, 7, 12, 20, 26, 30, 41–62, 67, 73, 93, 170–72, 177–81, 183, 184, 190–92, 194; advocacy of fast growth, 41–42; consolidation of power, 53–55; death of, 54; political struggles with rival leaders, 47–52, 184; "Southern Tour," 49, 178; success in policy implementation, 60–62

depoliticization of public, 6, 27
Doi Moi reforms, 20

economic growth, 1–2; political legitimacy and, 18; politics of, 4, 7; types of growth, 3
elite opposition, 10, 24, 29; control of wealth, 10, 24–26; disposition towards policy, 10, 25–26; horizontal collusion, 10, 25–26; vertical collusion, 10, 25–26; weak and strong, 26
elites, 4, *21*, 24; Leninist regimes, in, 6; noncompliance with central directives, 7, 29; opposition to growth, 4; political advantages over leaders, 9; strength, 10, 24
enabling condition, theory of, 9–10, 17–38, 187; case overview, 36–38; combination possibilities, 31–32, *33*; external developments and, 35; failure of policy and, 30; ideology and identities, 36; operation of, 29–31; political actors, 17–28; political strategies, 31–35; repression and coercion, 190–91; timing, 30
extensive economic growth, 3

Fang Fenghui, 113

Germany, 70, 102
Glasnost reforms, 29
Gorbachev, Mikhail, 13, 20, 29, 35, 145, 147, 152–59, 162–64, 170, 172, 173, 176, 181, 190, 193; "acceleration" reforms, pursuit of, 148; failure to carry out upgrading policies, 162–63; Glasnost reforms, pursuit of, 158–59, 170, 190; perestroika reforms, pursuit of, 153; purges, 154–55
Great Leap Forward, 6
Guo Boxiong, 105, 110, 113

Ho Chi Minh, 6
Hu Jintao, 12, 29, 35, 37, 67–93, 101, 105, 107, 170–72, 174, 176, 181, 184, 193, 195; consolidation of power, 73–74; efforts to discipline party, 78; failure in policy implementation, 89, 170–71; political strategies of, 69, 91–93; repression of public, 184; scientific development concept, 67, 78, 80
Hu Yaobang, 45

information asymmetry of bureaucracies, 8
Institute Revolutionary Party (Mexico), 5
institutions, 4, 6, 27
intensive economic growth, 3–4, 6–8

Japan, 70, 76, 108
Jiang Zemin, 12, 45, 50–52, 71–73, 91, 120, 195; "Three Represents" ideology, 74, 91

Kosygin, Alexei, 146
Kruschev, Nikita, 163
Kuomintang (KMT), 6, 23, 36, 129, 130, 132–40, 191, 192; erosion in capacity of, 140; factions, 132, 133; ideology, 132, 133; mainlander members, 129, 130; organization, 132; recruitment, 136, 138–39; repression, 133; Taiwan-born members, 132, 133

Lenin, Vladimir, 5, 6, 163
Leninism, 5–6, 23, 37
Liberal Democratic Party (Japan), 5
Ling Jihua, 107, 113

Mao Zedong, 2, 6, 8, 36, 92, 114, 194
Mexico, 122
"middle income trap," 3
modernization, 2

policy change, 18–20, *20*; major, 19; minor, 18; revolutionary, 19
policy implementation, 18

political actors, 20–21
political mobilization, 9, 26–28
political party, 23
political strategies, 32–35; administrative measures, 34; centralization, 34; coercion, 34; liberalization, 34; mass mobilization, 35
political violence, 8–10
principal agent problem, 7
productivity, 1–2; contrast between democratic and authoritarian states, 2; definition and types, 3–4; low productivity, 3, 11–12; "low productivity trap," 3; political dilemmas for autocrats, 7
public cohesiveness, 9, *21*, 26, 29–30; economic, 10, 26, 27; fragmentation, 26, 28–29; political, 10, 26–28; social, 10, 26, 29

Russia, 21, 43, 122

selectorate theory, 7
Singapore, 2, 83
single party, authoritarian regimes, 1–5; definition of, 4
South Korea, 2, 83, 108
Soviet Union, 1, 12–13, 27, 29, 37, 42, 169, *170*, 180–83, *184*, 187–88, *189*, 194; agriculture sector, 147, 150, 160; case study comparison, 181–82, 187–88, *189*; corruption, 148, 155; Council of Ministers, 149; coup in 1991, 145, 161, 191; debt, 145–46, 160; economic performance of, 1, 145–47, 159, 162–63, 169; elections, 162; elites, 148, 157, 160–61, 171, 173 (collusion, 148, 157, 171, 173; share of wealth, 149, 161, 173); energy sector, 150; Glasnost policies, 158; gray market, 150, 159, 162; inflation, 156, 159–61; military, 148, 150, 156, 160–61, 163; perestroika reforms, 145, 153, 154, 158; price liberalization, 154; productivity, 146, 154, 163; public cohesiveness, 150, 157–58, 161–62, 174 (economic conditions, 158–59, 162; ethnic fragmentation, 150, 158, 162; inequality, 150, 162; political opportunities, 150, 162); republics, 159, 160; state owned enterprises, 146, 160, 162–63, 183; State Planning Committee (Gosplan), 149; Thirteenth Five Year Plan, 154; war in Afghanistan, 156, 160
Stalin, Joseph, 6, 8, 149, 163
Su Rong, 113

Taiwan, 2, 12, 29, 36–37, 83, 102, 129–56, 176–81, *184*, 187–88, *189*, 192; case study comparison, 180–81, 187–88, *189*; economic performance of, 2, 131, 140, 141; elections, 133, 136; elites, 130, 133, 136–37, 138, 177–79, 181, 184 (differentiation, 133, 136–37, 139, 141; opposition to reforms, 155; political differences, 140; share of wealth, 133, 136, 139, 179, 184; support for KMT economic strategy, 139–40; worker health, 147); enabling condition, achievement of, 135, 137, 140–41; land redistribution, 130; middle class, 139; military, 15, 135–36, 138, 179; productivity, 131; public cohesiveness, 133, 137, 140, 141 (business sector linkages, 133, 137, 141; ethnic relations, 129, 133–34, 137, 140; formal workforce, 137, 140, 141; inequality, 134, 140, 141; political involvement, 134, 137, 140, 141); Republic of China government, 130; small to medium enterprises (SME), 130, 136, 137, 180; state-owned enterprises (SOE), 130–32, 136, 156, 180; Tang-Wai, 136, 139–41; Ten Major Construction Projects, 129, 131, 136, 140

Tencent, 114
Tiananmen Square Massacre, 41, 42, 45
Trump, Donald, 119

United States, 11, 43, 70, 102, 131, 194, 196

Wang Qishan, 118
Wan Li, 44
Wen Jiabao, 71, 85, 90, 102
World Trade Organization, 69

Xiaomi, 114
Xi Jinping, 2, 12, 18, 36, 37, 93, 101–23, 170–72, 174, 176, 181, 184–85, 191, 193–95; control of military, 105; "core" of leadership, designated, 118; cult of personality propaganda, 111, 115, 185; failure to implement intensive growth policies, 120, 169–71; nationalist diplomacy, 115–16; political centralization, 2, 101, 109–10, 116, 170; political strategies, 184–85; purges of senior leaders, 110; term limits for PRC president removed, 118
Xu Caihou, 105, 110, 113

Yang brothers, 50

Zhao Ziyang, 42, 44, 45
Zhou Yongkang, 105, 110, 112–13, 193–94

About the Author

Timothy R. Heath is a senior international defense researcher at the RAND Corporation who previously served in the US government as an intelligence specialist on China. He has authored dozens of reports, articles, and commentaries, as well as the 2014 book, *China's New Governing Party Paradigm: Political Renewal and the Pursuit of National Rejuvenation* (Ashgate). He has a PhD in political science from George Mason University and lives in Alexandria, VA, with his wife and two sons.

Milton Keynes UK
Ingram Content Group UK Ltd.
UKHW011837301123
433557UK00004B/95

9 781666 947397